WORSHIP

i

WHAT THE
BIBLE SAYS
ABOUT

WORSHIP

By

Lynn Hieronymus

College Press Publishing Company, Joplin, Missouri

Printed and bound in
United States of America

Library of Congress Catalog Card Number: 84-072576
International Standard Book Number: 0-89900-097-5

DEDICATED to the memory
of Elbert and Edith Hieronymus, faithful members
of the Atlanta (Illinois) Christian Church,
who led their sons to meet the Lord in holy worship.

Table of Contents

PART ONE: "HOW WE GOT HERE"

TABLE OF CONTENTS

Chapter *Page*

Introduction

Praise ye the Lord. Sing unto the Lord a new song, and his praise in the congregation of saints (Psalm 149:1).

Praise ye the Lord indeed! Yours is perhaps the most joyous avenue of service in the church. Only the one who initially announces the Good News has a more important role. You as a worship leader—whether you be a minister, elder, deacon, teacher, or hold no other position of leadership—are guiding the people of God in learning to do well that which they will do throughout all eternity! Think about it! How competently are you guiding in this most important area of maturation? This book is written for you!

Leaders of the Christian Churches/Churches of Christ in fact have a philosophy of worship that guides their actions in devising and conducting services of worship of the assembled congregation. This philosophy was formulated in the early decades of the nineteenth century when the Restoration Movement came into being in frontier America. This philosophy has been refined—but scarcely altered—with the passing of the years. This book is written to analyze the formation of this philosophy, to evaluate its relevancy for our day, and to consider ways of giving expression to corporate worship as one of the ultimate encounters of the church with the Lord of the church!

The author writes from the perspective of twenty-five years in pastorates and from a position of teaching courses for over a decade in both the areas of worship and the history of the Restoration Movement at Lincoln Christian College and Seminary. The author feels a strong identity with the past as the congregations that he has served average well over one hundred thirty years of age. Yet as an educator at college/seminary level he feels the necessity of guiding

Christian workers to a role of relevancy in the present. As a concerned student of the history of the Restoration Movement he feels that present-day leaders of the churches are often unnecessarily confined to certain worship practices of the past history of these churches—certain practices that are not necessarily a mandatory part of the biblical model. Being freed from these inhibiting practices and yet faithfully loyal to the biblical model, he believes, will provide a new vitality and vibrancy to the worship of these churches today.

Abraham Lincoln in his famed "House Divided" speech stated that if we could know first where we are we could then know better what to do and how we should do it. I would adopt that homespun logic to our study of worship. Therefore this book is structured in two parts. The first part, "How We Got Here!," is a careful examination of the worship practices past and present of the Christian Churches/Churches of Christ as well as an elementary study of the biblical model of worship and a simple formulation of a biblical theology of worship for today. The second part of the book, "Where We Can Go!," is a study at the very practical level of improving the worship services today. In this latter section are considered such topics as the public presentation of the Word, observing the Lord's Supper, developing congregational participation, and the planning of an actual service of worship.

The author is indebted to the elders of the Eminence Christian Church, rural Atlanta, Illinois, where he presently serves, especially to those men who were able to substantiate from experience several of the deductions he had made. He is appreciative of the administration of Lincoln Christian College for released time to pursue those studies in a doctoral program that led to the writing of this book. He is appreciative also of Dr. Keith Watkins and Dr. Lester G. McAllister of Christian Theological Seminary who gave initial encouragement to undertake the writing of this book. He acknowledges the gracious assistance given by Gwen Hicks and Donna Brumfield in typing portions of the manuscript.

The author's doctoral paper, "A Study of the Openness of Bible College Students of the Christian Churches/Churches of Christ to Change in Worship Practices," from which parts of Chapters One and Two of this book were adapted, rests in the library of Christian Theological Seminary, Indianapolis, Indiana, and the author acknowledges the approval of the administration of that seminary and the support of the librarian, Leslie R. Galbraith, for the publication of this selected material.

Part One — "HOW WE GOT HERE"

Chapter One

CONSIDERING THE HERITAGE OF THE PIONEERS

Leaders of the Christian Churches/Churches of Christ today, mirroring the custom of the earlier period, prefer to refer to themselves as a part of a movement rather than to their churches as a part of a denomination. That movement or fellowship—the Restoration Movement—is traced to the activities of a number of like-minded individuals of the early nineteenth century. Outspoken preachers, including such personages as Barton Warren Stone, Walter Scott, Thomas and Alexander Campbell, championed the cause of the quest for a united church on the basis of the restoration of what they deemed to be New Testament Christianity. It was the intent of these men to organize congregations that would practice only those simple rudiments of the Christian faith as they believed were plainly evident within the pages of the New Testament. Congregations with similar witness and expectation would thus find a certain compatibility with one another and Christian unity would be a reality at the grass roots level. An oft-spoken slogan was indicative of their doctrinal quest, "Where the Scriptures speak, we speak; where the Scriptures are silent, we are silent." Located as it was in the rugged setting of frontier America the movement captured the imagination of many people and the churches of these reformers grew rapidly.

The Influence of Alexander Campbell

Emerging from this group as the principal leader and the most signal influence was Alexander Campbell. From the early 1820s to the time of his death in 1866 he was without

1

peer as the revered spokesman and leader of the movement. It is with interest therefore that we search out his views concerning worship for those views were indeed normative for these churches of that period.

In 1828 Alexander Campbell commented:

> The New Testament contains no liturgy, no congregational service, as did the Old Testament. In the writings of the great Jewish apostle, Moses, there is a ritual, a liturgy, a tabernacle or temple service laid down; but no such thing is found in the apostolic epistles.[1]

While one must consider with reservation some of the opinions expressed by Campbell during this period of his life (as the critical iconoclast of the *Christian Baptist*) yet this particular statement does seem indicative of Campbell's life-long attitude toward the use of liturgy in respect to worship.

Basically Campbell's view was that the local congregation must be free to express its own wishes, needs, and interests in corporate worship. Yet while there is to be no prescribed liturgy it is imperative that all be done in decency and order. Campbell commented that whether the church "should first pray, sing, or read the Living Oracles; and at what period of her worship she should do this, or that, are matters left to the discretion" of the congregation and added that it was important "that all the ordinances shall be solemnly attended to, and that perfect order shall be preserved in all her worship."[2]

Campbell did state a simple philosophy of worship in his observation that when the congregation assembles, "that joy

---

1. Alexander Campbell, "Review of the History of Churches. No. II," *Christian Baptist* 5 (June 1828): 254.

2. Alexander Campbell, "Order of the Church as Respects Worship," *Millennial Harbinger* Extra—No. 8 (October 1835): 509.

in the Lord, that peace and serenity of mind, that affection for the brethren, that reverence for the institutions of God's house, which all feel, should be manifest in all the business of the day."[3] Therefore, "what is passing in the minds of all the worshippers" ought to determine the order of the worship itself.[4] Certain aspects of worship will take place, and these include "singing, praying, reading, teaching, exhorting, commemorating, communicating."[5]

In the mid 1830s a correspondent from Iowa, Francis W. Emmons, proposed that Acts 2:42 ("And they continued steadfastly in the apostles' doctrine and fellowship, and in breaking of bread, and in prayers,") presents a mandatory order of worship for those churches committed to restoring the New Testament pattern. Alexander Campbell objected editorially to Emmons' proposal. (This exchange is significant in light of the effort of a number of contemporary churches— see Chapter Two of this work—to utilize the same passage as a model for worship.) We note the brusqueness of Campbell's rejection of the proposal as he stated that "it would give to the Christian worship a liturgy, a ritual form like the Jewish, wholly incompatible with the genius of Christ's religion" and thus would make it "an intolerable idea, and hostile to the spirit and scope of the evangelical economy."[6] Rather various factors (as the "localities of particular communities, as to country, village, or city residence") will determine the sequence of what is done in worship, and that

---

3. Alexander Campbell, *The Christian System*, 4th ed. (Bethany, Va.: Printed by Alexander Campbell, 1857), p. 283.

4. Ibid.

5. Ibid.

6. Alexander Campbell, "Order of Worship," *Millennial Harbinger* New Series, 2 (June 1838): 247.

3

everything is "done decently and in order" it is necessary that the elders "have an understanding upon the time and place for everything; and then to have every thing in its proper time and place."[7] But always the criteria for structure is that there be freedom and performance within decency and order. Campbell enjoined: "It is pleasing, indeed, to see the brethren freely unite in one harmonious and general outline of worship in public assemblies."[8]

Thomas Campbell, Alexander's father, had stated much earlier in the monumental document, *Declaration and Address*, that "the New Testament is as perfect a constitution for the worship, discipline and government of the New Testament church . . . as the Old Testament was for the worship, discipline and government of the Old Testament church" (proposition 4). Alexander Campbell was in agreement with this—but he and the others saw the New Testament as a "constitution for worship" only in that it clearly set forth the essential aspects of worship, such as prayer, reading, singing, and the observance of the Lord's Supper.

Two distinct characteristics of the worship service stand out in Alexander Campbell's thinking. (1) The observance of the Lord's Supper is central to it all (that is, in terms of priority, not necessarily in fact of sequence). There could in fact be no legitimate worship after the New Testament model without the observance of the Lord's Supper. (2) The sermon was intentionally missing from the service of worship of the assembled congregation. Campbell made a sharp distinction between the role of preaching (*keryssein*) and that of teaching (*didaskein*). He viewed himself as a teacher

---

7. Ibid., p. 250.
8. Ibid.

and his own ministry as that of teaching. To be sure the evangelist had his proper, important role (as witness the success of Walter Scott with the full approval of Campbell) but it was not before the congregation assembled in Sunday worship. The Scriptures were indeed to be expounded on that occasion but in a manner suitable for edification and not with a view to evangelism.

Alexander Campbell, having said all this about his reluctance to utilize any particular liturgy, nonetheless did present a notable illustration about an order of worship that surely must have served as a model for early pioneer congregations. He commented, in the pages of *The Christian System* (first published in 1835), about a congregation that he had visited: "The following extract from my memorandum-book furnishes the nighest approach to the model which we have in our eye of good order and Christian decency in celebrating this institution." That service may be summarized as follows: a call to worship, a hymn, a reading from one of the Gospels, a prayer, a reading from one of the Epistles, a communion hymn, a statement about the Lord's Supper, a prayer for the bread, the breaking of the bread and distribution, a prayer for the cup and distribution, a prayer, the offering, the sharing by various members toward "the edification of the body" (this was the closest semblance to a sermon), several songs, and a benediction. My own impression of Campbell's lengthy description of the model worship is that it reminds me of the agenda of a modest business meeting.

The Contribution of Frontier Primitivism

For three decades and more from the time of their earliest beginnings the churches of the Restoration Movement—or

5

Disciples of Christ, as they were frequently called—were generally oriented in the frontier culture of the midwestern region now identified as Kentucky, Tennessee, Ohio, Indiana, Illinois, and Missouri. This frontier culture was in fundamental contrast to that of the inhabitants of the Eastern seaboard. A brief but adequate description of this simplistic society would be that of primitivism. Even as the area progressed deeply during the next half century into a rural-oriented society, simplicity of life-style remained as a clinging vestige of an earlier day.

Frontier life was simple, earthy, and emotional by its very nature, and this was reflected in the area of worship. Viewing religion as personal, free forms of worship were preferred. In a manner similar to that of the New England Puritans one hundred and fifty years earlier they desired such freedom of form that the Spirit might have liberty to work within the service.

The economic life of the frontier functioned at almost the lowest of levels. Much of the daily exchange was barter and trade. Precious little coinage was available for even the simplest of accoutrements of liturgical worship let alone the erection of buildings even modestly appointed for such a form of worship.

While in reality primitivism and simplicity do not always go together I believe that the assumption that they do is adequate for this study. One of the major proposals for the investigation of American history, that championed by Frederick Jackson Turner, suggests that the era of the American Frontier correlated directly to a certain phase of the westward migration of the early settlers. Therefore while some of the congregations of the Restoration Movement may have existed in conditions of frontier primitivism until the time of the Civil War yet it is my opinion that the decade of the 1840s marks the time when most of these congregations advanced to the next step of social development. Therefore we can establish a period of perhaps three decades —the formative decades indeed—in which a large percentage of the early members of the congregations of the Disciples (the Campbells) and the Christians (Stone) were influenced by the conditions of primitivism of the frontier.

A simple life, limited literacy, meager economy, geographical isolation, all were social factors that contributed to a simple worship style. This, plus the example of their respected leader, Alexander Campbell, established a style of simplicity in order of worship. I would make two further observations. (1) I believe that the particular interpretation of the nature of worship in the apostolic period which was held by these early nineteenth century Restorationists was in reality significantly influenced by the cultural conditions of the frontier. (It is my studied opinion that in contrast the first century Christians on occasion both used fixed forms of prayer and practiced a liturgical worship). (2) While the passing of the years brought a drastic, significant alteration of the once-primitive frontier society Disciples of Christ continued to cling to the simplistic worship styles because they had, I believe, adopted an incorrect biblical assumption for their actions, thinking that their worship practices were a very near approximation to the first century model rather than recognizing the influence of the frontier society.

Reliance on a Lay Ministry

In his early days as an editor Alexander Campbell had been extremely critical of the professional clergy. This helped establish a view of ministry among the Disciples that would endure for a generation or more. Limited educational facilities and a general economic impoverishment contributed to it. The outcome was that the ministry of the early Disciples was located in the "teaching elders," men who commonly were farmers by occupational status. As in all other things this was viewed as conforming to biblical precept. Always there was a plurality of elders—or "shepherds"—over a local congregation, though if the congregation was small the "plurality" might number no more than two. Election to the eldership was usually followed by a simple ceremony of ordination. Among the duties of the eldership was that of officiating at the observance of the Lord's Supper. In the early period one of the elders would be selected to serve on a given day (or one of the other men if there were no qualified elders) and that individual was called the "president of the day."

The early churches of the Disciples of Christ practiced "close communion," that is, only members of the general fellowship of the Disciples were permitted to commune with the local congregation. A statement by Isaac Errett in 1861 suggests however that by that time perhaps no more than a third of the congregations strictly observed "close communion."[9]

Alexander Campbell's First Hymnal

One of the first significant hymnals to be used by the Disciples of Christ was published by Alexander Campbell in 1828. It was entitled, *Psalms, Hymns, and Spiritual Songs,*

---

9. Isaac Errett, "Letter from I. Errett," *Millennial Harbinger* (December, 1861): 711.

Adapted to the Christian Religion, and bore the appended title, *Selected by Alexander Campbell.* The choice of the title is indicative of Campbell's biblical literalism, as Campbell himself observed that the choice of words was in reference to Paul's admonition: "TEACH and admonish one another in psalms, hymns, and spiritual songs."[10] Further, Campbell used these three groupings as the threefold division for the contents of his hymnal.

Of interest is the listing of certain recognizable hymns in the three categories he selected. In the section Psalms he included, "Jesus Shall Reign Where e'er the Sun," and, "Christ, the Lord is Risen Today." The only familiar Hymn was "All Hail the Power of Jesus' Name." Spiritual Songs included, "Come Ye that Love the Lord," "Glorious Things of Thee Are Spoken," "O God Our Help in Ages Past," and, "On Jordan's Stormy Banks I Stand." Included also in this latter section were thirty-two songs from the "Scotch version of David's Psalms." The hymnal was similar to several others of the period to which I compared it.

The Rise of a Professional Ministry

The first three decades of the history of the Disciples of Christ are unique in that they evidenced a general absence of any sort of a professional ministry. As we have noted, the function of teaching, the administration of the ordinances, and the shepherding of the flock were tasks performed by the elders of the local congregations. This was a non-professional role, for which the only training was a thorough, though elementary, study of the Scriptures. By the middle

10. Alexander Campbell, ed., *Psalms, Hymns, and Spiritual Songs, Adapted to the Christian Religion* (Bethany, Va.: By the Editor, 1828), p. ii. (The reference is to Colossians 3:16).

of the nineteenth century however a professional ministry began to rise. D. S. Burnett and Isaac Errett were perhaps the first men of this new breed of full-time pastors.

One consequence of this is of significant importance. The congregations therefore, in a sense, had a dual ministry, that of the pastors and of the elders. Today, elders of the Christian Churches/Churches of Christ are no longer considered "ministry" and yet almost without exception it is yet their responsibility and prerogative to preside at the Lord's Table.

A second consequence of this rise of professional ministry is that the sermon became a part of the Sunday morning worship service. While this was not unique to Protestant (or Roman Catholic) worship it was to the Disciples. With the sermon came the addition to the worship service of the invitation or the call to membership. (Please understand there had been preaching—much preaching—before but not in the gathered Sunday morning assembly.)

A Rising Awareness of a Need for "Order"

The changing nature of the ministry, plus the gradual but sure urbanization of midwestern society, emphasized the need for attention to order in worship in the maturing Disciples churches. This is reflected in articles appearing in the journals of the time. An editorial in the *Christian Standard,* in 1891, evidently written by the editor, Hugh McDiarmid, commented sarcastically that the usual order of worship (which he outlined as a hymn, reading of the Scriptures, prayer, hymn, and notices) merely served as introductory to "the great thing," the sermon. He concluded: "The idea of a grave, decorous, ornate, spiritual, helpful, devout ministration throughout, from opening hymn to

10

benediction, does not seem to occur to many leaders of Christian assemblies."[11]

B. A. Abbott, writing in *The Christian Evangelist* in 1907, commented that "the order and nature of the forms of public worship will be determined by the ends sought in the assembly" and added, "if conducted in the right way it will be of distinct value in the extension of the kingdom of God." He observed that an order of service "is the contribution of culture through art to the endeavor to make God and our fellowmen more real and precious to our own souls."[12]

The role of the local congregation as an institution was changing, as well as the physical facility of the local congregation to serve that institution. For example pipe organs were added and the one room buildings were being replaced by multi-room structures.

A Period of Change in Worship

The decades between 1880 and 1940 saw a number of changes in the worship customs of the churches of the Disciples of Christ. I shall note five of the more significant.

(1) Something of a change is noted in respect to the prominence accorded the celebration of the Lord's Supper as an act of worship. The respected Isaac Errett wrote in 1872 that the Lord's Supper was not viewed with the "awfulness of a sacrament" but rather as a "sweet and precious feast of holy memories" and a "joyful and refreshing feast of love."[13] By 1910, however, the sermon had replaced communion as the high point of worship, even though Disciples

---

11. [Hugh McDiarmid], "Order in Public Worship," *Christian Standard* 27 (July 11, 1891): 582.

12. B. A. Abbott, "Enriching the Order of the Services," *The Christian Evangelist* 44 (April 18, 1907): 496.

13. Isaac Errett, *Our Position*, cited in, James DeForst Murch, *Christians Only* (Cincinnati: Standard Publishing Company, 1962), p. 175.

continued to give lip service to communion as the "central act of worship." Consequently the sermon was moved to the end of the service, in the climactic point of worship. Many congregations made this very significant shift in the order of worship. While varying explanations are offered to account for this change in order I believe that one contributing factor was the fact that the people—at least the preacher—viewed it as most important.

(2) Worship manuals began to appear among the congregations. Perhaps the first such manual was one published in 1884 by John Burns, entitled *The Christian Minister's Manual*. In 1890 W. W. Dowling released *The Christian Psalter: A Manual of Devotion Containing Responsive Readings for Public Worship*. In 1904 James A. Lord, then editor of the *Christian Standard*, prepared *On The Lord's Day*, a book especially designed for small, isolated groups.

(3) The publication of new hymnals as useful manuals of worship became significant. Such a hymnal was William E. M. Hackleman's *Gloria in Excelsis—A Collection of Responsive Scripture Readings, Standard Hymns & Tunes, and Spiritual Songs*. Appearing in 1905, it was published jointly by the Christian Board of Publication, St. Louis, and the Hackleman Music Company, Indianapolis. The contents of the hymnal are most impressive and certainly illustrative of the interests that some congregations held in regard to worship: suggested orders of service, sentences for opening service, invocations, responsive readings (choral), the communion service (biblical texts), the baptismal service, baptismal chants (choral), the offering (biblical texts), offertory prayers, offertory sentences (choral), selections from the Psalms, responsive readings, eight indexes, eight hundred fourteen songs, five doxologies, benedictions and twenty-one ancient chants and canticles.

(4) The worship service was shortened from two or three hours to approximately one hour. This was done to accommodate the expansion of the Sunday school program which in turn fulfilled the purpose of the exposition of the Scriptures of Campbell's day.

(5) The widespread use of the mimeograph in the 1920s contributed greatly to the structuring of worship. Each worshiper could have in his or her hands a concise, manageable order of worship.

Division and Its Consequences for Worship

A movement committed to the quest for unity found itself confronted with the threat of division. By the mid 1920s members (and congregations) of the Disciples of Christ found themselves gravitating toward one of two positions—one that acknowledged the responsibility and integrity of an integrated national organization and one that emphasized the priority of local autonomy in respect to the polity of the congregations. (An earlier division in the late nineteenth century had seen the more conservative brethren go their separate way as the non-instrumental churches of Christ.) Underlying this polarization was the increasing focus on attachment to either a literal or liberal view of both the Scriptures and the historic principles of the Campbellian movement. By the mid-twentieth century lines would be drawn between the Christian Church (Disciples of Christ) and the independent Christian Churches/Churches of Christ. The Christian Church (Disciples of Christ) has been increasingly involved in the quest for liturgical renewal as evidenced by the appearance of *Christian Worship: A Service Book* in 1953 and more recent attention to the worship studies of the Consultation on Church Union (COCU).

In distinct contrast independent Christian Churches/ Churches of Christ however continued to follow the worship practices of an earlier generation of Disciples. Through the years of the 1940s and the 1950s the congregations of the Disciples and the independents at worship took divergent paths. Gradually the day came when a member of one branch of the national fellowship attended the worship services of a congregation of the other he or she would feel a certain unfamiliarity if not uneasiness with participation in the worship.

The leadership—both elders and ministers—of these independent congregations today (as for the past forty years) share a high view of inspiration that exalts the Bible and especially the New Testament as a unique directive from God—a veritable manual-of-arms for the guidance of the churches. Subsequently the leaders of these churches, anchored in this biblical view, have frequently identified the traditions of an earlier generation of Restorationists as a rather exacting correspondence to the first century practices—the inevitably correct scriptural norm.

Elders and ministers alike are committed to maintaining the orthodoxy of the institution. Ministers especially feel the need to conform to peer pressure, and in this instance to be as loyal to the sacrosanct traditions as are their colleagues. It is for this reason that the worship practices have been maintained so unvaryingly. Thus a paradox occurs. The reality of local autonomy as expressed and practiced by independent congregations normally provides an unrestrained freedom in which each local congregation can "do its own thing" with no sense of need for conformity to any outside pattern or trend. And yet at the same time ministers feel a need to conform to one another's expectations lest they be considered unfaithful to the Restoration heritage.

The truth remains that ours is a heritage of freedom in Christ. Let us use that freedom to prepare services of worship that adequately meet the spiritual needs of our people in these waning years of the twentieth century! We are dependent upon nineteenth century models only as long as they are pertinent to our needs. We are committed to the timeless model of the Scriptures which is always relevant!

Questions and Projects

1. Do some research to attempt to determine the nature of the worship of the Seceder Presbyterians in the early 1800s. (This is the church from which Thomas and Alexander Campbell exited.)
2. Write a brief essay on the meaning and significance of the slogan, "Where the Scriptures speak, we speak; where the Scriptures are silent, we are silent."
3. Why was there no place for a sermon in Alexander Campbell's Sunday morning worship order?
4. Why did Alexander Campbell object to making Acts 2:42 a mandatory model for an order of worship?
5. To what does the term "close communion" refer?
6. Examine carefully a copy of a hymnal that is at least one hundred years old. (Such can be found in the Lincoln Christian College library—as well as other facilities housing rare books.)
7. Why did the pioneers use a single, large communion cup and why did later generations change to the use of multiple cups?
8. Talk to an alert senior citizen who can remember worship services dating prior to 1900.

Chapter Two

SURVEYING THE PRESENT PRACTICES

Almost no serious attention has been given to a study of the worship practices of the Christian Churches/Churches of Christ. With this recognition in mind the author undertook such an investigation in 1980 as a part of his doctoral studies at Christian Theological Seminary. The study was limited to selected congregations in the states of Illinois and Indiana for the reasons that (1) this is the area of his personal experience and observation, and that (2) the churches of this two state area are representative of the heartland of the Restoration Movement both in point of origin and numerical strength today.

Two simultaneous avenues of research were undertaken. The first was the preparation and distribution of a survey to determine the attitudes and practices of the leaders of the churches. This survey was mailed to forty-nine ministers in Illinois and thirty in Indiana. Eighty-two percent of the people queried replied.

In the second phase of the study 119 worship bulletins were collected from seventy-two Illinois congregations and forty-seven in Indiana. These bulletins were analyzed in view of forty-four carefully prepared questions.

The Ministers' Sensitivity to Worship Precepts

This is perhaps the most difficult phase of this particular study to put in proper perspective. As a general observation I may note that ministers are not particularly sensitive to or appreciative of a study of worship practices though they are concerned that a joyful, legitimate worship takes place when the congregation assembles on Sunday morning.

As might be expected the traditional language of liturgics is shunned by ministers of these churches—not surprisingly,

16

for they have long been admonished to refer to "Bible things by Bible names." For example, the word "sacrament" is seldom used by the ministers and the word "fraction" never appeared in the bulletins. Only six ministers acknowledged that they used frequently one or more of the following prayers, collect, introit, litany, or bidding prayer, in the morning worship hour. Five ministers responded to the query that they had worn a pulpit robe—but only at the occasion of a wedding.

A considerable number of the ministers use on occasion a worship manual—though it is not likely they would refer to it as such as perhaps even recognize it as such. A principal manual may be identified as James DeForest Murch's *Christan Minister's Manual.* (It should be noted that a basic purpose of this particular manual is to provide information and resource material for weddings, funerals, and other special services, and it is quite likely that the manual is most often used in this fashion.)

Ministers were asked to give a word association for two ideas, "liturgy" and "high church." The response to the second idea is interesting as twenty-six replied with the word, "formal." Three suggested "highly structured" and two each put forth the words, "cold," "Catholic," and "episcopal." I think this is significant because one could, with a proper understanding of the phrase, identify Alexander Campbell with a high church position.

My conclusion from all this data coupled with my candid observation of these churches for over twenty-five years in a ministerial role is that while the ministers are becoming somewhat increasingly sensitive to an awareness of sound worship practice yet their attitude is to be distinguished sharply from that of their counterparts in the mainline denominations including those of the Disciples of Christ with whom they share a common historical development. Ministers of the Christian Churches/Churches of Christ view their role in Sunday morning worship as prophetic and not priestly. They are preachers—proclaimers of the Word— and not clergypeople in the traditional sense.

The Order of the Morning Service

Seventy-seven percent of the ministers noted that the sermon followed the Lord's Supper in the order of worship, and the Sunday worship bulletins confirmed an even higher ratio of eighty-five percent for the sermon coming after the Lord's Supper. This order of sequence may reflect an earlier day when a minister was not always available and the sermon was appended on those occasions when one was present— or it may reflect something of priority attached to the sermon (as we shall note later in this chapter). In sixty-four percent of the congregations the offering follows the Lord's Supper in the order of worship.

I attempted subjectively to classify the 119 worship services as portrayed in the bulletins as to the nature of order they seemingly present. Sixty percent simply presented the items of worship in sequence as one might prepare an agenda for a business meeting. (And this is not unlike the example established more than a century ago by Alexander Campbell.) Thirty-two percent presented an order of worship where a deliberate attempt has been made to structure the sequence of the respective acts of worship under an outline of subheadings. In eighteen instances of this latter group— or almost half—the effort has been to embody those features stated in Acts 2:42. In others the effort has been to focus on the major themes of worship, to be provocative, or perhaps to present an attention-catching format. Let us first focus our attention on the more frequent pattern above.

Acts 2:42 states of the early Christians that "they continued steadfastly in the apostles' doctrine and fellowship, and in breaking of bread, and in prayers." While most scholars of either the New Testament or of worship would not see this passage as a pattern for the sequence of worship, eighteen congregations use these four subjects as subheadings under which the various items of worship are listed. For example, one church simply lists three subheadings as, "In Fellowship and Prayers," "In the Breaking of Bread," and "In the Apostles' Doctrine."

Ten other congregations follow a similar yet distinctly different sequence of subheadings. In these instances the subheadings are such as, "Worship in Praise and Song," "Worship in Breaking Bread," "Worship in Giving," and "Worship in Message and Decision." Four services apparently attempt to capture in the subheadings something of the movement of worship. For example, one service lists quite dramatically, "Vision," "Confession and Renewal," and "Commitment." Another presents, "We Approach God in Praise and Prayer," "God Approaches Us Through the Preaching of His Word," "We Respond to God," and "We Fellowship with One Another."

The worship bulletins, selected at random as they were, present a total of twelve baptismal services as listed in the order of worship. Of these ten came at the close of the worship—probably for the convenience of the minister and those who made physical arrangements for the opening of the baptismal facility.

Place of Priority—Lord's Supper or Sermon?

When queried as to what they viewed as "most significant

19

at the Sunday morning worship hour" forty ministers selected from among "Lord's Supper," "sermon," "prayer," and "scripture reading" the Lord's Supper as most significant. Fourteen responded with the sermon. Seven respondents footnoted that the Lord's Supper and sermon were equally significant, and another six (there was some duplication in answering) said that while in theory it was the Lord's Supper in actual practice it was the sermon.

Two other pertinent questions were directed to the ministers in the Congregational Worship Awareness survey. In response to, "Would the congregation consider it to be a complete worship service if there were no sermon on a particular Sunday morning?," twenty ministers replied, yes, but more than twice that many—forty-four—replied, no. This is interesting, especially in light of Alexander Campbell's position that there was no place for a sermon in the Sunday worship assembly. The ministers responded to the question, "Do you consider the sermon an integral part of worship, or is it rather in a sense a very important act appended to the worship hour?" Fifty-nine answered that it was an integral part, thus making an emphatic affirmative for the validity of preaching as inherent to worship. Four stated that it was an appended act.

I have observed for years that the members of these churches and especially the leaders of these congregations have given lip service at least to the position that the observance of the Lord's Supper is the most important act that is observed when Christians gather together. (In fact I am surprised that only sixty-two percent of the ministers list it as most significant.) I have noticed on many occasions that worshipers when departing early from the services will choose to leave immediately after the observance of the Lord's Supper.

20

I believe that ministers of the Christian Churches/Churches of Christ do consider—subconsciously perhaps—the act of preaching to be more important than that of the observance of the communion. Time and time again I have sensed the momentum of worship rise as the minister takes his place behind the pulpit. Similarly, I have noted on numerous occasions a routine, if not unimaginative, approach to the celebration of the Lord's Supper. I have perceived the over-riding theme of many Sunday services of these congregations to be evangelism (or at least exhortation and teaching) and not worship. The very position of the sermon at the climactic point of the service is indicative of this. (Recall that this position in the order occurred from seventy-seven to eighty-five percent of the time in the two surveys I conducted.) There are other factors that might explain the appearance of the sermon in this position but I do not believe that these factors totally account for the situation as we find it. It may be that frequent positioning of the sermon in this place of climactic prominence accounts for its significance but I rather think it is the significance attached to the sermon by the ministers that causes it to retain its place at the climax of the service. I am confident that the reality of the situation belies that to which these surveys attest, that at least for the ministry of Christian Churches/Churches of Christ the sermon is the most significant aspect of the worship service.

The Use of the Scriptures

It was in this area of my research that I received the greatest surprise. A survey of the worship bulletins indicated that twenty-nine percent of the congregations listed no scripture reading at any point whatsoever; there was no mention of a

call to worship, scripture at the celebration of the communion, or scripture in connection with the sermon—simply
none at all! It would be my assumption that in most of these
instances the reading of scripture did occur and that the
evidence at my disposal represents nothing more than an
omission in the printed order. (However four ministers
responded to one question of the survey by specifically
answering that no scriptures were read in the Sunday service.)
Nonetheless the situation is rather startling in view of the
preponderance of acclaim that the leaders of these churches
place on being a "people of the Book," a "true to the Bible"
fellowship, etc. Also it is to be noted that only one minister
selected the scripture reading as the most significant act
of the Sunday morning worship.

On a more positive note however, in response to the
survey eighteen ministers said one passage of scripture was
commonly read, twenty-one indicated two passages, nine
replied with three passages, and twelve with more than
three. The survey of worship bulletins revealed that forty-
eight percent of the congregations have a scripture lesson
in the course of the morning worship. Further, the average
number of verses read—inasmuch as it was possible to determine from the information presented in the bulletins—
was slightly more than eight. The survey also indicated that
only two congregations used a responsive reading on that
particular Sunday.

People of these congregations have little appreciation for
the traditional practice of standing at the reading of the
words of Jesus. When questioned none of the ministers said
that the people did so exclusively though in nine congregations the people stand for the reading of scripture in
general.

Prayer

One of the areas of strength within the worship service of the Christian Churches/Churches of Christ is that of the significance attached to the role of prayer. A tabulation of the worship bulletins indicated that seventeen percent of the congregations specifically provided an opportunity for prayer requests during the morning assembly. (Other congregations might do that without notation appearing in the printed order.) Several worship bulletins listed names of those who were to be mentioned in prayer. Twenty-eight percent of the congregations provided an opportunity in the order of worship for silent prayer. Only four bulletins had mention of congregational recitation of the Lord's Prayer. It is my recollection that these churches at a time twenty and thirty years ago made much more frequent use of the Lord's Prayer in public worship.

Music

Singing is a significant part of the services of these churches. An effort is made to involve people in the singing through special music as well as through careful attention to congregational singing. The mood of the musical portion of the service is determined by the predominant selection of gospel songs—and yet this is somewhat balanced by the use of the Doxology and the occasional use of hymns.

Examining those bulletins where the selected songs were named it is to be noted that only fifteen percent might be classified as hymns—the remainder being gospel songs or, in some instances, choruses. Included among those hymns that occurred more than once in the worship bulletins were "All Hail the Power of Jesus' Name," "Amazing Grace,"

"Rock of Ages," and "When I Survey the Wondrous Cross." The songs that appeared most frequently in the services were "How Great Thou Art" (nine times) and "Trust and Obey" (seven times). Songs selected for the celebration of communion included "Break Thou the Bread of Life," "Near the Cross," and "'Tis Midnight." Most of the congregations used a closing chorus which consisted of such songs as "Blest be the Tie that Binds," "The Family of God," "Follow, I Will Follow Thee," and "God Be with You til We Meet Again."

In a different mood of music forty-seven percent of the congregations used the Doxology. Six congregations used the Gloria Patri. In only four worship bulletins were "anthems" actually mentioned. Only two services made mention of organ selections such as Bach.

The nature and mood of music as used in the Christian Churches/Churches of Christ is thus clearly defined. The old hymns of the church are respected but yet rather infrequently used. Much more common is the use of gospel songs. Enthusiastic, robust singing is encouraged and even considered to be a good mark of worship.

Officiants in the Service

Of interest at this point is the way the congregations view the role of the ministers, the elders, and others in the ministration of the services. Are there duties that are peculiarly those of either the minister or the elder? Who serves at the Lord's Table? Who officiates at the rite of baptism? Is ordination a prerequisite to the performance of any function?

A survey of the worship bulletins indicates that in twenty-six congregations a worship leader is listed in addition to the minister. In other instances presumably a worship leader served though unmentioned in the bulletin. In a number of instances an associate minister was also listed as participating in the service.

When queried as to who presides at the communion service during the Sunday morning worship hour, fifty responses indicated that it was an elder. Another ten responses indicated that it was someone other than the minister. The question was posed, "Who would serve at the table (Lord's Supper) if no elders were present?" Ten answered that the minister would, while six more suggested that a deacon would. The majority however answered that "any member" could preside, as forty-five answers listed this alternative. (Some felt the need to clarify this point by adding such notes as "all our men take turns at the table," "it would have to be a male," and "any male.")

The ministers were asked if an elder of the congregation had performed a baptism in the period of the last five years. The responses were that in forty-six congregations elders had and in the other nineteen they had not. All this is not to suggest that the practice of laypeople administering baptism is widespread among these churches, for commonly it is the minister who performs the act of baptism.

It is apparent that there is in the thinking of these people a division of function established by custom—and not by the Scriptures—between the duties of the elders and the minister. The minister's task, at least in respect to the worship assembly, is to proclaim the word, to preside at the worship service (excluding that portion which is the celebration of the Lord's Supper), and to baptize, and the elders' task is to preside at the celebration of the Lord's Supper. In instances of necessity the roles can be reversed.

The Layperson's View of Worship

Ministers were asked to express an opinion as to what

the people of their congregations viewed as the most significant aspect of the morning worship hour. As might be anticipated the leading answer was the Lord's Supper, indicated by thirty-four respondents. Twenty-four named the sermon and one suggested prayer. No one selected the reading of the Scriptures.

However when asked for what aspect of the worship service people most frequently express appreciation, the answer came back, music (as "music," "special music," and "songs"), forty-two, and prayer, twenty-one. The Lord's Supper was mentioned only nine times and fellowship received one mention. (Respondents were instructed to respond to this query with an answer other than "sermon" that a more realistic appraisal might be obtained).

A rather telling response came from the reply of the ministers to the questions, "Do you think that the structure and mood of the Sunday morning worship is influenced more by adherence to New Testament example or by the needs and requests of the people?" Thirty-three responded that it was the needs and requests of the people while only twenty-six stated that it was adherence to New Testament example. Given the historic emphasis of these people for the restoration of New Testament Christianity and considering the biblical literalness of their approach to the Scriptures, one might expect a far higher percentage selecting the former answer, adherence to New Testament example.

Children and Worship

An examination of the worship bulletins indicates that the services are not generally structured with the children in mind. Nor are the songs selected with a view to appealing to youthful interests. Correctives were noted however. Sometimes youth choirs contributed to the worship hour. Six services did indicate that a children's sermon was delivered in addition to the morning message. Seventeen percent of the congregations did list a separate children's church. In some instances elders and deacons appear before these children, duplicating some of the features of the adult worship.

It is my observation and estimate that the majority of all congregations of the Christian Churches/Churches of Christ, at least those in the midwest, now employ a youth minister, in sharp contrast to three decades ago when one minister was responsible for all activities of the congregation. Thus I assume that more options for worship experience for the youth are available than are indicated in the bulletins.

The Bulletin as an Aid to Worship

After examining the worship bulletins I have the definite impression that ministers pattern these services after one another's models. This tends to produce a certain uniformity of order.

In half of the bulletins people are given instructions as to when to stand during the service. In forty-five percent of the bulletins instructions are printed to guide people in participation in the communion service. (Customs vary so much from congregation to congregation that information of this sort is appreciated by the one who is a stranger to the service.) Twenty-four percent of the bulletins offer guidelines to the non-member for responding to the invitation for membership.

A definite effort on the part of the minister and the congregation to be friendly is evident in the worship bulletins. Fifty congregations have a period when a welcome is extended to all. In fourteen bulletins a definite time is included in the order for the recognition of visitors. Twenty-six bulletins designate a time within the limits of the worship period to sign roll call cards. Three bulletins list the recognition of birthdays during the worship service—and other congregations include this in the announcements.

Summation

Leaders of the Christian Churches/Churches of Christ interpret the Sunday morning congregational assembly as basically an occasion for proclamation of the Word and for fellowship. This is in sharp contrast to mainline protestant bodies that view the same hour as one of praise and the reception of grace through participation in the sacraments.

With that interpretation of the worship hour in mind the leaders of the Christian Churches/Churches of Christ are consistent in their liturgical view of worship. Such a view supports doctrinally (content) what they believe to be the major priorities of the mission of their churches and carries out structurally (form) a sequence of acts of worship that undergirds and emphasizes those priorities.

Certain weaknesses are inherent in this view of worship. The use of music is for purposes primarily other than that of being expressive of adoration to God. There is a potential risk of failing to grasp the full sacramental meaning of the celebration of the Lord's Supper and to relegate it to a position of less than major priority. The reading of the Scriptures—traditional to protestant worship since the earliest days of the Reformation—may be minimized or even neglected, and there is no surety that a balanced program of the public reading of the Scriptures will be followed. The service of worship has a tendency to become human-oriented rather than God-centered.

There are, however, strong points observed in this particular view of worship. There is powerful proclamation of the Word, motivated by a biblical imperative for evangelism. There is a strong celebration of the Lord's Supper as a remembrance of the Lord's death. There is a robust, personal involvement of the laypeople in the activity of worship, reflecting an awareness of the concept of the priesthood of believers. There is a strong sense of the family of the congregation, as evidenced both in the attention to personal prayer requests and the expressive words of the closing choruses.

Questions and Projects

1. Examine carefully James DeForest Murch's book, *Christian Minister's Manual.*
2. Give your own word association for "liturgy" and "high church."
3. Does the observance of communion precede or follow the sermon in the order of worship of the congregation you attend? Do you know why?
4. What do you consider the more important in the morning worship, the observance of the Lord's Supper or the sermon?
5. At how many different places in the order of worship of your congregation is the Bible read?
6. Does the Sunday morning worship service of your congregation make provision for prayer requests? If so, how?
7. List your ten favorite songs of worship and then attempt to categorize them as hymns, gospel songs, or choruses.

Chapter Three

EXAMINING THE BIBLICAL MODEL

Christian Churches/Churches of Christ maintain a strict, traditional interpretation of the historic principles of the nineteenth century unity movement initiated by Thomas and Alexander Campbell and Barton Warren Stone. Their continuing emphasis on the restoration of New Testament Christianity was among the contributing factors that led to their separation from the national body of the Disciples of Christ in the mid-decades of the twentieth century. Their cry for the restoration of New Testament Christianity remains as a significant rallying point for their leaders today.

Such a quest is certainly legitimate at the present time. Thus it is well that individuals of the Christian Churches/Churches of Christ pursue the search for a better understanding of those matters that relate to the essential life, doctrine, and mission of the primitive church. Basic to such study would be an investigation of the worship practices and beliefs of that early church.

It is the opinion of this writer that many—if not most—of the leaders of the Christian Churches/Churches of Christ assume that worship in the first century was characterized as simple and informal, with prayers offered extemporaneously, and certainly non-clerical in its nature. In a word, at least in respect to structure and order, they view that early worship as non-liturgical. I believe however that this view of the worship life of the early church is in reality the inheritance of these people from an earlier day of frontier primitivism. It was the rejection by the Campbells of creeds, clericalism, and the physical accoutrements of luxuriant worship facilities coupled with the simplistic life-style of frontier America (where these churches thrived) that produced a view of worship that subsequently was equated with the disposition of worship of the first century.

With this assumption in mind we turn to an examination of worship in the first century period. A cursory survey indicates that only minimal information can be gained from the New Testament Scriptures about the actual order of the services of the churches. Rather therefore our purpose is to concentrate on those aspects that relate specifically to an appreciation of the temperament and disposition of those worship services. Such a study includes an examination of the relevant biblical texts and the commentaries on those texts as well as the available literature by noted scholars on the subject. Some attention is given to the entire panorama of Israelitish and Jewish worship for it was in this milieu that the church was brought into existence.

Worship in the First Century Synagogue

Though there is considerable question about the origin of the institution of the synagogue it was apparently in existence as early as the Exile as a substitute for religious expression for a people no longer able to participate in the Temple worship. With the eventual return to Jerusalem and the rebuilding of the Temple the synagogue continued to perform an important role as an institution for worship. By the time of the first century of the Christian era the Temple became little more than a symbol for the great majority of Jews who did not live in Jerusalem. Most of the people simply did not register attendance at the Temple service. Distances and modes of transportation made it difficult if not impossible. This is further evidenced by the fact that at the time of the cessation of Temple worship (A.D. 70) the Talmud indicates there were three hundred ninety-four synagogues in Jerusalem. Eventually the Temple was destroyed but corporate worship continued. It was this

31

corporate worship—in the synagogue—that is significant to the origins of the worship of the church.

The synagogue came out of the effort to give religious expression to the masses. The worship was structured to meet their needs. Thus the worship was twofold: to provide an opportunity for a public expression of praise and to provide an occasion for the study of the Scriptures.

The synagogue itself was usually a simple building appointed with minimal, necessary items for worship, a raised podium, a seat for the learned teacher, and an "ark" to contain the sacred scrolls. The offices of the synagogue were lay positions: a president (or "ruler") selected by virtue of his age and integrity from among the male company of the synagogue, and his assistant (or "minister"). Priests served only on such occasions as they were invited to do so by the president—and even then certainly not in the traditional priestly role.

While there was a daily synagogue service it was the longer, morning sabbath service that is of particular interest to us. It is generally agreed that through most of the first century of the Christian era the liturgy was not fixed, so only general observations about the order and content can be noted here.

The service was opened with psalms, such as especially Psalm 19, 32, 34, 90, 91, 92, 135, and 136. Then the *Shema* was recited by the congregation, consisting of the texts of Deuteronomy 6:4-9; 11:13-21; and Numbers 15:37-41. The main prayer followed, called the Eighteen Benedictions or the Eighteen Blessings. It was offered by a man appointed by the "minister." (Note: the word "minister" is used here in the sense of "assistant," not as "clergyman" according to our modern usage.) Next came the readings in the Hebrew text from the Law and the

Prophets. Various members of the congregation participated in this. Following this was the translation of these same passages into the Aramaic of the audience (i.e. their normal, conversational language). Then, often but not always, an expository address on the text (probably the Prophets rather than the Law) was delivered to the congregation by a male participant selected by the "ruler." (Thus Jesus so spoke at Nazareth, Luke 4:21ff., and Paul at Antioch in Pisidia, Acts 13:15ff.) If a priest were present he would close the service with a benediction or blessing. A doxology might be used.

The synagogue service of Jesus' day might be characterized as offering freedom within a somewhat structured framework. Within this flexibility there was a certain compulsory definiteness as the Eighteen Benedictions must be used (though in turn the text for these benedictions was not yet fixed during the first century). Thus there was a certain rigidity in the order (*Shema*, prayer, reading, translation, exposition, and benediction) and yet flexibility as regards content within that order.

The Eighteen Benedictions prayer is recognized as a classic example of Jewish petitionary prayer. During the first century the text of that prayer was indeed both variable and adaptable. (For example in "emergency situations" a greatly abbreviated form might be used.) Though the text was not fixed nonetheless any recitation of it would indicate deliberate preparation and reflection on the part of the one praying as well as reverent reliance on the traditional texts shared with so many other worshipers. Thus one notes in the prayer something of the stateliness of the presentation as well as the majesty of the God revealed. These prayers are words of beauty, struck with a note of solemnity.

The synagogue worship was, as we have noted, essentially a lay religion. There was no necessary ordained clergy nor a hereditary priesthood. A synagogue could be formed wherever as few as ten Jewish males gathered for worship. Any one with adequate learning could lead the synagogue in prayer and in the reading of the Scriptures or the exposition thereof. Both men and women participated in the congregational response to the worship though they were segregated as to their stance in the building. (Further, the men were bareheaded and the women veiled.) All stood for the prayers and all responded to each individual segment of the Eighteen Benedictions with a vocal "amen."

It has been noted above that the scripture reading, delivered from the Hebrew text, was to be translated publicly into Aramaic that there might be actual communication of the message. Any competent person—even a minor—was permitted to do this. The translator, though permitted to translate the text at a prior time, was expected to follow the original text at the time of the public reading. The translation was to be accurate to the original text and yet not follow it in a woodenly literal way. It is obvious from this that the first century Jewish worshipers did not hold a particular translation of the Scriptures sacrosanct in the fashion that an earlier generation of twentieth century American Protestants revered the King James version. Some have suggested that an early lectionary was used to select the passages that were read but the evidence is scanty and inconclusive.

Worship in the First Century Church

The earliest constituency of the Christian community was predominantly Jewish. These were a people who shared a

34

heritage for a millennium of the Temple worship and its significance for their historical development. The participation of their parents in the synagogue institution extended for some three centuries or more. It seems rather unrealistic at first thought that a people with such a rich experience should suddenly reject that manner of worship and embark on a different passage. Such of course is possible however and the next phase of our investigation will be to consider the worship of the first century Christians with a special view to their Jewish backgrounds.

It is seemingly apparent from the New Testament narrative that the early Christians did reject the Temple cultus. There is for example no mention in the Acts of the Apostles of the Christians being involved in the daily sacrifices. That they were present at the hours of sacrifice is evident, but it was for purposes other than that of actual involvement in the service.

The attitude of the early Jewish Christians toward the synagogue worship is, I believe, a different matter. The very purpose of the public assembly was similar to that of the synagogue—to provide both for public prayer and for public instruction in the Scriptures. (Though more extensive than this, the outline suggested in Acts 2:42 for the church is not incompatible with the description of the function of the synagogue.) James 2:2 may reflect something of a sense of this interrelation between the two as it is noted that the "assembly" of the Christians is actually "synagogue" in the Greek text (eis sunagogēn)—though admittedly this is the only reference in the New Testament where that word is used in reference to the church.

The early Christians gathered for worship at dawn and at sunset, perhaps following the Jewish custom of gathering at similar times as the designated hours of prayer. Later as the church spread into the Gentile world different social pressures came to bear on the designated periods for assembly for worship.

It is difficult to ascertain precisely how closely the early church followed the model of the synagogue though the general consensus of the authorities that I have examined is that the early church was strongly influenced by the pattern of synagogue worship. Nothing in the New Testament texts significantly contradicts this basic assumption. This is not to suggest that the early church adopted verbatim the prayer texts of the synagogue. There is no evidence to suggest this—and certainly the Jewish texts were not fixed during the period. The influence of the synagogue is one that lies in the areas of the basic components of worship and the general disposition of worship rather than that of the actual sequence and/or the adoption of liturgical texts.

There were no service books during this period in either the church or the synagogue. Prayers were recited from memory and thus were transmitted in the church even as they had been for generations in the synagogue. Worshipers conformed to the proven liturgies of the day and yet were open to the working of the Spirit. I would characterize the period as one of the synthesis of structure and flexibility.

It is doubtful that the four points of the corporate life of the church as mentioned in Acts 2:42 actually constitute an outline for the sequence of worship. Though these four points are surely embodied in the movement of worship in any specified service it is much too simplistic to suppose that they actually constitute a statement about the sequence of worship. The worship of the early church included these four aspects even as it included the aspects of worship found in the synagogue service but the aspects themselves do not inherently suggest an outline of worship.

That the eucharistic meal was central to the worship of the early church is readily apparent. (Incidentally the word *eucharist* is derived from a word the early Christians used to refer to the Lord's Supper, from "thanksgiving.") It seems evident—at least in the Jerusalem church—that the Lord's Supper was observed on a daily basis at the beginning, even as Jews had attended daily to the services in the synagogue. The passing of the years coupled with the adversity of physical conditions saw this daily worship observance erode to a weekly celebration situated on the "day of the sun"—the day commemorating for the early Christians (among other reasons) the resurrection of the Lord. A few additional points may be surmised from evidences (both biblical or historical) of the day. First, the synoptic gospels and I Corinthians contain accounts of the observance in the Upper Room (see Matt. 26:26-29; Mark 14:22-25; Luke 22:17-20; and I Cor. 11:23-25) that may have served as words of institution or consecration in the worship of the first century eucharistic celebration even as the reading of these texts serves such a purpose in the worship of many churches today (Christian Churches/Churches of Christ included). Second, it is quite likely in the first century that the actual elements of bread and wine were contributed by the participants in the service. Thus the celebration of the Lord's Supper would include among other aspects a sense of stewardship—an awareness long since misplaced by the church. Third, the use of a single cup by Jesus in the observance in the Upper Room was no doubt perpetuated by the early church even as it would be by the church in medieval and modern times. (Senior citizens in the Christian Churches/Churches of Christ today have related to me on several occasions that the single cup was yet used in their memory and eliminated only for hygenic purposes in the early years of the twentieth century.)

Several scholars affirm that the Lord's Prayer (as Christians have familiarly named the prayer recorded in Matthew 6:9-13 and in abbreviated form in Luke 11:2-4) performed a significant role in the early liturgy of the church. They testify that it is a most excellent example of proper Jewish prayer form. Thus it is suggested by some that the Lord's Prayer served essentially the same purpose for the early church as the Eighteen Benedictions did for the synagogue, and that further, this was a conscious substitution.

It is my impression from surveying the New Testament that the Jewish custom of public reading from the Law and the Prophets was quickly adapted by the young church. It is evident that the New Testament authors made a conscious effort to show the fulfillment of prophecy (from the Old Testament writings) in the life of Jesus. Further, the recitation of the Psalms long used by the Jews as acclamations of praise surely replaced the readings from the Law for the Christians, in light of the latter's attitude toward the Temple worship. (In this instance I believe that recognition of the significance of long-standing historical custom must be the determinative factor in ascertaining the practice of the early church.) As apostolic writings became available it is quite apparent that they were read in the public Christian assemblies.

Jewish worshipers had long practiced the custom of standing for prayers with their hands lifted towards heaven. This custom was continued by the early Christians and followed until perhaps A.D. 200, and even then it was continued on Sundays and festivals. Similarly, as had the Jews, the Christians stood for the sermons, though Augustine at a much later time recommended sitting if possible. Paul admonished the women to be silent in the church, as I Corinthians 14:34 records. ("Let your women keep silence in the churches: for it is not permitted unto them to speak; but they are commanded to be under obedience, as also saith the law.") This followed precisely the custom of the synagogue. This attitude would continue for centuries in most societies into which the church was extended. It is suggested by some that the appearance of the "Holy Kiss" in the New Testament (Rom. 16:16; II Cor. 13:12; I Thess. 5:26; and I Peter 5:14) indicates that this act was a fixed worship practice.

There are a number of brief passages within the New Testament texts that scholars have identified as fragments from hymns or liturgies of the early church. Such a passage is Ephesians 5:14, especially obvious when it is read in the text of the New English Bible. (Indeed the verse is such as might be used in a present day baptismal service.) Other passages that may well be excerpts from early hymns (or perhaps doctrinal statements) include I Timothy 1:17; 3:16; II Timothy 2:11-13; Colossians 1:15-20; Philippians 2:6-11; Hebrews 1:3; Romans 11:34-35; I Corinthians 15:3-5; and Ephesians 1:11-13.

It is of course quite evident that benedictions appear in the New Testament text, and we may here note: "The grace of our Lord Jesus Christ be with you" (I Cor. 16:23); "Brethren, the grace of our Lord Jesus Christ be with your spirit. Amen" (Gal. 6:18); and, "The grace of our Lord Jesus Christ be with you all. Amen" (Rev. 22:21). Possible doxologies may be found in Romans 11:36; II Corinthians 11:31; and Ephesians 1:3. The very use of a doxology suggests Jewish origin. Explicit reference to the congregational "amen" is made in I Corinthians 14:16.

Certain passages as the *Magnificat* (Luke 1:46-55), the *Benedictus* (Luke 1:68-79), the *Gloria in excelsis* (Luke 2:14), and the *Nunc Dimittis* (Luke 2:29-32) are unique in the worship use of the historic church. The only question would be as to how early they were first utilized in that fashion.

Our purpose in presenting the above texts is to make manifestly obvious the majestic beauty of the passages. Consider the rhythm, the mood, the solemnity, the grandeur, the lyric quality of the readings. They strike a joyous chord. Admittedly such characteristics could be found in biblical writings that were not used in liturgical fashion and yet the presence of such qualities in obvious contrast to the adjoining texts certainly supports the thesis that they represent significant glimpses of the worship of the first century church.

Conclusion and Summation

The worship experience of the early church was both rich and warm. Of it we may make these observations:

(1) The earliest Christian community was predominantly Jewish in its ethnic and cultural makeup. It shared a tradition that was rich in experiences derivative from both the Temple worship and the synagogue. Further, it is the consensus of present scholarship that the worship of this Christian community was influenced significantly by its Jewish backgrounds. It would be illogical, so it seems to me, to reason otherwise.

(2) That aspect of the Jewish background which was especially significant to the worship life of the early church was that of the synagogue. Worship of the synagogue is characterized as being within a framework that was both

flexible and yet structured. It was marked by its constant attention to praise and scripture. The disposition of the mood of that worship may be described as truly liturgical— traditional, theologically expressive, moving and lyrical.

(3) The New Testament records bear only minimal references to the actual structure of the worship of the first century church. Yet such evidences as are to be observed indicate that a vital corporate worship experience was shared by the early Christians. It was a worship experience that utilized the same basic components of expression as the synagogue yet with no particular regard that the order of the synagogue service be maintained. It was a worship that, like the contemporary synagogue service, featured no fixed liturgical texts or service books yet was quite sensitive to traditional practices. It was a service that centered around a eucharistic meal—and in this indicated a departure from the Jewish norms. It was a service that perhaps at points made conscious substitutions for the Jewish precedents, as the Lord's Prayer for the Eighteen Benedictions and a credal statement (e.g., I Cor. 15:1-5) for the *Shema*. It was a service that reflected the leaders' concern for the vocal recitation of the sacred texts—though the selection of those texts was drastically altered by the Christian community.

(4) A careful consideration of the supposed "hymn fragments" to be found in the New Testament texts reflects the remarkable quality of the Christian worship. That worship at least in some measure followed the temperament if not the content of its synagogue antecedents. Such temperament is marked by the joyous, lyrical, and solemn majesty of the personal encounter with the Father.

Thus in conclusion I affirm that the historical quest of the Christian Churches/Churches of Christ for the restoration

41

of New Testament Christianity is most definitely a legitimate one, especially in this present day of renewed witness for the unity of the church. It is quite likely that leaders of these churches have previously made incorrect deductions about the nature of the worship of the early church. Basic assumptions can be investigated and where necessary corrected. Further studies along lines suggested here can provide both an increasingly rich experience for worshipers within the Restorationist fellowship as well as the opening of avenues to a closer realization of the unity of the universal church.

Questions and Projects

1. What is the single, basic principle by which the worship services of Christian Churches/Churches of Christ are patterned?
2. Does the New Testament give explicit information about the order of worship in the first century church?
3. Was the "minister" of a first-century synagogue a clergyman?
4. Visit a synagogue; talk to one of its leaders about their worship today.
5. What was the pattern for the selection of scriptural readings in the synagogue and the early church?
6. Read the book of Acts and/or the epistles noting every reference that illuminates the first century practice of worship.
7. Locate and read Justin Martyr's account of worship in the second century church.

Chapter Four

DEFINING A BIBLICAL VIEW OF WORSHIP

Before one can prepare that culinary delight, barbecued smoked pheasant, one must have a rather precise knowledge of and cultivated taste for barbecued smoked pheasant. (The recipe calls for chopped onions, chili powder, brown sugar, and catsup. Nebraska readers who wish to pursue this cooking venture are urged to invite the author to their home—preferably on opening day of the hunting season!) Similarly if we are to commit ourselves to the preparation on a regular basis of a worship service that adequately meets the definition of a model of biblical worship we must first have a rather precise and knowledgeable understanding of what constitutes biblical worship.

To undertake such an examination is especially relevant for leaders representing a fellowship of congregations committed to the restoration of New Testament Christianity. In fact to do otherwise would place one in the position of being unfaithful to the heritage of those congregations.

The biblical record contains ample evidence for an examination of this fashion. An appropriate place to begin is with a dictionary study of the words used for "worship" and "prayer."

The Word "Worship" in the New Testament

Basically there are three words in the Greek text of the New Testament that are used to express the idea that is conveyed in the English translations by a single word, "worship." Each of these Greek words carries a shade of meaning distinct from the other two.

The word most frequently used in the New Testament is the word *proskuneo*. It is traced to an early Greek word that indicated the act of bowing to the earth in reverence to a deity. In the Septuagint (that Greek Old Testament also called the LXX) the word translates Hebrew words that have the basic sense of "to bow" and is usually in reference to veneration of the true God (or for that matter false gods, or angels, and sometimes kings or other rulers). Its usage in the New Testament always conveys the idea of reverence (that is, the act of bowing) to an object either actually or supposedly divine.

This word is used almost sixty times in the New Testament with more than half the instances occurring in the writings of John. (The word is common in the Gospels, in Acts, and in Revelation but appears only most infrequently in the Epistles.) Often the verb is used in connection with the verb *pipto* ("fall") and is translated, for example, in Matthew 2:11, "They saw the young child with Mary his mother, and fell down, and worshiped him." It is this word *proskuneo* that appears repeatedly in the account of Jesus' encounter with the woman of Sychar (John 4:20-24). The word is not reserved for reference only to worship of Jesus. Luke records that Cornelius, meeting Peter for the first time, "fell down at his feet, and worshiped him" (Acts 10:25).

A second word, appearing twenty-one times in the New Testament, is the word *latreuo*. This word came in the early Greek from the noun *latron*, "reward" or "wages" and hence had the idea of serving for reward (sometimes even of serving without regard to reward). The labor was in reference to bodily services. The word appears ninety times in the LXX and connotes the idea of performing ritual acts of worship, especially those of sacrifice.

The essence of this word is in its reference to the acts or duties that one performs in the overall role of worship, for

44

example, the act in the ancient day of offering sacrifice or burning incense. The word as used in the New Testament reflects this cultic worship though it is a spiritualized service. For example the writer of Hebrews records, "How much more shall the blood of Christ . . . purge your conscience from dead works to serve the living God?" (9:14) and "Whereby we may serve God acceptably with reverence and godly fear" (12:28). See also in this respect Acts 7:7 and Revelation 22:3. The word relates the activity of worship to the activity of service. In this sense it seems to be almost a synonym for the more familiar New Testament word, *diakoneo,* to which the words "servant" and "deacon" relate.

On two occasions in the New Testament the word is used in close relationship with another word for worship. Hence we note Jesus' reply to Satan during the temptation experience: "Get thee hence, Satan: for it is written, Thou shalt worship [*proskunēseis*] the Lord thy God, and him only shalt thou serve [*latreuseis*]" (Matt. 4:10). In a similar structure Paul speaks of those who "changed the glory of the uncorruptible God into an image made like to corruptible man": they "changed the truth of God into a lie, and worshiped [*esebasthēsan*] and served [*elatreusan*] the creature more than the Creator" (Rom. 1:25).

A third word, used ten times in the New Testament, is *sebomai.* The original meaning of the noun was "to fall back before." Hence it refers to that bodily movement that is associated with an inner feeling of respect, respect for God, gods, or man, as the case may be. (The most vivid description of this word that comes to my mind is the experience of observing my wife's reaction when she unexpectedly found herself face-to-face with a campaigning candidate for the office of the President of the United States. She was suddenly, utterly speechless!) The word eventually comes to refer to an act rather than an attitude. In the LXX the word is used to express the idea of "serve," the honoring of divinity by the doing of that one's will. In the New Testament it implies more than just the attitude of being impressed by another; one must in fact perform certain acts.

The word appears in Matthew 15:9 (and the parallel passage, Mark 7:7) as Jesus quotes Isaiah (29:13): "But in vain they do worship me, teaching for doctrines the commandments of men." In the remainder of the instances the word appears in Acts where it is used several times to describe a Gentile who believes in God. On another occasion (Acts 18:13) the Jewish accusation was leveled against Paul: "This fellow persuadeth men to worship God contrary to the law."

On rare occasions yet other words appear in the New Testament conveying the sense of worship but little is to be gained by our further pursuit of these words. In summary rather we may note that the New Testament writers seem to refrain from selecting any one word as the correct or official word to describe worship. As far as the language of the New Testament may be understood, the worshiper is to be found within a perspective of freedom of expression. The worshiper may feel humbled, awestricken, or even motivated in some meaningful activity.

The Word "Prayer" in the Bible

The word *euchomai* is a verb meaning "to speak out" or "to utter aloud." Hence it has two basic ideas: "pray" in the sense of worship, and "wish," as a reflection of the soul. In the former connection we consider Paul's statement,

"Now I pray to God that ye do no evil" (II Cor. 13:7) or James' injunction, "Confess your faults one to another, and pray one for another, that ye may be healed" (James 5:16). In the latter sense is John's admonition, "Beloved, I wish above all things that thou mayest prosper and be in health" (III John 2). There is only a close line of distinction between these two ideas, and some of the modern English translations for example proceed to translate the "wish" of III John 2 as "pray."

A related form is the noun, *euchē*, "prayer." James writes: "And the prayer of faith shall save the sick, and the Lord shall raise him up" (5:15). This noun also may have the meaning of a "vow" or "oath." For example Paul had his hair shorn in Cenchrea as the result of a vow. (See Acts 18:18.) But what is a vow if not a prayer in which one purports to take a certain course of action?

A derivative yet distinct word, *proseuchomai*, appears many times in the New Testament with the essential meaning of "pray." For example, Jesus said: "Love your enemies . . . and pray for them which despitefully use you" (Matt. 5:44); and, "After this manner therefore pray ye: Our Father which art in heaven" (Matt. 6:9). See also Matthew 14:23; 19:13; 24:20; 26:36, 39, 41, 42, 44; Mark 1:35; 6:46; 11:24, 25; Luke 1:10; 3:21; 5:16; Acts 1:24; 6:6; 8:15; I Cor. 11:4, 5, 13; and numerous other references.

The related noun form is *proseuchē*, and is translated "prayer" in such passages as, "My house shall be called the house of prayer" (Matt. 21:13). Other references include Mark 9:29; 11:17; Luke 6:12; 19:46; 22:45; Acts 1:14; 2:42; 3:1; 6:4; etc. The significance of *proseuchē* is that it is used only as an address to God, never to any other one or thing.

47

A third verb, *deomai*, has the meanings of "to need," "to want, or lack," "to desire, or long for," "to ask, or beg," or "to pray, or make supplication." Thus we may consider such passages as: "And when they had prayed, the place was shaken where they were assembled together" (Acts 4:31); "Pray God, if perhaps the thought of thine heart may be forgiven thee" (Acts 8:22); and "I have prayed for thee, that thy faith fail not" (Luke 22:32). The word is sometimes used in a sense not relevant to prayer, as the eunuch's words to Philip, "I pray thee, of whom speaketh the prophet this?" (Acts 8:34).

The noun form is the word, *deēsis*, and has the meanings of "need," "seeking," or "entreating." Consider, "Brethren, my heart's desire and prayer to God for Israel is, that they might be saved" (Rom. 10:1). See also I Peter 3:12 and II Timothy 1:3. This word is not specifically a religious word as is *proseuchē* (above). It is frequently used in that sense but not necessarily so.

Yet another word with a different shade of meaning is *entugchano*, with the meaning of going to a person for the purpose that consultation or supplication may be carried on. In this way the word conveys the idea of praying, entreating, or making petition. Thus we appreciate the words of Paul: "It is Christ that died, yea rather, that is risen again, who is even at the right hand of God, who also maketh intercession for us" (Rom. 8:34).

The related noun is *enteuxis* which came to have the particular meaning of a petition addressed to one of royal stature. This reflects both the boldness of the one making the request as well as the potential of that request being granted. Thus we consider the passage, "It is sanctified by the word of God and prayer" (I Tim. 4:5).

There are other words broad in their general meaning that appear occasionally in the New Testament in the sense of prayer. Such a word is *parakaleo,* which means "to call to one's side" or "to beg, entreat, or beseech." See the passage, Matthew 26:53. Also there is the word *erotao,* which means "to question, ask, or beseech." See John 14:16; 16:26. Apparently this word is used in the sense of prayer only in reference to the prayers that Christ offered. Yet another word is *aiteo,* which means "to ask for one's self." This gives clarification to Martha's words to Jesus: "I know, that even now, whatsoever thou wilt ask of God, God will give it thee" (John 11:22).

Rounding out our examination of words translated "pray" or "prayer" are several from the Old Testament. The most common noun is *tephillah* which is derived from a basic root meaning "to cut." (See the incident of Elijah and the prophets of Baal at Mount Carmel: "And they cried aloud, and cut themselves after their manner with knives and lancets, till the blood gushed out upon them," I Kings 18:28). Examine the translation of this word as "pray" in Genesis 20:7 or Job 42:10. Other words have the idea of "pray" through the use of one of several words meaning "call." (This use is perpetuated in the New Testament as *epikaleisthai to onoma,* "call upon the name," see Acts 2:21 or 9:14.) In this sense consider such passages as Genesis 4:26; Judges 3:9; Psalm 17:1 or 72:12. Yet other words offer the meaning of prayer as "seek." See Amos 5:4 or Hosea 5:15.

Selected Biblical Examples of Worship

The biblical narrative records numerous incidents of worship, both private and public. Though many of these may not be relevant as models for our practice today, nonetheless an examination of selected incidents should prove

49

beneficial to our growing awareness of that which constitutes legitimate worship.

As a guide in focusing on that which is important, we should pose certain questions in our examination of each incident. Such questions might include:

What is the occasion?
Who is involved in the worship?
What is the apparent primary objective?
Who is the leader?
Are there prerequisites for leadership?
What is the role of the general participants?
Is there a special time for the worship?
Are there special facilities? special utensils?
Are there unique ordinances?
What is the order?
How may the mood of worship be described?

One of the earliest accounts of worship in the Bible is that of Noah immediately following his exiting from the ark. (See Gen. 8:20-22.) The worship was simple—the erection of an altar and the offering of animal sacrifice (not just any animal, but specifically "clean" animals). God's response was a recorded blessing for Noah and his descendants. Later in Genesis (28:16-22) is recorded the experience of Jacob following his traumatic departure from his brother Esau. Awakening from the dream that conveyed a heavenly revelation, Jacob declared: "Surely the Lord is in this place; and I knew it not . . . How dreadful [or read, awesome] is this place! This is none other but the house of God, and this is the gate of heaven" (vs. 16-17). His response was to erect a simple altar, to offer sacrifice (in this instance, oil) thereon, and to make a vow to take the Lord as his God and to give a tenth to Him. (Strangely enough, in light of the desperate circumstances confronting Jacob, it was a provisional vow; "If God will be with me, and will keep me . . . .")

Whereas these Genesis accounts speak of simplicity and individuality in worship, the book of Leviticus (especially for our purpose, chapters one to eleven) and sections of the books of Numbers and Deuteronomy speak of the splendor, complexity, and ritualism of the worship prescribed for the corporate body of Israel. Here is a model of biblical worship surely foreign in its magnitude, intricacies, and sacerdotalism to the worship experience of most of us. Yet it is indeed a prescribed biblical worship and one that must be appreciated if not modeled.

Again an interesting contrast is to be observed between the somewhat parallel accounts of the worship expressed by David as he escorted the ark of the covenant into the city and the worship rendered on the occasion when that same ark at Solomon's command was placed in the Temple. In the former account (II Sam. 6:12-19) we note that David went "with gladness," that he sacrificed "oxen and fatlings" and offered "burnt offerings and peace offerings," and "danced before the Lord" to the accompaniment of shouting and trumpeting. Also David pronounced a blessing on the people "in the name of the Lord of hosts." In the latter account (II Chron. 5:1-14), the occasion of transferring the ark to the Temple, the disposition of the occasion is much more sacerdotal as well as exaggerated in its magnificence. We note the suggestion of a processional (v. 5), the offering of innumerable sheep and oxen (v. 6), the participation of the Levites "arrayed in white linen" assisted by 120 trumpeter-priests (v. 12), and the unified vocal expression of praise (v. 13). The Lord in turn filled the Temple with a cloud (v. 13) and His glory (v. 14) in such a manner that the priests had to withdraw.

Luke records the account (Luke 4:16-21) of an occasion when Jesus visited a synagogue in Nazareth. (The incident is of particular interest in light of our consideration in Chapter Three of synagogue worship.) We note both that it was Jesus' "custom" to attend and that it was on the sabbath day. As a guest dignitary he was invited to read—and he "stood up for to read." A book (read, "scroll") was given to him—that of the prophet Isaiah. With the reading of the passage Jesus gave the scroll back to the synagogue assistant ("minister," a lay position) and sat down to speak. The account of the order is indeed scanty but it does coincide with that which is otherwise known about worship in the first century synagogue.

Luke also records (Acts 20:7-11) the interesting account of Paul at worship at Troas. We may simply note that the worship occurred on the "first day of the week," that the disciples were assembled to "break bread," and that Paul "preached" at quite some length. In reality the word "preached" (*dielegeto*) might more properly be translated "discussed" as we would make again the distinction regarding the word *keryssein* (see Chapter One).

Paul's account (I Cor. 11:17-34) of the proper observance of the Lord's Supper merits our attention. It is to be noted that it is a discipline of worship received from the Lord (v. 23) and that it is a highly symbolical one at that (vs. 24-25). The Christian through a legitimate exercise of observance makes proper testimony to the grand truths of the gospel (v. 26). It is a time for extremely guarded self-discernment (vs. 27-29). A proper observance holds priority among the reasons for the corporate assembly of the congregation (v. 34).

Surely the most staggering view of worship in the Scriptures is that described in the book of Revelation. While this is visionary—the worship is depicted as taking place in heaven—it is nonetheless a magnificent demonstration of that which is truly the eternal function of God's saints in glory! Consider carefully, prayerfully these passages: Revelation 4:2-11; 7:9-12; 15:2-8; and 19:1-8. Contemplate especially the magnificent strains of worship reflected in these phrases: "And all the angels stood round about the throne . . . and fell before the throne on their faces, and worshiped God, saying, Amen: Blessing, and glory, and wisdom, and thanksgiving, and honour, and power, and might, be unto our God for ever and ever. Amen." (7:11-12).

The Movement of Worship

Perhaps the classic example of worship is that recorded in Isaiah 6:1-8. In this visionary experience Isaiah describes his personal, overwhelming confrontation with the Almighty God! Aside from the role of this particular passage as devotional material we are able to gain from it something of the proper dynamic of legitimate worship.

The worship experience to be complete—and thereby totally valid—must proceed along a certain psychological course. The worshiper need not be consciously aware of this course though certainly such a knowledge would facilitate the experience. Is this strange to suggest? Does not the young lad in love pursue a definite pattern of increasingly developing patterns of emotion? Does not the would-be purchaser of a new automobile follow ever-intensifying patterns of desire?

Read carefully these opening verses of the sixth chapter of Isaiah and note the movement of worship. Initially there must be an awareness of God's presence and the significance of that presence. Isaiah records: "I saw also the Lord sitting upon a throne, high and lifted up, and his train filled the temple. Above it stood the seraphims . . . . And one cried unto another, and said, Holy, holy, holy, is the Lord of hosts: the whole earth is full of his glory. And the posts of the door moved at the voice of him that cried, and the house was filled with smoke" (vs. 1-4). In language not unlike that of the above-mentioned passages in Revelation, Isaiah graphically attempts to describe what it is like to meet God in a place appointed for worship. Without this first experience worship can proceed no further; other things perhaps can—fellowship, education—but not worship! Even Christ Himself could do nothing for the self-righteous.

The second experience follows naturally from the first. Isaiah continues: "Then said I, woe is me! for I am undone (read, lost); because I am a man of unclean lips, and I dwell in the midst of a people of unclean lips: for mine eyes have seen the King, the Lord of hosts" (v. 5). To stand in the presence of Him who is the Creator of the universe, Him by whom all goodness is measured, can only cause one to consider hopelessly one's personal and utter inadequacy.

But God would not leave us in this utterly dejected condition. Isaiah proceeds with joyful words: "Then flew one of the seraphims unto me, having a live coal in his hand, which he had taken with the tongs from off the altar: And he laid it upon my mouth, and said, Lo, this hath touched thy lips; and thine iniquity is taken away, and thy sin purged" (vs. 6-7). Though the full significance of this imagery escapes adults who live in the age of antibiotics yet it is very apparent

that a confrontation with God which brings total self-humili-
ation also brings complete purification, or in a theological
sense, redemption.

Filled with a sense of renewal the worshiper desires to
express his gratitude. Isaiah recalls: "Also I heard the voice
of the Lord, saying, Whom shall I send, and who will go
for us? Then said I, Here am I; send me" (v. 8). The one
who has confronted God desires to share that confrontation
with others who as yet know Him not!

Here is the classical movement of worship—awareness of
God, confession of inadequacy, sense of restoration, and
commitment to witness. Call the movements what you wish.
Select other words if you will so that the movement can
be described in three—or in five or even six—acts. But one
cannot rearrange the movements. Commitment cannot
come before awareness of God. Sense of restoration cannot come before the reason for the need of restoration.

Aiming at Biblical Worship

Our study has indicated that there is freedom from pattern
in biblical worship. There are almost as many variables as
there are incidents of worship. Yet there is an overriding
awareness of being in the presence of God and there is one
identifiable factor common to worship, that of praise to God.
And what praise it is! We hear a shout of acclamation (that
scarcely changes from the words of Isaiah to the visions of
John) of His majesty and glory. We would not dispute that
humankind has several claims on its stewardship on earth
but surely to be numbered among the priorities is the responsibility—the privilege—of worship.

Worship after the biblical model then we may define as
a deliberate, reverent attempt at confrontation with God

as revealed through Jesus Christ with a committed effort on our part to make our lives totally conformable to His will. Thus each act of worship in a sense is a re-enactment of our initial commitment to God through His Son. In worship we measure our lives against the eternal standards and vow to yield to Him who is able to make total restoration.

This is biblical worship, but is it our worship? Do the congregations in which we participate exemplify these principles at the assembled worship hour? Have we who would restore New Testament Christianity actually restored something of the mood and spirit of New Testament worship? Is an 11:00 service oriented toward preaching necessarily fulfilling the requirements of worship? Is the congregation who in singing is instructed to "raise the roof" with its volume (or even more preposterous, add twenty-four "powers" to "Power in the Blood") really falling to its face before the throne? Is the congregation who is queried, "Is everybody happy?" really aware that "the Lord God omnipotent reigneth"? There is indeed a biblical model for worship. The mandate for us is to prioritize, practice, and perpetuate that model!

Questions and Projects

1. Name the three major words that are translated as "worship" in the English New Testament and differentiate the uniqueness of each word.
2. After examining a number of scriptural references to prayer write a brief statement about the nature of biblical prayer.
3. Using several New Testament commentaries write a brief analysis of the Model Prayer, Matthew 6:9—13.
4. What questions should one ask in studying an example of worship recorded in the biblical narrative?

5. Memorize Isaiah 6:1-8.
6. Write a brief statement that defines biblical worship.
7. Using books on comparative religion note that which distinguishes the Judaeo/Christian practices of worship from those of the major world religions.

Chapter Five

ESTABLISHING A BIBLICAL PERSPECTIVE

I vividly recall life on a central Illinois farm during that eventful period when farming made the transition from the use of horses to that of tractors as the basic mode of power for the farming operation. It was a significant yet traumatic period. Significant, because the farmers could cultivate more acres of land with a more satisfactory point of cost efficiency with at the same time the exercise of less physical exertion. (Also the land that once had been set aside as pasture for the horses was now put into grain production.) Traumatic, because for more than two centuries horses had constituted an integral part of the American farm homestead and now old, familiar friends were disappearing. It was a sad day for me personally when the last two horses left our farm. They were named Tom and Bob—all horses had names for they were part of the farm family. I had driven them, ridden them, and fed and cared for them as though they were pets. (I recall that on more than one occasion during this period of transition from horses to tractors we had to use the horses to extricate those early tractors—quite small and lacking in power when compared to today's equipment—from muddy fields.)

There are those today of the Campbellian heritage who say that the idea of restorationism, like the American farm horse, is obsolete, worthy of its day in the nineteenth century but irrelevant in an age rapidly approaching the twenty-first century. Nonetheless the foundational principles of the Restoration Movement demand that we turn to those Scriptures that record the life and witness of the early church in an effort to observe today that which was essential then. It is imperative therefore in a study such as this, "What the Bible says," to establish that the principle of restorationism is indeed valid for our day.

The Relevance of Restorationism

The fundamental truths that I believe as a Christian may be summarized as follows: I believe that Jesus Christ is Lord, that the Scriptures are the inspired Word of God, that I am saved by grace, that there is no salvation outside the church, and that the church is the bride of Christ. But these five truths are not unique to Christian Churches/Churches of Christ; they are held by most Christians and most churches around the world. What then is unique to Christian Churches/Churches of Christ? It is the thesis that the much-desired unity of the church may be acquired through the means of restoring New Testament Christianity. (Many have sought unity, others have attempted restorationism, but perhaps no one else has attempted to combine the two ideas.)

Historically the Restoration Movement was in the minds of Thomas and Alexander Campbell (and in the actual practice of the Christian Association of Washington) a body of believers committed to the restoration of the essential teachings and practices of the New Testament church in order that Christians in modern times might achieve a common unity. Leaders of the Restoration Movement have formulated these three goals/values. (1) The church of Christ upon earth is essentially, intentionally, and constitutionally one and the quest for that oneness within the reality of human experience is of utmost priority. (2) Such a quest can be conducted most effectively and legitimately on the basis of the restoration of the essentialities of the first century church. (3) That expression of the life and faith of the early church is to be sought within grammatical/historical parameters. (Many other groups speak of restoring New Testament Christianity but mainline denominations attempt it theologically and pentecostal churches attempt it experientially. The former is not practical, the latter is not realistic. Both then in turn are divisive!)

Some in positions of leadership among Christian Churches/ Churches of Christ today have noted that there is a decline in the restoration emphasis. Such a decline may be attributed to a number of pressures that have compromised what was once a stalwart witness. Many local congregations today have become miniature "melting pots" (even as the United States was once described as a "melting pot" in its assimilation of people of many nations). People are motivated to membership in the local congregations because their partner in marriage is a member, because of the youth activities, or because of the excellent musical offerings in the services. Doctrinal instruction or personal intellectual assessment has played only a minor role in the process of accepting membership. Little more is done to inform these people of the rich heritage of the movement of which they have become a part. People are active in positions of leadership who evidence little persuasion in following what Alexander Campbell called the "search for the ancient order of things."

So for various reasons many are ignoring the restoration emphasis and its complementary procedure of the careful examination to the customs and teachings of the first century church.

There are surely others who simply fail to see the relevancy of the old principles in this modern day. Though conservative in their theological stance they nonetheless have reached the same conclusion as their more liberal counterparts in the Campbellian heritage, namely that restorationism no longer meets the need of the modern church. But there is the oft-told story of the pilot of a sailing ship who, tired from hours at his post, turned the wheel over to the hands of a novice with the instructions to "head toward that star." Returning later he found the ship off course and the inexperienced navigator explaining that he'd sailed past that particular star. We have not sailed past the star! The old truths are still valid! Restorationism is yet relevant!

I believe that there is a strong biblical precedent for restorationism, though surely not a clearly stated, "Thus saith the Lord." In the time of King Josiah when the temple was being repaired the "book of the law" was discovered by the high priest, Hilkiah, who excitedly took it to the king's scribe, Shaphan, who in turn read it to the king. The king in sorrow ("he rent his clothes") responded: "Go ye, enquire of the Lord for me, and for the people, and for all Judah, concerning the words of this book that is found: for great is the wrath of the Lord that is kindled against us, because our fathers have not hearkened unto the words of this book, to do according unto all that which is written concerning us." (See II Kings 22 for the complete account.) In the New Testament we note Paul writing to the churches of Galatia: "I marvel that ye are so soon removed from him that called you into the grace of Christ unto another gospel" (Gal. 1:6). While the "gospel" here spoken of (see verses 6-12) is a verbal one the transition to a written gospel is applicable. Or again, consider the words of John to the church of Ephesus: "Thou hast left thy first love. Remember therefore from whence thou art fallen, and repent, and do the first works" (Rev. 2:4-5). The call is to the Ephesians to turn again to an earlier—and superior—level of Christian conduct.

The idea of restoration is sound and workable. The great reform movements of history within the church have been almost without exception movements either initiated by or accompanied with people turning to the Scriptures.

The Restoration Movement itself originated on the American frontier. Members of these congregations—like frontierspeople everywhere—wanted something that was simple, good, and workable. (These same people built log cabins often with chimneys that in the event of fire could quickly be pulled away from the main structure to control the spread of the flames. They built chimneys this way because the idea was simple, good, and workable.)

I believe that there is great validity in maintaining continuity. One characteristic of the integrity of the church today is its continuity with the church of the first century—and restorationism contributes to the achievement of that continuity. (This is a continuity of faith and not one of ministry.) In one sense therefore restorationism equates with continuity.

A dear friend, and my former minister, observes with his homespun Hoosier logic: "You can't change the rules every time you play checkers!" No, you can't! I think of this often as I reflect upon the social and theological pressures that are brought to bear upon congregations of the Restoration Movement. Long ago our leaders selected a perspective within which to work for the unity of the church. It seemed to them the only tenable procedure. Time has not altered this premise—nor must we change the rules! Restorationism is scriptural, workable, and relevant. It is imperative that we continue our task. It is imperative that we carefully explore what illumination the Scriptures cast upon worship.

The biblical basis for continuity in faith and worship is found in the unchanging nature of God and the immutable quality of His steadfast love. We will do well now to explore this relationship between worship and steadfast love.

The Foundational Relationship of Steadfast Love

Words are amazing! The skillful use of words can create imaginative landscapes, destroy idols, motivate armies, or woo a lover. Words can be harsh as granite or as soft as a rose petal. Well-chosen words can stand as seemingly eternal directives of conduct. And yet how quickly hostilities become intensified when antagonists fail to grasp the meaning of the speech of one another.

Consider the word "snowbound." For some—myself included—it evokes memories of the serene aftermath of the winter blizzard. The raging wind and snow of the night before have subsided. All is quiet. The sun is shining brightly. The youthful resident awakens with the exhilarating feeling that comes with the knowledge that today there will be no school. Opportunities exist for tracking rabbits in the fresh-fallen snow perhaps, but certainly no school. There is a refreshing sense of isolation from the problems of the world. There is the penetrating comfort of warmth from the open fire in the fireplace and the diffusing aroma of good things cooking that wafts from the kitchen. There are books to be excavated from the pile of things in the closet and to be read. And, eventually, there is the restlessness of confinement that is alleviated only when the township snowplow and its crew of men from the roadway maintenance department emerges into view. All this from the word "snowbound." One can similarly play with the words "county fair" or "homecoming" or "toothache." Truly, words are amazing vehicles of communication!

With the exception of the proper name "Jehovah" surely the grandest word in all of the Old Testament is the word *hesed*. No single word can correctly translate it. The familiar "mercy" of the Authorized Version (the King James Bible) is so inadequate—however more modern translations serve only little better. (But is the inability to find a single, correct word so rare? The traveler in the southern part of West Germany sees a neatly lettered sign at the entrance to a restaurant, "Kaffee und Kuchen." "Kaffee" is readily recognized—but "Kuchen"? A glance at the tourist dictionary reveals that the words means "cake"—but, believe me, if that particular "Kuchen" happens to be Black Forest Kuchen then one single word or even one single sentence is woefully inadequate as a description of even a small morsel of that tantalizing confection.) A short, well-stated paragraph can perhaps be used to translate the world *hesed* but as that would be most unmanageable in the printed text the Bible student must be content with a translation such as "steadfast love." Thus for our study here this particular translation will perhaps be adequate.

"Steadfast love" (*hesed*) is the highest degree of good will. Though it is within the capability of mortals to exhibit "steadfast love," ultimately it is the prerogative of God—and so the word is commonly associated with Jehovah in the Old Testament. The word "steadfast love" conveys the idea of pardoning without respect to merit. One does not earn "steadfast love" by meritorious acts performed before an exacting Sovereign. In this sense the word "steadfast love" is similar to the idea of "grace" in the New Testament. The word "steadfast love" combines both the dynamic concepts of "kindly affection" and "loyalty." One party in the relationship has made a commitment to the other party (or perhaps both parties make this commitment reciprocally) and this commitment transcends or endures beyond that point at which "kindly affection" ceases. Yet an enduring relationship can be passionless and so "kindly affection" is imperative to this unique association.

The translators of the Septuagint (the early Greek version of the Old Testament, commonly called the LXX) invariably used the Greek word *eleos* (mercy) to translate the Hebrew word *hesed*. But in reality *hesed* covers more than that because it conveys the idea of *charis* (grace) and *eirēnē* (peace) as well as *eleos* (mercy).

"Steadfast love" is limited by God's justice because if God is to be God He must be just as well as loving. Yet justice is always subordinate to *hesed*. Whatever God may be, and however minimally mortal mind can comprehend the grandeur of that Being, God is love (or, as we are suggesting, "steadfast love"). In summary it is "steadfast love" that is God's constant support of stumbling, blundering mortals that provides the only possibility of their eventual salvation. Hear again the opening words of the hymn:

> Amazing grace! how sweet the sound,
> That saved a wretch like me!
> I once was lost, but now am found,
> Was blind, but now I see.

"Steadfast love" can be expressed on occasion in a person-to-person relationship. This may be illustrated biblically with reference to the instance of David and Jonathan (see I Sam. 20:14). But much more commonly it is a God-to-person relationship. "Steadfast love" is an essential attribute of God. It is inconceivable to envision God as God or to define God as God without this attribute of "steadfast love." Further, "steadfast love" commonly goes with the concept of "truth" in the Scriptures. It is within this relationship that truth has substance.

A person must first know "steadfast love" if that one is to exhibit love to another. The Old Testament furnishes excellent example of this in the experiences of David. Convicted of guilt in his adulterous interlude with Bathsheba, grieved at the loss of his child, he came to know of the forgiving love freely given by a gracious God. Then and only then could he be in a frame of mind as to love his own errant son, the usurper of the throne, Absalom. (Among the most tragic lines of the Scriptures are those of David, "O my son Absalom, my son, my son Absalom! would God I had died for thee, O Absalom, my son, my son!" II Sam. 18:33b.)

One's attention is drawn to Psalm 136. As the psalmist ventures forth the words of praise, "O give thanks unto the Lord; for he is good . . . O give thanks unto the God of gods . . . O give thanks to the Lord of lords . . ." always there comes the response, "for his steadfast love endures forever." In fact this particular phrase, "for his steadfast love endures forever," appears over forty times in the Old Testament.

In the ever-popular animated cartoon the cautious cat with increasing bravado pokes the sleeping dog. What were initially gentle jabs become violent blows. But then the dog awakens and—POW! Or in the drama of real life a child offends the parent again and again and again. For a time the parent is patient and is seemingly willing to take the continuing rebuff. But the child continues until the parent can endure it no more. Once again, in a spiritual sequel, a rebellious child of God turns against the Creator and offends that Creator again and again and again. How long does a forbearing God tolerate this insolence? To know the answer is to understand the nature of "steadfast love."

The beloved dean emeritus of Lincoln Christian Seminary has on more than one occasion been asked to repeat for the student body one of his favorite sermons on the topic of love. The message is high-pointed with the recitation of the illustration of a man who again and again received back with forgiving love his wandering, unfaithful wife. Why do you do it, brother, are you crazy? But the answer rings forth clearly, Because I love her! (In a similar vein our Master challenges us. See Matt. 6:14-15; 18:21-35.)

The point to which we have been leading is this: the *hesed* relationship is foundational to a valid worship experience. The one who more fully understands and appreciates the significance of the *hesed* relationship is the one who more fully understands and appreciates the worship experience. This is not to say that the one who does not know or does not experience *hesed* cannot worship. It is to say simply that the *hesed* relationship is foundational to the valid worship experience. Worship outside that relationship is certainly limited if not meaningless. Worship on any other premise is truncated or illusory.

Worship is a natural reaction of response to the *hesed* relationship. Worship is most meaningful in this context. Legitimate worship is based primarily on love and not on fear or duty. We may indeed stand in awe of God and we may indeed serve him as a sense of fulfillment or obligation but we worship God because we love Him and because we respond to His love for us. Worship may be performed that is based on fear or duty rather than love but it is a worship lacking those inherent qualities that in essence rightly define worship. Thus, for example, to give praise to God for the "steadfast love" that He exhibits to us is a most appropriate expression of worship.

Because *hesed* is continuing experience ("his steadfast love endures forever") so worship is a continuing experience.

It is not simply a once-in-a-lifetime shout of thanksgiving offered at the time of one's initial acceptance of the Master. Nor is it a joyful acclamation given annually on the anniversary of some occasion of dramatic note. It is not even just a weekly experience shared with the corporate body of believers. It is that but it is also more. Even as "steadfast love" is a continuing relationship so is worship a constant attitude of mind and soul, an attitude that does indeed erupt at periodic intervals as at the Sunday corporate experience of worship.

The *hesed* relationship provides an openness and freedom to the structure of worship. For some, worship that acknowledges *hesed* is free, unfettered and joyous. For others such worship to provide valid expression is fixed, formal and solemn. Whatever the form it must be harmonious to the mind of the worshiper. All is valid worship as long as the forms enable the individual to give expression to the acknowledgement of the overwhelming influence of "steadfast love" on the individual's life.

To know the Lord in the meaningful way is to be strengthened for all the exigencies of life, to walk, if needs be, "through the valley of the shadow of death." How grand it is to grasp, even in small measure, the meaning of the *hesed* relationship and to be able to express that in the praise language of worship. "O give thanks unto the God of heaven: for his mercy endureth for ever" (Psalm 136:26).

The Tension Between Form and Content

There are important, enduring tensions in the physical world. One such tension is the resulting balance between gravity and centrifugal force that keeps the moon either from flying off into space or from falling on one's head.

The Chinese speak mythologically of some such tensions in descriptive terms of Yin and Yang.

A most significant tension that concerns us within the field of worship is that between form and content. Content is the sum of what one expresses in worship. Form is the vehicle within which and by which that content is communicated. A brief if not superficial observation from the vantage point of Christian Churches/Churches of Christ is that the mainline, liturgically oriented churches emphasize form through carefully prescribed use of historic ritual and that the pentecostal churches abandon the use of form that the Spirit might be free to work. Christian Churches/Churches of Christ formulate their worship on the premise that there is a proper balance between a form compatible with the biblical model and a content consistent with apostolic teaching. Such worship, thus balancing form and content, is both biblical and apostolic, functional and authentic.

It must be recognized initially that form is very important. (How else does one manage a large, frozen custard cone on a hot July day?) From a biblical perspective the books of Exodus, Leviticus, Numbers, and Deuteronomy provide extensive instruction for appropriate acts of worship for virtually every occasion of life, both daily and seasonal, of the worshipers of Israel, both individually and collectively. These acts of worship were designed to make restitution for sin. The acts were mostly sacrificial in nature. The priest was the important, central figure in all this. Heavy emphasis was placed on the ritual—or as we suggest here, the form— of worship. We must therefore establish a premise that ritual in worship is both biblical and valid.

In the survey that I conducted of a number of midwestern ministers I asked for a word association to be matched with the word liturgy. The most frequent response was the word

69

ritual. Yet ritual is basically repetition. When a seemingly simple worship service, consisting of three songs, a prayer, and a sermon, is used again and again that simple service becomes a ritual, a liturgy.

The use of ritual can be self-defeating. Driving to the college each day I commonly take an inter-state for several miles and then exit to a service-road. On one such recent journey I found myself on the service-road without the faintest recollection whatsoever of having taken the very prominent exit ramp. Why? I had made that same trip over five hundred times—and now I had gone through the process without any apparent conscious involvement. This is the ever-present threat of risk with the use of ritual. But it need not be. As the old expression goes, we need not throw out the baby with the bath.

Though a significant portion of the Pentateuch called for the carefully prescribed use of ritual in the acts of worship the intervening years saw that worship come to be badly distorted. Hence one of the central features of the reformatory message of the Old Testament prophets was a call for genuineness in worship.

The prophet Isaiah participated in the worship of the day. (See Isa. 6:1-8.) In his view worship rites are good and acceptable if performed by people whose actions reflect their commitment. But on the other hand if they did not, Isaiah denounced:

> To what purpose is the multitude of your sacrifices unto me? saith the Lord: I am full of the burnt offerings of rams, and the fat of fed beasts; and I delight not in the blood of bullocks, or of lambs, or of the he goats. . . . Your new moons and your appointed feasts my soul hateth: they are a trouble unto me; I am weary to bear them. . . . Yea, when ye make many prayers, I will not hear: your hands are full

of blood. . . . Learn to do well; seek judgment, relieve the oppressed, judge the fatherless, plead for the widow (Isa. 1:11-17).

Hosea was talking covenant language when he demanded unswerving loyalty of the people to God. "For I desired mercy, and not sacrifice; and the knowledge of God more than burnt offerings" (Hos. 6:6). Yet no one stated the case more strikingly than did Micah. He asked:

Wherewith shall I come before the Lord, and bow myself before the high God? shall I come before him with burnt offerings, with calves of a year old? Will the Lord be pleased with thousands of rams, or with ten thousands of rivers of oil? shall I give my firstborn for my transgression, the fruit of my body for the sin of my soul? (Mic. 6:6-7).

Then comes the ringing answer: "He hath shewed thee, O man, what is good; and what doth the Lord require of thee, but to do justice, and to love mercy, and to walk humbly with thy God?" (Mic. 6:8). The prophets were so committed to their position that they were willing to die for it (and die they did; read Heb. 11:32-38).

In large measure the warning of the prophets went unheeded. Centuries later Jesus continued their emphasis, the total involvement of heart, soul, and mind in the quest to be obedient to God. In His majestic Sermon on the Mount Jesus proclaimed: "Therefore if thou bring thy gift to the altar, and there rememberest that thy brother hath ought against thee; leave there thy gift before the altar, and go thy way; first be reconciled to thy brother, and then come and offer thy gift" (Matt. 5:23-24). On another occasion He strongly rebuked certain religious leaders with the words: "Woe unto you, scribes and Pharisees, hypocrites! for ye

71

pay tithe of mint and anise and cummin, and have omitted the weightier matters of the law, judgment, mercy, and faith: these ought ye to have done, and not to leave the other undone" (Matt. 23:23). In neither instance does Jesus urge the abandonment of form. Rather He puts it into proper perspective with content. Clearly, at least in these instances, content is the more important of the two.

Both the prophets and Jesus were calling for the return to the old values. To call again for the old values is precisely what restorationism is. (This is significant to those who seek as a people collectively to be the Restoration Movement.)

The burden upon the worship leader therefore is to attempt to attain a proper tension between form and content in worship. There are those people—frequently of the pentecostal persuasion—who would enter the post of leadership in a service of worship trusting the Spirit to guide them spontaneously in the selection both of the order of worship and of the elements that support that order. Such a position is untenable to Restorationists however who have been taught for generations that everything should "be done decently and in order." For worship leaders in the Restorationist heritage this entails thoughtful preparation of the worship service.

Leaders of the Christian Churches/Churches of Christ surely emphasize content more than form. They have learned well the message of Jesus and the prophets. Unfortunately many of these same leaders have been prone to criticize those who are liturgically oriented. Such critics ought to be patient however with those who lean to the use of liturgy for there is certainly ample biblical precedent for the actions of the latter. The right to consider and evaluate the use of liturgy in worship is inherent within the rights of Restorationists for Alexander Campbell maintained that "the spirit and soul of all reformation is free discussion."

The traditional position historically of Christian Churches/ Churches of Christ has been to seek a legitimate balance between form and content in worship with the preponderance of attention being focused on the maintenance of proper content. It is well that Restorationists maintain both this tradition and this balance for such a procedure has served us adequately in the past. It is also well that worship leaders ever keep a watchful eye for contributions of others that will enhance a biblical approach to worship. It is just quite possible that all such truths have not yet been apprehended and appropriated.

The Significance of Continuity

The significance of the church's observance of the Lord's Supper lies in part at least in its historic origin in the observance of the Passover feast by Jesus and the Twelve. That the Lord's Supper was first celebrated on this occasion is attested to by the three Synoptic Gospels. (See Matt. 26:17-30; Mark 14:12-26, and Luke 22:7-39.) The various incidents relating to the first Passover form the basis for our study of this topic. (The reader should carefully examine the record of Exodus, chapters 7-12.)

Time and time again Moses and Aaron, commissioned by God, went before the pharaoh of Egypt demanding the release of the Hebrew people. The continuing injunction was, "Let my people go, that they may serve me." To support this demand nine plagues were directed against Egypt— the river turned to blood (7:20), frogs covered the land (8:6), lice were throughout the land (8:17), a vast swarm of flies (8:24), the death of the cattle (9:6), the presence of boils (9:10-11), destructive hail (9:23), the devastation brought by locusts (10:13-15), and darkness over the land (10:22-23). Repeatedly the pharaoh yielded to Moses' demands—but then prior to the implementation he relented ("the heart of Pharaoh was hardened") and prohibited the release.

At that point Moses was instructed to make careful plans for an exodus. ("Speak now in the ears of the people, and let every man borrow of his neighbour, and every woman of her neighbour, jewels of silver, and jewels of gold," 11:2.) A tenth and final plague—a plague of death—was to come upon the land (11:4-6). The people of Israel could avoid that calamity by following strictly a carefully prescribed ritual. That ritual may be summarized as follows: The people were to participate by families or in small groups (see 12:3-4). Each unit was to take a yearling lamb "without blemish" (v. 5) on the tenth day of the month. On the fourteenth of the month this lamb was to be slaughtered. (This month, Nisan, was to be a special month, for from this point on, "This month shall be unto you the beginning of months: it shall be the first month of the year to you," 12:2.) The blood of the Lamb was to be used to mark "on the two side posts and on the upper door post of the houses, wherein they shall eat" (12:7). Concerning the lamb itself: "They shall eat the flesh in that night, roast with fire, and unleavened bread; and with bitter herbs they shall eat it" (12:8). The marked doors would provide asylum when death visited the land. "When I see the blood, I will pass over you [hence the name Passover], and the plague shall not be upon you to destroy you, when I smite the land of Egypt" (12:13). The reader is surely familiar with the events that transpired in the immediate aftermath (see 12:21-51).

God's initial instructions to Moses continued: "And this day shall be unto you for a memorial; and ye shall keep it a feast to the Lord throughout your generations; ye shall keep it a feast by an ordinance for ever" (12:14). Moses assembled the people and, relaying the divine instructions, admonished the people: "Ye shall observe this thing [the Passover feast] for an ordinance to thee and to thy sons for ever" (12:24). The words of Moses continued:

> And it shall come to pass, when ye be come to the land which the Lord will give you, according as he hath promised, that ye shall keep this service. And it shall come to pass, when your children shall say unto you, What mean ye by this service? That ye shall say, It is the sacrifice of the Lord's passover, who passed over the houses of the children of Israel in Egypt, when he smote the Egyptians, and delivered our houses (12:25-27).

(I would call the reader's attention to the emphasis—as clearly stated in the texts above—on the repeated observance of the feast through the centuries as both a memorial and an instructional device.)

The people of Israel were by no means faithful to their continuing obligation to keep the Passover feast. There were many extended lapses through the centuries. Yet as we examine the record of the New Testament Scriptures we note that the Passover was being observed. Thus we read: "Now the first day of the feast of unleavened bread the disciples came to Jesus, saying unto him, Where wilt thou that we prepare for thee to eat the passover?" (Matt. 26:17, compare Mark 14:12 and Luke 22:7-8).

The customary ritual during the first century of the observance of the Passover meal was after this fashion: There was a benediction, the washing of hands, the eating of bitter herbs dipped in sauce, the explanation of the origin of the feast, the making of a sop from the lamb and bread and herbs, the eating of the sop, and the eating of the lamb. Interspersed throughout the ritual—and an essential part of it—was the consumption of four cups of wine and the singing of the Hallel (Psalms 113-118).

The gospel records do not contain an exacting account of the last Passover in which Jesus participated. We can only surmise that it followed the customary ritual as described above. John does describe Jesus' act of the washing of the feet (hands) and the act of the dipping of the sop (John 13:26, compare Matt. 26:23 and Mark 14:20). Also Matthew (26:30) and Mark (14:26) mention the singing of a hymn, surely a reference to the Hallel.

It was in the traditional setting that Jesus instituted a new memorial meal:

> And as they were eating, Jesus took bread, and blessed it, and brake it, and gave it to the disciples, and said, Take, eat; this is my body. And he took the cup, and gave thanks, and gave it to them, saying, Drink ye all of it; for this is my blood of the new testament, which is shed for many for the remission of sins. (Matt. 26:26-28; compare also Mark 14:22-24 and Luke 22:17-20; Paul adds his own testimony, I Cor. 11:23-25).

The hours that immediately followed brought the arrest, trial, and crucifixion of Jesus. Then there was the resurrection, the glorious resurrection. The disciples began to comprehend the full significance of those last words of Jesus—and a new memorial, the observance of the Lord's Supper, became the appropriate focal point of the worship of the early church.

The Lord's Supper was to the early Christians many things. It was a medium of unity as believers came together. It was a

76

memorial. It was, to some, an avenue for grace. And, it was a means of witness, for Paul had said, "As often as ye eat this bread, and drink this cup, ye do shew the Lord's death till he come" (I Cor. 11:26).

I have recalled these accounts of the institution of the Passover feast and the Lord's Supper for one reason basically. I wish to call attention to—and stress—the idea of continuity. God commanded Moses that the former feast was to be observed "for ever" and that through that perpetual observance they were to teach future generations. Jesus said of the new memorial, "This cup is the new testament in my blood: this do ye, as often as ye drink it, in remembrance of me" (I Cor. 11:25). Paul affirmed, "As often as you eat this bread, and drink this cup, you do shew the Lord's death till he come" (I Cor. 11:26). Continuity? Yes, continuity. As a professor of church history I believe that I can correctly observe that somewhere on earth Christians have gathered every single day since that first celebration to remember once again our Lord's death. They may have gathered and participated in a liturgy of communion celebration not to our liking, but nonetheless the celebration was observed and the continuity was continued. It is my position, in light of the historic precedent as attested by the Exodus account, that such continuity is very significant and that it composes an essential part of the framework of worship today! And it may be that if continuity is important here then continuity may be appropriate in respect to other acts of worship as well.

Questions and Projects

1. State three goals/values of the Restoration Movement.
2. Has a class on the Restoration Movement been taught in the last three years in the church that you attend?

3. Over a period of several weeks read the Psalms in the Revised Standard Version reflecting upon the use of the words "steadfast love" as they appear in the text.
4. Write a brief statement about the meaning of the word, *hesed* ("steadfast love").
5. Examine several extensive passages from the books of Exodus, Leviticus, Numbers, and/or Deuteronomy. Who authorized the acts of worship described therein? Who were the officiants? Who were the principal benefactors?
6. Memorize Micah 6:6-8.
7. In what ways is continuity significant to the observance of the Lord's Supper?

Chapter Six

EXPLORING BIBLICAL THEMES

I can readily recall a time three decades ago when conservative Christians gathered and burned at public bonfires copies of the Revised Standard Version of the Bible. This was considered by the participants to be the deserved fate of a liberal, unacceptable translation of the Holy Scriptures. Yet I must admit I was surprised when a student told me in recent months that he was severely chastised by an elder for using something other than the familiar King James version in the pulpit. Most of us who have attended Bible college or seminary have heard the oft repeated witticism about the King James Bible: "If it was good enough for the Apostle Paul, it is good enough for me!"

I believe that Christians today would be strengthened in their worship experience if they were more fully aware of the attitude with which the first-century Christians viewed the authority of the Scriptures which they possessed. It will be our purpose to make such an inquiry at this point.

The First Christians and Biblical Authority

Realize, of course, that the "Bible" of the first century Christians consisted primarily of the Old Testament writings plus those of the manuscripts of the gospels and the epistles that were even then being circulated. These people had no "New Testament" (at least not as we know it) for the writings of John were composed at the end of the first century and the actual compilation of the New Testament came later than that.

In fact it could be correctly observed that the first century Christians had two "Bibles." One was the cherished Hebrew text of their fathers. (In its later variations it is presently referred to as the Masoretic text.) In one sense the Hebrew language was no longer a "living language" for the ancestors of these people, those exiles who had returned from the captivity, had brought with them a corrupted, common variation of Hebrew that is called Aramaic. It was this Aramaic that was used by Jesus and His disciples in everyday parlance.

A second and more commonly used "Bible" of that day was the Greek (or Alexandrian) text, now designated as the Septuagint. The Septuagint was a translation of the Hebrew Bible into the Greek language, a task initiated in Egypt during the reign of King Ptolemy (285-247 B.C.) and finished prior to 132 B.C. This Greek translation, often called the LXX (the designation being a reference to the supposed seventy scholars who shared in the task of translation), was widely circulated throughout the Greek-speaking world and was commonly used in Palestine at the time of Jesus.

There are several significant differences between the Hebrew and the Greek texts that should be noted. (1) The Septuagint often contained several books that are not to be found in the Hebrew text—including such books as Judith, Tobit, Baruch, and the four books of the Maccabees. (2) The sequence of the books in the Septuagint did not follow the order or the classification of the Hebrew text, i.e., Law, Prophets, etc. (3) The actual content of the text of the Hebrew and the Greek Bibles is not identical. Both Bibles have a significant number of passages that are not to be found in the other. (Interestingly that portion of the text which is most consistent is the Pentateuch—that part of the Bible most important to the Jews.)

Thus we can make certain observations about the Bible of first century Judaism. It was a Bible whose canon was not officially finalized. It was a Bible that was extensively circulated in two well-known tongues. It was a Bible whose different versions disagreed with one another both in respect to the order of the books as well as to the actual content of those books. It was a book that was regularly interpreted by the allegorical method (in contrast to the grammatical-historical method commonly used today). This was the Bible of the Jews of the first century of the Christian era. That the Jewish worshiper of the day readily accepted such a condition (i.e., varying canons, varying orders, and varying texts) indicates that the emphasis of approach to the Scriptures must have focused on the spirit of the writings and not in a legalistic approach to the text.

The earliest Christians—themselves Jewish as well by birth—naturally initiated their own spiritual pilgrimages from this same perspective. In the intervening years additional revelatory writings were accepted and these eventually became the New Testament. The Holy Scriptures continued to be the priceless possession of these believers. The Christians, as their Jewish predecessors in the faith, recognized that these writings were in a unique sense the Word of God. The writer of the epistles to the Hebrews declared, "God, who at sundry times and in divers manners spake in time past unto the fathers by the prophets" (Heb. 1:1), and Paul affirmed, "Well spake the Holy Ghost by Esaias the prophet unto our fathers" (Acts 28:25).

The early church recognized that the intervention of the Holy Spirit was the causative factor in inspiration. "For the prophecy came not in old time by the will of man: but holy men of God spake as they were moved by the Holy Ghost" (II Peter 1:21). All sacred writings were thus inspired, for Paul stated, "All scripture is given by inspiration of God, and is profitable for doctrine, for reproof, for correction, for instruction in righteousness" (II Tim. 3:16). Further, the New Testament writers had a special awareness of both the completion of Judaism and the need to indicate the fulfillment of the Old Testament prophecies in the life of Jesus. Peter's declaration, "Men and brethren, this scripture must needs have been fulfilled, which the Holy Ghost by the mouth of David spake before," is representative of many similar claims that appear in the New Testament (Acts 1:16).

The early church containing such a high percentage of Jewish people among its early membership found it natural to adopt the common version of the Scriptures of the day, the Septuagint. In fact there was such a general acceptance of the Septuagint by the early church that the Jewish community in its developing hostility to the church came to repudiate the Septuagint during the second half of the first century of the Christian era. It is to be noted that the quotations from the Old Testament that appear in the New Testament texts are largely derived from the Septuagint. But more than that the theological presuppositions of the New Testament writers are more often posited on the Septuagint rather than the Hebrew text. There can be no question but that the New Testament writers had access to the Hebrew and Aramaic writings; the inference is rather that the early Christians, like their Jewish counterparts, had little concern about the variations that were to be found within the existing texts.

Hopefully the relevance of this investigation will become apparent to us as we reflect upon these two summations. (1) The early church—the church of the first century period—did not have a definitive, "official" Bible. Rather the Bibles they possessed were to be found in different texts, with differing sequence of order of the contents, and even with variations between the texts themselves. Nonetheless the Christian of the first century was unconcerned with these factors. That which the individual read or heard was recognized to be the inspired Word of God and that was unquestionably sufficient for the believer. The early Christian was much more concerned with the spirit of the message than with the exactness of the letter. To that individual the significance of the Book was that it so boldly presented the Man of the Book, Jesus the Christ! (2) The first century Christians because they viewed the sacred writings as uniquely the revelation of God cherished them indeed as the Holy Scriptures. These writings, both the Old and the New Testaments, were read in their public assemblies and, when available, in their homes. These Holy Scriptures were both studied in serious investigation and reflected upon in private meditation. They were committed to memory. They served as a major motivational resource for the evangelistic mission of the church. They became the primary source-book of preaching (especially as the apostolic witnesses passed from the scene). They constituted the single, tangible, most glorious possession of the church.

Cannot we learn a very important truth for worship today from the life and witness of these early believers? When we divert our energies to probing discussions of particular theories of inerrancy, when we quibble with one another about the legitimacy of a particular version for public worship, when we sever fellowship with other believers because we cannot agree on the resolution of these matters, we cause the communicative powers of the Holy Spirit to become ineffectual in our lives. We who would restore New

Testament Christianity ought to be earnest in our efforts to capture the attitude of the first century worshipers in this respect.

We possess significant spiritual advantage over those early worshipers. In our day the canonization of the Holy Scriptures has long since been completed. The technology of modern printing has made the writings readily available. The exactitude of modern scholarship has assured us a text more complete and of surpassing accuracy to that possessed by the early Christians. Having this unique blessing we ought surely to commit ourselves—as did those early Christians—to the study, the proclamation, and the utilization as a primary worship resource, of the Holy Scriptures of God. As Restorationists we have no alternative but to be true to our principles of procedure. It is within this perspective that our whole approach to the Word in worship must be implemented.

The Day of Worship

Memories of the Sundays of my childhood come flooding back to me. Always there was the morning services of the local church. Then sometimes we stopped at the local drugstore—one of the few establishments open on Sunday in those days—to buy a copy of the Sunday newspaper and a quart of ice cream. (In the winter months we huddled around the coal stove to eat the ice cream because it was cold and there was no central heating!) But always we attended the services of the church. My family never even considered the option of not attending. It was Sunday and Sunday was a day of rest and worship.

The creation account records: "And on the seventh day God ended his work which he had made; and he rested on the seventh day from all his work which he had made. And God blessed the seventh day, and sanctified it: because that in it he had rested from all his work which God created and made" (Gen. 2:2-3). The die was cast; God had rested on the seventh day and man ever after was to observe it as a holy day of rest as well.

This seventh day is properly called the Sabbath. The word comes from a Hebrew root from *SBT* which bears the meanings of "cease, desist, rest, come to an end, and inactivity." Hence the word "sabbath" may be properly translated as, "day of rest." The book of Exodus records an interesting verse that might be translated literally, "For in six days the Lord made heaven and earth, and on the seventh day he rested, and *caught his breath* (Exod. 31:17b; the major English translations are not quite so descriptive, reading rather, "he rested, and was refreshed").

During the period of the wilderness wanderings God provided generously for the physical sustenance of the people in sending an abundance of quail and manna. (See Exod. 16.) This manna was an interesting substance. It is described as "a small round thing, as small as the hoar frost on the ground" (v. 14) and "it was like coriander seed, white; and the taste of it was like wafers made with honey" (v. 31). Careful instructions were given to the people that they were to gather a double portion on the sixth day of the week for on the seventh there would be none. There were those folk though who disregarded the instructions of the Lord; "there went out some of the people on the seventh day for to gather, and they found none" (v. 27). The Lord rebuked them through Moses, and at last "the people rested on the seventh day" (v. 30).

In this context was issued the commandment—one of ten —to the Israelites: "Remember the sabbath day, to keep it holy" (Exod. 20:8). The explanation was added:

> Six days shalt thou labour, and do all thy work: but the seventh day is the sabbath of the Lord thy God: in it thou shalt not do any work, thou, nor thy son, nor thy daughter, thy manservant, nor thy maidservant, nor thy cattle, nor thy stranger that is within thy gates: for in six days the Lord made heaven and earth, the sea, and all that in them is, and rested the seventh day: wherefore the Lord blessed the sabbath day, and hallowed it (Exod. 20:9-11).

The purpose of the day was clearly one of rest. "Six days thou shalt do thy work, and on the seventh day thou shalt rest: that thine ox and thine ass may rest, and the son of thy handmaid, and the stranger, may be refreshed." (Exod. 23:12; again, the word "refreshed" is literally "catch one's breath," compare Exod. 31:17, as mentioned above.)

With the creation of the synagogue during the Exile as an institution, the Sabbath became a day of worship and study of the Scriptures as well as a day of rest. While there is no biblical injunction for the establishment of the Synagogue the authentication of its worthiness is attested by the regular presence of Jesus at its services. "And [Jesus] taught in the synagogues, being glorified of all. And he came to Nazareth, where he had been brought up: and, as his custom was, he went into the synagogue on the sabbath day, and stood up for to read" (Luke 4:15-16). Synagogue sabbath services were designed to provide an opportunity for praise and singing as well as the study of the Scriptures. Fellowship was a significant aspect of the assembly.

Unfortunately and tragically, through the centuries the Jewish rabbis had made the Sabbath an end in itself. While the purpose of the Sabbath was clear enough—the cessation of all labor—the rabbis had gone to great lengths to define precisely that which constituted work and that which did not. Numerous interpretations and regulations were declared. Many were so extreme that they bordered on the ridiculous. (For example, if a person suffered from a toothache on the Sabbath that person might gargle with vinegar—a common remedy of the day. To gargle was not an infraction of the sabbath law; to spit out the vinegar was, for this was considered an act of labor and all labor was prohibited! The hapless toothache sufferer had no alternative but to swallow the vinegar!) The situation was so desperate that in the time of Antiochus Epiphanes thousands of Jews were slaughtered in the streets of Jerusalem rather than taking action on the Sabbath to fight back in defense!

This needless perversion of the Sabbath had not abated by Jesus' day. Some at this time maintained that even the act of walking on the grass on the Sabbath was wrong because in so doing one would crush the grass seed from the stems and this constituted a threshing-of-sorts (and, clearly, threshing was wrong).

Thus Jesus, in His continuing efforts to bring divine illumination on the understanding of God's will for the well-being of His supreme creation, focused many of His teachings on this perversion of the Sabbath. With perhaps the single exception of the conflict with the Jews about His Messiahship Jesus took sharpest issue with them on this issue of the true nature of the Sabbath.

On one Sabbath Jesus and His disciples were walking through a grainfield. His disciples were hungry and they (not Jesus) ate some grain from the field. On any day but the Sabbath this act was both legal and acceptable. But on

87

this occasion the ever-present watchdog Pharisees commented, "Behold, thy disciples do that which is not lawful to do upon the sabbath day" (Matt. 12:2). Jesus answered them (which answer we shall shortly note) and proceeded on to their synagogue (v. 9) where He was shortly embroiled in controversy again, this time over the issue of healing a person on the Sabbath. Jesus' response was: "What man shall there be among you, that shall have one sheep, and if it fall into a pit on the sabbath day, will he not lay hold on it, and lift it out? How much then is a man better than a sheep? Wherefore it is lawful to do well on the sabbath days." (Matt. 12:11-12; Jesus then healed the man's withered hand, v. 13). On another Sabbath He healed a woman who had an "infirmity eighteen years, and was bowed together, and could in no wise lift up herself" (Luke 13:11). In this instance the ruler of the synagogue with indignation challenged Jesus' act of compassion: "There are six days in which men ought to work: in them therefore come and be healed, and not on the sabbath day" (v. 14). Jesus rebuked the man as a hypocrite (v. 15) and after giving a rebuttal similar to the one recorded in the twelfth chapter of Matthew it is noted that "all his adversaries were ashamed: and all the people rejoiced for all the glorious things that were done by him" (Luke 13:17). On yet another Sabbath Jesus healed a man who suffered from dropsy. On this occasion His opponents "could not answer him again to these things." (See Luke 14:1-6.)

When the church came into being shortly after the resurrection the accepted day for worship underwent a transformation. Sunday (the Roman "day of the sun") became the special day of the church—the day when Christians gathered around a table for a simple, common meal "in remembrance of Him." Sunday was determined as the special day primarily because it was the day the Lord arose. Through the passing years as the membership of the church became increasingly non-Jewish there was a gradual disassociation from all things Jewish. The Sabbath was no longer significant to the church; the Lord's Day (Sunday) was. (Even yet one occasionally hears Sunday referred to as the Sabbath but this is no more than the incorrect usage of a figure of speech.)

Ironically however during the intervening centuries leaders of the church slipped into the errors of their Jewish for-bearers. Acceptance of a mode of Sunday worship followed a pattern not unlike that of the Jewish Sabbath. Stringent rules were set up to regulate human actions and behavior on the Lord's Day. Oftentimes these regulations applied to all the population and not just to those who were actually members of the church and therefore worshipers of the Lord of the church. For example in the first English-speaking colony in North America, Virginia, a group of harsh dictates were set forth in 1610 by Sir Thomas West. Re-established the following year by Sir Thomas Dale they are known to-day as "Dale's Laws." One of these laws, the sixth, attempted to establish regular attendance at the two Sunday services. The first infraction of the attendance policy was to result in the forfeiture of the provision allowance for the week (these early settlers shared a common store). A second infraction brought a similar forfeiture for another week plus a whipping. If a settler missed a third time the law said that "for the third to suffer death." (Brutal? Do you think it actually needed to be enforced?) It is important to note that this was civil law for thus had the church so permeated society. A generation or so later in Massachusetts a law was passed (1653—again this was civil law) that made it illegal to cook, clean house, or even go for an extended walk on Sunday! The spirit of the first century rabbis was alive and well—and to be found in the early American church! In reality it is only within the lifetime of most of the readers that the vestige of the old, harsh "blue laws" (as they are broadly called) have been eliminated or moderated.

Yet the truth of the matter is that the Lord's Day—or the Sabbath—exists to give God's people a richer, fuller existence. Human need always takes precedent over ritual observance. When Jesus' disciples plucked grain from the field through which they were passing the Pharisees objected to Jesus, "Why do they on the sabbath day that which is not lawful?" (We refer now to the account of this incident as it is recorded in Mark 2:23-28 rather than the parallel passage in Matt. 12:1-8.) Jesus responded: "Have ye never read what David did, when he had need, and was an hungred, he, and they that were with him? How he went into the house of God in the days of Abiathar the high priest, and did eat the shewbread, which is not lawful to eat but for the priests, and gave also to them which were with him?" (Mark 2:25-26, compare to I Sam. 21:1-6). How was David able to eat this shewbread? Noblesse oblige? No! The answer is simple yet pertinent and far reaching in its consequence. "The sabbath was made for man, and not man for the sabbath" (Mark 2:27). A sacred thing is never so sacred as when it is used to help a needy, desperate individual!

The Lord's Day is for the spiritual benefit of God's people. It is yet a day of rest and worship and Bible study. It is a day when all members of the family ought to enter joyfully into the pursuit of these objectives. My parents did not hold a threatening cudgel over me respecting church attendance. Rather church attendance was the accepted high-point of

90

the activities of the Lord's Day. It was the time we gathered with our larger family and our friends to join in a joyful worship of our Lord!

Americans make much of recreation today (and spend billions for it as well). Now admittedly there is vast distortion of the recreation emphasis, especially in respect to Sunday activities. Nonetheless the fundamental concept of recreation is both good and holy. The word means to re-create in the sense of restoring or refreshing. I once served for some weeks as the interim preacher of a rural congregation whose house of worship was located just a short distance from a strip mine. I observed there two of the largest cranes I have ever seen. An elder of the church informed me that each of these cranes was operated by three men on eight hour shifts, seven days a week, fifty-two weeks a year. The only shutdown was breakdown! But the human body and soul cannot endure such an ordeal. There must be re-creation and that re-creation comes most beneficially in the form of worship on a regular basis on the Lord's Day! The Sabbath was made for man!

I live in a rural farming community. On a recent Sunday in the midst of a busy harvest-time I voiced my commendation to a farmer friend for his attendance at the worship services. His reply was: "If we're too busy to take Sunday off for worship we're too busy." Admittedly we live in a highly complex industrial society where there are indeed exorbitant demands on our time and energies. Yet I recall one elder who though he had to work at a nearby factory on Sunday morning actually clocked out long enough to come to church to serve at the Lord's table!

Making Sunday a day of family worship involves family planning. Saturday evenings ought not be so busy that the family is still tired on Sunday mornings. Sunday morning worship should be a joyful family occasion. Sunday afternoon family activities ought not be so hectic that they place undue pressure on family members to conform. (I believe that re-creation is a God-ordained enrichment.) And then how about an early Sunday vesper hour service so that the family is free to spend a relaxed Sunday evening together at home?

Edward Taylor was a minister of a Congregational church in colonial Massachusetts. As death came to him in 1729 when he was in his mid-80's clearly he was a part of an American culture that gave serious (though distorted) attention to proper Lord's Day osbervance. Being a minister of a denomination that celebrated communion on a monthly basis, Taylor took his role as the officiant very seriously. He devoted long hours on Saturday evening and night to meditation and prayer in preparation for the task that would be his on the morrow. Often times he set down his devotional thoughts in poetic form—and out of this experience came some of the greatest spiritually-oriented poetry in the history of American literature!

How wonderful that a worship experience can be life-transforming! And it can be—and ought to be! This is the Lord's Day, a day for praise and worship of our Lord and a day for life-restoring and soul-transforming for each of us both individually and in our various family relationships! Make the most of the Lord's Day!

Places of Worship

I greatly enjoy the opportunity to go hiking through the autumn woods. It is an unmatched thrill to view the fall foliage with its many breath-taking hues. I often carry with me a squirrel call—a small, brass plate on a wood device that produces a rasping sound—with which I can "talk" to the squirrels. (I may even carry a rifle to satisfy the expectations of curious neighbors—but I wouldn't think of firing it and spoiling the tranquility of the occasion.) Why then do I venture out in this manner if I'm not going to hunt? Because I love the sheer beauty, the solitude, of the woods. It is the perfect place and occasion to commune with God.

But don't kid yourself (and many evidently do), such an experience alone does not satisfy the basic worship requirement. Make no mistake about it, there must be a corporate worship experience—the individual must worship with the body of believers. The psalmist declares the joy of such a worshiper in the house of the Lord:

> How amiable are thy tabernacles [or translate, dwelling place], O Lord of hosts!
> My soul longeth, yea, even fainteth for the courts of the Lord: my heart and my flesh crieth out for the living God.
> Yea, the sparrow hath found an house, and the swallow a nest for herself, where she may lay her young, even thine altars, O Lord of hosts, my King, and my God.
> Blessed are they that dwell in thy house: they will be still praising thee. . . .
> For a day in thy courts is better than a thousand. I had rather be a doorkeeper in the house of my God, than to dwell in the tents of wickedness (Psalm 84:1-4, 10).

We now direct our attention to make some observations on the basis of what the Bible says about the appropriateness of the place of worship.

A very significant achievement of the Jews during the period of the Exile was the establishment of the synagogue as a continuing institution. When they returned to Palestine at the close of the Exile the synagogue went with them. From there the synagogue was taken to almost every city around the world where emigrating Jews took residence. The significance is that the synagogue was very much the center of Jewish religious, educational, and social life for centuries. There they worshiped, there their children assembled for study, there they gathered for fellowship. The synagogue was very much the focal point of the community.

It is no wonder then that when the church came into being it also was the religious, educational, and social center for the people. Consider the following narration: "They continued steadfastly in the apostles' doctrine and fellowship, and in breaking of bread, and in prayers . . . And all that believed were together, and had all things common; and sold their possessions and goods, and parted them to all men, as every man had need. And they, continuing daily with one accord in the temple, and breaking bread from house to house, did eat their meat with gladness and singleness of heart, praising God, and having favour with all the people" (Acts 2:42, 44-47). Clearly the church was very much the focal point of the Christian community. Though there were surely no church buildings as we know them today yet such places of worship as they used came to fill the same, essential role as had the physical facility of the synagogue.

One of the very first buildings that the earliest English settlers in New England constructed was the church. It was a simple structure, made of logs, and walled about as a stockade. Because they also used it for other purposes—a courtroom, town hall, temporary residences, and a fort to ward off Indian attacks—it was called a "meeting house" rather than church, but church still it was! It met the criteria of being the place of gathering for worship and the focal point of community activities.

It is no mere coincidence that the church buildings of Europe with their magnificent spires dominate the landscape of the communities that house them. This is most appropriate. The church building ought to be the one thing that towers over the community. The little rural church that I serve meets in a building that has a splendid white spire that can be seen from almost every area of the township. (In fact I can see the spire from the college chapel that houses my office, eleven miles away!)

The house of worship is many things to many people. But among other things it is to serve as the center of community. It is most unfortunate that in many major American cities today the skyline is dominated by strictly secular structures.

We may also observe from our examination of the Scriptures that the place of worship is representative of the people's love of God. Yet it needs to be stated that the assessed value of the place of worship is of no immediate relevance. On the one hand the construction of the Tabernacle (see Exod. 25-40) and the Temple (see II Sam. 7, I Kings 5-6, I Chron. 21-22, 28-29, and II Chron. 2-4) in the Old Testament period was accompanied by the expenditure of funds almost beyond comprehension. On the other hand Jacob worshiped by a pile of rocks (Gen. 28:10-22), Moses worshiped by a burning bush (Exod. 3:1-5), and Jonah from the fish's belly (Jonah 2:1)—all places, we presume, constituted at a minimal outlay of money! In the New Testament we note of Jesus that He worshiped in the wilderness (Matt. 4:1-11), on a mountain (Matt. 17:1-9), in an upper room (Matt. 26:17-30), and in a public park (Matt. 26:36-46). Paul worshiped in many places it is recorded, not the finest of which was a prison cell (Acts 16:25). John's grand experience of worship came when he was in exile on the isle of Patmos (Rev. 1:9-10).

I have seen places of worship that contained furnishings plated with gold and complemented with intricately hand-carved sculpturings of wood, marble, or ivory. Yet I have also seen places of worship constructed of plywood and cinder block, even ormanented as it were with barbed wire!

Thus it matters not as to what is the economic value of the structure being used for worship. After all it is worship directed to One who owns "the cattle upon a thousand hills" (Psalm 50:10). It does matter that the physical structure should reflect the measure of the love of the individuals who worship there. The economic value of the church building should correlate directly to the mean per capita wealth of the congregation. To put it simply, as assessment of the autos in the church parking lot should be indicative of the relative value of the building. (The church budget for mission and Christian education should be commensurate as well.)

We may also observe from the Scriptures that the place of worship is purposeful to the needs of the people who gather there. It is quite significant I believe that reference is frequently made in the New Testament to "house churches," that is, congregations that gathered for worship in the homes of individuals. Consider, for example, Acts 12:12; Romans 16:5; I Corinthians 16:19; Colossians 4:15; and Philemon 2. (As the Romans permitted no construction during the first century for what we would consider conventional church buildings what other options were there then? Christians either met in the existing synagogues, out-of-doors, or in people's homes.)

Aquila was a man who shared a common profession and acquaintanceship with Paul (see Acts 18:3). He along with his wife, Prisca, opened their home as a meeting place for the church (Rom. 16:5), evidently doing this in both Rome and Ephesus. Being a tentmaker he probably needed—and had—large accommodations for a dwelling place. (One just doesn't lay out a tent in any old corner of the house!) The fact is noted that in four of the six times the couple is mentioned, Prisca is named first. She must have been quite a lady! Does this suggest anything to those of you who know wives well? "Aquila, do I have to clean the entire house again this Saturday? Have you invited the whole church for worship?"

The charter members of the congregation where I worship first met in 1838 in people's homes. After about a year a simple building was erected near a creek that intersected the township. This pattern of the "house church"—like that of New Testament example—would be duplicated in many, many communities across the American frontier. It was a simple, necessary expedient. And, it was adequate to the needs of the people.

Paul's usual approach to evangelism was to address first the Jewish synagogue in a city. In one instance (Acts 16:12-14) we read of a Jewish community so small that all of the active worshipers, in this case, women, gathered by the river bank. (If a few as ten Jewish men lived in a community a synagogue was to be established. Apparently less than that number lived in this city.) "And on the sabbath we went out of the city by a river side, where prayer was wont to be made; and we sat down, and spake unto the women which resorteth thither" (Acts 16:13). The city was Philippi; the leader among the women was named Lydia. A riverbank served the needs of the people, so by the riverbank the local church was started (see Acts 16:15).

The first permanent English settlement in North America was in what is now Virginia. (The village was named Jamestown, the river was called the James River. Why not? The king that authorized this expedition was James I; his name is also affixed to the familiar translation of the Bible.) The first English settlers, including the Anglican minister that came with them, shortly improvised a chapel from an old sail from the ship that brought them. Rough hewn planks and logs served as pews and pulpit and altar. It was a crude arrangement indeed but it met the immediate needs of the worshipers. Later, more elaborate functional structures for worship were erected.

Perhaps the most amazing worship experience of which I have heard in the twentieth century took place in a prison camp during the Korean War. Ironically it was a prison camp operated by our military forces and the worshipers were captured North Korean troops. (Who is to say one has to be a communist just because he was drafted into the North Korean army!) One of my friends was there (as an observer, I might add) and he saw thousands of North Korean prisoners gathered for the purpose of the singing of hymns and prayer. It was a self-initiated revival—American (or U.N.) forces had nothing to do with it! The surroundings were austere but the circumstances of worship met the needs of the people.

Jesus gives us a further, important insight into the nature of worship when He says: "But thou, when thou prayest, enter into thy closet, and when thou hast shut thy door, pray to thy Father which is in secret; and thy Father which seeth in secret shall reward thee openly" (Matt. 6:6). This is in sharp contrast to the hypocrites who love to pray in prominent public places that they "may be seen of men" (Matt. 6:5). Our destination then in worship is the "closet" (from the Greek *tameion,* literally the innermost or otherwise hidden room of the house), that is, any place where we may worship unpretentiously. The place of worship is to meet the spiritual needs of the people.

In summation we may observe: (1) A place of worship should reflect the majesty, the grandeur of God. It may be old, historic Kings College Chapel at Cambridge—or it may be a simple chapel in nature (as the beautiful "Temple of the Trees," a scenic spot in central Illinois where an outdoor chapel is framed entirely and exclusively by the towering maple trees of a virgin timber; there is no building, one sits on logs in a cathedral of nature!). Wherever, however, the building must call attention to the holiness of God! (2) A place of worship must be conducive to meeting the needs/experiences of the corporate body of believers. Nothing less is adequate, nothing more is necessary. (3) A place of worship must not be secondary to any other purpose of the congregation. Yet I see church structures that house basketball courts, stainless steel kitchens, and flowing fountains—and I wonder what are the priorities of the congregation.

Carl Ketcherside suggests that the church of the twenty-first century might just be a church that gathers around the kitchen table—a return to the "house church" concept. But wherever the church of the future chooses to worship—or is forced to worship—there are certain biblical guidelines to be observed. And when those guidelines are followed biblical worship will occur.

The Practice of Fasting

It is an interesting phenomenon that people observe those rules they wish to observe and ignore those rules they do not wish to observe. For example, umpires in major league baseball call some rules closely, others not at all. Illustrative of this was a controversial play at third base in a recent National League game. The baserunner slid violently into third base, escaping the tag. With minimal assistance from the third base coach he arose and continued his dash for home plate. He was immediately called out. Though the rules of baseball clearly indicate that the umpire's action was correct the irate team manager responded that this was the only time in his thirty years in baseball that he had actually observed an umpire enforce the regulation.

Christian Churches/Churches of Christ are a part of a movement of churches committed to the restoration of New Testament Christianity. A faithful attempt has been made to practice those customs and to perpetuate those teachings that are considered essential to the nature of the church as it was established by Christ and the inspired apostles in the first century. Hence the practice of believer's baptism by immersion is followed today. Biblical names—Christian, Church of Christ, Disciples—have been appropriated. A weekly observance of the Lord's Supper, administered by lay leaders, is everywhere observed. Church polity places authority for governance of the local body in the hands of the eldership of the congregation in question. Other facets of New Testament practice and teaching are faithfully followed. But has everything of note of the first century church been adopted by today's churches? Surely not! The author has long puzzled over the observation that these churches, given their priority emphasis of restorationism, have not added the observance of footwashing and/or fasting to the worship agenda of today. (Admittedly Walter Scott of noted nineteenth century achievement did on occasion practice

100

footwashing—even as some black congregations do yet to-day.) But fasting? Fasting is simply not compatible with the contemporary American life-style and no amount of clamor about restorationism is likely to alter that fact.

Nonetheless as fasting was definitely a biblical mode of worship careful attention shall be given to the subject here. Make no mistake about it, the author is by no means advocating the acceptance of the practice as a regular (or even occasional) feature of the worship of today's church. He is however suggesting three things about it. (1) It is clearly both a biblical and a legitimate contribution to worship. The Old Testament and the New Testament alike make that clear. (2) It is a practice that has meaning for today's Christians and one that could be utilized to much greater advantage by today's churches than is commonly done. (3) Even if a local congregation at no point whatsoever chooses to observe the fast still there is at least one very important truth to be gained from a consideration thereof. That truth is this: the Christian must take advantage of every means at his/her disposal to focus on the priorities among those things enumerated as spiritual. These reasons are clearly of sufficient importance to merit our attention to the study of fasting.

The word "fast" (and variations thereof) appears in both the Old Testament and the New Testament. The words most commonly used in the Old Testament are the Hebrew verb *sûm* and the Hebrew noun *sôm*. The Greek words regularly used in the New Testament writings are the verb *nēsteuo* and the nouns *nēsteia* and *nēstis*. (The reader sufficiently skilled in the biblical languages may wish to pursue further study of these words in the appropriate lexical dictionaries and concordances.)

Even a casual examination of a comprehensive concordance will indicate that fasting was indeed a recognized biblical practice. Indeed there are numerous such references to fasting in both the Old and the New Testaments. Consider, for example, David fasting in sorrow at the deaths of Saul and Jonathan (II Sam. 1:12). Ezra fasted because of his awareness of the sins of the people (Ezra 10:6). Nehemiah fasted in sorrow when he received news of the "great affliction and reproach" of the remnant at Jerusalem and of the condition of the wall and the gates of Jerusalem (Neh. 1:3-4). In the opening chapters of Luke's gospel we are introduced to the prophetess Anna who "departed not from the temple" and who worshiped God there "with fastings and prayers night and day" (Luke 2:37). On one occasion followers of John the Baptist came to Jesus with the query, "Why do we and the Pharisees fast oft, but thy disciples fast not?" Jesus' answer consisted of a brief statement of explanation and not a voiced abandonment of fasting. (See Matt. 9:14-15.) Positive statements by Jesus to be found in the Sermon on the Mount indicate rather His support of the practice. (See Matt. 6:16-18.)

From these and other references to fasting in the Scriptures we can make certain observations: (1) Fasting could be partial abstinence from food or total abstinence. (If fasting is to be practiced for an extended period of time it is generally recognized that the regular intake of fluids is exempt from the fast.) (2) Fasting could be of short or long duration. One might fast for a few hours or a day or so, but on the other hand are the examples of Moses and Jesus abstaining from food for a period of forty days. (Accounts in other literature—including contemporary events—cite instances of individuals fasting for much longer periods than this.) (3) Fasting was commonly practiced as an individual experience but it could be observed by a congregation collectively or

102

even by a nation. (See first Acts 13:3 and 14:23, then Judg. 20:26.)

It is evident from various passages in the Scriptures that certain individuals wished to give testimony to the public of the intensity of their personal experience of fasting. To do this they frequently refrained from washing, adorned their heads with dust or ashes, and exhibited pious countenances. Jesus was openly critical of such a public display of piety. (See Matt. 6:16-18.) Hopefully present leaders of the church who might advocate the practice of fasting would prescribe measures of conduct that would be more socially acceptable than those denounced by Jesus as hypocritical! (The appearance of such a disheveled caricature in the assembly of the congregation today would be more than most fastidious folk could tolerate!)

While there are a number of references in the New Testament to fasting the only regular fast of the Jewish people mentioned therein is that of the Day of Atonement (Acts 27:9). Perhaps the major sources of encouragement for the Christians in adopting the rite of fasting were that of the example of the synagogue and that of the personal enrichment that the practice of fasting affords. That the early Christians fasted is evident as is the fact that Christians through the centuries continued to observe it. (It is interesting to note that the *Didache*—an early Christian document dated just barely beyond the first century period—bids Christians to fast on the fourth and the sixth days of the week rather than to follow the practice of the unworthy folk who fasted on the second and fifth days! (See the *Didache*, 8:1.)

We note in the Scriptures that great distress in an individual's life can cause loss of appetite (as with Hannah at the frustration of being childless, I Sam. 1:7). So also great anger can cause one to abstain from eating (as Jonathan in his anger at his father's conduct toward David, I Sam. 20:34). More properly, however, fasting was intended to accomplish one of several distinct purposes. We may note four of these: (1) Fasting served as an expression of grief. Consider David's sorrow at the death of Abner (II Sam. 3:35). Any among the readers who has experienced the loss of an extremely dear friend can readily identify with this lack of desire for nourishment. (2) Fasting served as an expression of confession of sin. This was the reaction of the wicked king Ahab when he was confronted with the soul-searching words of Elijah (I Kings 21:27). To go without eating was also the reaction of Paul when he became painfully aware on the road to Damascus of the error of his actions (Acts 9:9, though the word "fast" does not appear in this passage). (3) Fasting served as a means of humbling oneself, or in some instances of bringing self-inflicted punishment in a futile attempt to do penance for sin. (One is reminded of the experience of Martin Luther in those precipitous days prior to the nailing of the ninety-five theses on the door of the Castle Church at Wittenberg.) (4) Fasting served as means of attempting to insure God's response to the individual's request. Thus David fasted in an effort to secure God's healing touch on his dying child. (Only when the child was dead and there was no point to prolonged fasting on David's part did he cease to fast, II Sam. 12:15-23.) There were those who thought that the act of fasting automatically brought a response from God but the prophets dramatically said "no" to this belief. (See Isa. 58:5-12; Jer. 14:11-12; and Zech. 7:1-13.)

Of particular interest to us are certain New Testament texts. On one occasion a father brought his demon-possessed

104

son to Jesus with the lament, "I brought him to thy disciples, and they could not cure him." Jesus later answered the query of the disciples concerning their futility that it was because of their unbelief. "If you have faith as a grain of mustard seed . . . nothing shall be impossible unto you." He then added, "Howbeit this kind goeth not out but by prayer and fasting." (Matt. 17:21, note that while this last verse is not to be found in some of the important ancient manuscripts, it was evidently considered to be a valid truth by the early Christians.) Further we note that the early church at least on occasion commissioned its missionaries with fasting and prayer (Acts 13:2-3, in this instance, Barnabas and Saul). Also there was a regular practice of ordaining elders in the churches to the accompaniment of prayer and fasting (see Acts 14:23).

The words of Jesus strike to the heart of the matter. "Moreover when ye fast, be not, as the hypocrites, of a sad countenance: for they disfigure their faces, that they may appear unto men to fast. Verily I say unto you, They have their reward." Rather His followers are admonished to seek a genuine relationship of piety toward the Father. "But thou, when thou fastest, anoint thine head, and wash thy face; that thou appear not unto men to fast, but unto thy Father which is in secret: and thy Father, which seeth in secret, shall reward thee openly" (Matt. 6:16-18). The correct conduct in fasting is essentially the same as that of the proper approach to stewardship. It is to be a private act of piety between the believer and God.

Fasting can be a valid religious experience. Basically fasting is the practice of self-restraint and self-restraint is fundamental to the disciplined Christian life. While on the one hand there is the inherent danger of excess discipline yet on the other hand without discipline there is no individual development to maturity and eventually, inevitably society collapses.

Again may I affirm that I am not advocating—nor even encouraging—fasting for today's churches. I simply observe that it is valid and it is biblical. The appropriate occasion for fasting today as in the first century period is at those times that are of momentous importance to the life of the congregation—ordination (the other participants and I fasted at the time of my ordination), those opportunities when the church may wish to initiate a bold venture in church growth or even perhaps the alleviation of world hunger, times of some extreme national crisis, or a period of intense, individual soul-searching.

Perhaps the most important single truth to be learned from this phase of our study is this: the Christian must always focus on priorities. The individual must always direct his/her energies toward that which is of ultimate value for the kingdom. This is the only thing upon which I insist, that we focus upon priorities. If fasting will enable us to focus upon priorities—and it could—then we should fast. But if there are other ways at our disposal of focusing on priorities then we have the privilege of pursuing those means and omitting the ritual of fasting.

Questions and Projects

1. What is the Septuagint?
2. Did the first century Christians more frequently refer to the Hebrew text or the Greek text of the Old Testament? What is the significance of this?

106

3. Describe Jesus' personal attitude toward the observance of the laws regarding the Sabbath.
4. What was the basis for the attitude of the early American colonists respecting the Sabbath?
5. Reflect upon the most worshipful experience that you have had in the last year. Did the physical facilities of the place of worship contribute to that experience? If so, how?
6. What is a "house church"?
7. How could fasting be incorporated into a service of worship by your congregation on a special occasion?

Part Two — "WHERE WE CAN GO"

Chapter Seven

DETERMINING PRIORITIES/OBJECTIVES

Perhaps the most relevant question that a person ever asks introspectively is, What is my ultimate priority on earth? We who are professed disciples of Jesus attempt of course to answer this question within the Christian context but even then the answer is not an easy one. Several obvious responses come to mind. Jesus has answered definitively, "and thou shalt love the Lord thy God with all thy heart, and with all thy soul, and with all thy mind, and with all thy strength: this is the first commandment. And the second is like, namely this. Thou shalt love thy neighbor as thyself" (Mark 12:30-31a). A second response is that each of us as Christians are obligated to make a faithful witness to others of the gospel that we ourselves have received. ("Gospel" here as elsewhere is defined as "good news"; Paul states specifically, "I delivered unto you first of all that which I also received, how that Christ died for our sins according to the scriptures; and that he was buried, and that he rose again the third day according to the scriptures," I Corinthians 15:3-4.) A third response—and one solidly supported by human reasoning—is that we are to perform that eternal stewardship of praise for which apparently Adam was created and which surely the saints in heaven do perform. (To support this I suggest that Adam was certainly a steward and that the ultimate objective of stewardship is to increase the glory of God. Further, the author of the book of Revelation relates, "I heard a great voice of much people in heaven, saying, alleluia; Salvation, and glory, and honour, and power, unto the Lord our God. . . . and the four and twenty elders and the four beasts fell down and worshiped God that sat on the throne, saying, Amen; Alleluia. . . . and I heard as it were the voice of a great multitude, and as the voice of many waters, and as the voice of mighty thunderings, saying, Alleluia: for the Lord God omnipotent reigneth," Revelation 19:1, 4, 6).

To rank further in terms of priority these above responses would indeed be difficult—and perhaps an unnecessary task. It should be obvious at this point in our study together that the act of worship is an absolutely essential aspect of the life of the Christian.

Establishing Priorities

That which is essential to the Christian as an individual is also important to the congregation as a corporate body. Thus the church to be the church must be faithfully involved in the functions of caring personal relationships (i.e. love of God and neighbor), evangelistic witness (sharing the good news), and worship. (It is certainly appropriate and scriptural to add to our objectives "education" as a responsibility of the church.) Again, to say that one of these functions holds priority over the others for the congregation is a questionable deliberation.

To turn to the more mundane level, however, of scheduling activities an individual or a local congregation may well designate priorities for the moment. Focusing our attention on congregations we may note that that which is the uppermost priority of a particular church this year might not be the same as that of the same congregation ten years ago. Further, the priority of a new congregation in a rapidly expanding urban area would surely differ from a long-established rural congregation. And the priority of a particular congregation at 11:00 on a specific Sunday morning might not be the same as the priority of that same congregation for its overall program of the decade of the 1980s. In fact the 11:00 Sunday morning priority of that congregation just might vary from Lord's Day to Lord's Day.

Sunday Morning at 11:00

Members of the congregation are aware that two activities of the church commonly take place on any given Sunday morning. It has been this way as long as they can remember. They assemble for an hour of Bible study—or at least they make certain that the children attend. Then, at 11:00 a.m., the congregation (or at least forty percent of it) assembles for worship. But what is this "worship" for which they come together? What is the purpose—or purposes—for which they meet? The author vividly recalls attending services as a youth and hearing church members refer to the absence of a vacationing minister with the words, There will be no church today. But was that a correct assessment of the situation? Were the people not gathered, and were they not gathered for a purpose? There was indeed "church"; worship was conducted, hymns were sung, prayers were offered, communion was shared. There was simply no preaching. (Apparently the people did not consider the brief homilies presented by the elders to be preaching.) But is preaching to be equated with worship? Cannot worship be conducted without preaching? (We use the word "preaching" here in the broader sense, not confining it to the word *keryssein* which implies evangelistic witness of the good news.) No one would question that preaching is a legitimate part of the activities of the gathered congregation nor that it is an inherent part of worship. (See again Chapters One, Three and

110

Four.) The author merely contends that worship can be conducted without preaching (though not without confrontation
with the Word) and preaching can be done at places other
than that of the gathered congregation (though it cannot be
done outside the perspective of a worshipful attitude at
least on the part of the preacher).

It is obvious from the author's survey (see Chapter Two)
that members of the Christian Churches/Churches of Christ
are not clear or united in their thinking in terms of the basic
priorities of the Sunday morning worship hour. They have
been told for several generations that the observance of
the Lord's Supper is the most important thing that Christians do when they come together as a congregation, and
yet they act as though preaching were that all-important
activity. In reality the basic nature of the activities of the
observance of the Lord's Supper and of preaching are different. The observance of the Lord's Supper is an act of
worship (and of course an act of fellowship as well). The
function of preaching on the other hand is that of evangelism
and/or edification. The minister by the act of the presentation of his sermon may perform an individual act of worship
(even as the soloist may, in the singing of a song, perform
an act of worship) but the presentation of that sermon
scarcely constitutes an act of worship for the congregation.
The sermon may lead or motivate the congregation to acts
of worship but it does not become for the congregation a
strong act of worship per se. (The proper hearing or reception
of the sermon could be an act of worship or contribute to
other acts of worship on the part of the listeners.) Basically
we must remember that worship is worship and it stands on
its own merit as an essential, integral part of the activities
of the assembled congregation. It may be supplemented by

and complemented by powerful biblical preaching but it is not dependent upon the latter. Worship is a priority of its own and the congregation at worship fulfills that particular priority.

Setting a Course of Action

I recall an event that took place at a week of summer church camp in central Indiana. Through the securement of a most generous provision of surplus food from a federal distribution program the camp cooks had provided all week long a nutritious and quite delicious menu of roast beef, Salisbury steak, beef and noodles, and baked ham. Remarkably though, some of the campers were unimpressed by these tasty dishes. Toward the end of the week, on a Thursday night, to vary the daily routine, a picnic meal was provided for the campers. One camper, with a hamburger in each hand, commented to me, "Now *this* is really eating!" We indeed relish that to which we have become acclimated and accustomed!

Unfortunately a congregation may seek in worship that which they want rather than that which they need. As with our camper they strongly desire that to which they have become accustomed. For example the congregation in worship may choose popular gospel songs that can be sung enthusiastically (there again is that seemingly important criterion for determining worship as successful) rather than the stately hymns that have withstood the test of the centuries. They prefer the old familiar Bible stories (provoking nostalgic memories of a happy childhood in Bible school) rather than the epistolary readings of the New Testament that prick (and rightly so) both soul and conscience. (We're disturbed enough by the events of the week without being disturbed on Sunday as well.) Sermons of twenty minutes are greatly to be preferred to those of thirty-five. (Guest speakers are duly apprised of this preference.) It is all right to rise from the pew to a standing position perhaps twice in the service but certainly not four or five times. Prayers are to be loud enough but not too loud, personal but not too personal. And, why doesn't the minister read from the translation that I'm using? Doesn't he know the Bible is hard enough to follow as it is?

There is a definite trend among many churches today to do things democratically—the majority rules, so to speak. After all, what could be more "American" (and hence presumably Christian) than to let everyone have their say and then to follow the wishes of the majority. So a worship committee is appointed, with members duly and representatively selected from the board of elders, the board of deacons, the high school youth department, the couples class, and the Loyal Workers. This committee meets at stated intervals and structures the worship program of the diverse segments of the committee. And everyone is pleased—partially—at the new worship service!

Now this procedure might be appropriate for some organizations. It might work well with a civic body, it might be quite acceptable for a parent-teachers organization of the local school. It might even serve expediently for some of the activities of the church. But the act of worship however is far too holy to be entrusted to the democratic process. Worship is a confrontation of the individual and/or the corporate body with Almighty God! And where a relationship exists that involves the personhood of God democracy ceases to exist. Monarchy, yes; theocracy, perhaps; but not democracy. The elders of the local congregation are selected as the spiritual overseers of the congregation and the oversight of worship is surely within their domain. They must of course be sensitive to the wishes and the needs of the diverse groups of the congregation (as for example the youth in the selection of music) but their priority of obligation is that the worship hour be consistent with the biblical model. It might be quite proper to have a representative worship committee structured along lines suggested above (the needs of the local congregation will determine this) but always the action of the committee is subject to the oversight of the elders. It is the responsibility then of the elders both to be conversant with the principles of the act of public worship and to be thoroughly knowledgeable of the biblical models of worship. The minister should be sufficiently informed and skilled as to be able to guide them in this quest.

What We Say to Others

We look to see what kind of car the automobile salesman purchases for his wife. We observe if the building contractor has aluminum siding on his own home. The aspiring high school athlete watches to see if the coach smokes. (One of my coaches enjoined, "Do as I say, not as I do.") I attempt to determine when my barber last got a haircut. Indeed Kipling was right; our actions often speak louder than our words.

In like manner our fundamental approaches to worship speak their own lessons to ever-observing attentive congregations. This may occur in many ways. For example, when entering the room where the congregation assembles for worship, what do we see? At what focal point do our eyes naturally come to rest? What item of furniture or motif of architecture do we first notice? Is the pulpit in a structurally central location? Or is that center rather the communion table or the baptistry? (Heaven forbid that it be some work of art that was dedicated to the memory of a departed loved one.) The functional design and arrangement of the existing worship facility speaks volumes to the worshiping attendant. Any of the features mentioned above—the pulpit, communion table, or baptistry—could properly be the center of focus but each would indeed convey its own unique message of centrality and priority. For example, a congregation may attempt to emphasize the preached word but the location of the choir—or the organ—may override that. A congregation may stress evangelism but a poorly designed or remotely located baptistry tends to nullify that emphasis. A congregation may talk about worship but the effectiveness of the worship service is minimized if the worshiper gets a crick in the neck turning toward the communion table.

I have worshiped with a congregation whose Sunday assembly area served during the weekday as a gymnasium. I have worshiped with people in barns, in kitchens, in motel rooms, and in national guard armories—but in every instance the natural surroundings were something else than conducive to worship. (Our Lincoln Christian College chapel for years met in the school basketball gym. I often had the uncomfortable feeling that I was standing in the three-second lane too long, and honestly, this distracted from my worship experience!)

Little can be done perhaps to move the location of an organ and surely not that of the baptistry. But the choir could be shifted or even moved so that the gaze of the congregation focuses elsewhere. (In more than one instance

115

I have observed the choir to be strategically and effectively situated in a balcony.) The communion table can be moved, placed farther back perhaps in a focally central spot or perhaps moved forward to be in the "midst" of the congregation —the family around the table, as it were. (In some instances where the pews are movable the communion table can literally be placed in a central area with worshipers seated all around.) Elevating the communion table on a firm, six-inch base might contribute significantly to the meaning of the observance. The pulpit can be moved and hopefully elevated. (The pulpits in the old Reformation churches were elevated—sometimes almost too high for the physical comfort of the worshipers—but preaching was emphasized in the process and great preaching came from those pulpits!) Some congregations use an additional item of furniture from which the Scriptures are read. This desk is called a lectern and is therefore distinguished from the pulpit. (The use of both a pulpit and a lectern creates a situation called a divided chancel.) The advantages of using a lectern include the focusing of attention on the reading of the Scriptures and the exalting of the Word. The disadvantages include the fact that the pulpit may be moved for architectural balance (though not necessarily so) to the side and thus shifted from a location of focal centrality.

The terminology we use is indicative of our views of worship. Most of us have long since learned that the edifice in which we assemble is rightly called the "church building" and not the "church." But what do we call the room in which the congregation gathers for worship? Is it the auditorium, the assembly hall, or the sanctuary? (What many of us call a sanctuary is certainly not called that by those knowledgeable of correct liturgical vocabulary.) The correct term is nave—but this word is so seldom used that it is little more than a meaningless entity (at best confused with "knave"). And the raised area where the pulpit is located, is it the stage, the platform, the rostrum, or what? The memorial meal we so faithfully observe—we call it the Lord's Supper or the communion, but what of the identifying terms, "eucharist" or "sacrament"? What about the congregation's seminary-trained leader? Even whether we call him pastor, preacher, minister, or brother (oldtimers added "parson") says something about both our view of worship and our view of the priorities of the church.

Alternatives

All of this is to suggest that the congregations must give serious attention to the matter of priorities and careful thought to the establishing of congregational objectives. To set forth on this course of action calls for strong biblical preaching, careful study of the Scriptures, and loving pastoral oversight from the elders. Even if the prior practice of the congregation has been inadequate or perhaps erroneous, change must be enacted ever so slowly and carefully. The traditional practice of a congregation is a strong thing and not one to be quickly set aside. Correct teaching, prayer, and loving administration will be necessary to bring change.

Even as there is no rigidly discernible order of worship set forth in the Scriptures so is there no reason to expect that two congregations today would come to precisely the same stance in respect to their views concerning worship. While this diversity of practice may be both confusing and frustrating to the individual who of necessity travels among the churches, still this is the nature of local autonomy—and

117

local autonomy is an important, if unpublicized, part of the heritage of Restorationist congregations. The important thing is that the congregation have a theology of worship and that it is consistent with the biblical model.

Thus a single congregation might confront the Sunday morning worship hour in one of several ways and yet still be consistent with the biblical model. (Even as in like fashion two congregations could be consistent with the biblical model and yet in some ways dissimilar to one another.) For example, a congregation might conduct two half hour services beginning at 11:00. The first service (or actually portion of the hour) would be a worship service centering around the Lord's Supper and complemented by the reading of the Scriptures and the singing of appropriate hymns, all of which focuses on a specific theme of worship appropriate to the Lord's Supper (as, sacrifice, love, redemption, or thanksgiving). Then the hour merges into a preaching service with another theme carried through in the songs, the readings, and the preached word (now the theme might be, commitment, evangelism, missions, or stewardship). The congregation need not be aware that a transition is taking place. On the other hand, of course, a single theme can be carried through the entire hour with the choice of songs, prayers, and even the communion meditation complementing the sermon. In a reverse approach, on another Sunday, the theme of the service might be one specifically appropriate to worship—and everything, including the theme of the sermon, leads in that direction.

Congregational worship is vital! It is the very heartbeat of the local body of believers! It is the initial act of a praise-pattern that will extend through all eternity! It is an extremely weighty responsibility therefore that falls upon the shoulders of the worship leader. It is of utmost importance that that person, with the full support and direction of the elders, knows what are the objectives of the occasion and how these objectives are to be attained within the perspective of worship.

Questions and Projects

1. Think about the Sunday morning service of the congregation you attend. What is the primary objective the congregation is attempting to accomplish? Is it worship, evangelism, education, fellowship, or something else?
2. Are Christian Churches/Churches of Christ agreed in their assessment of the ultimate priority to be emphasized at the Sunday morning assembly?
3. After reading the book of Revelation consider what seems to be the basic objective of the worship described therein.
4. Think about the interior architectural design and the placement of furniture in the church building where you worship. What is the priority that is emphasized by these physical features?
5. How determinative a factor is nostalgia in the worship services of your congregation?
6. Does the building in which your congregation worships have a divided chancel? Do you know why?
7. What do you call the room in the church building where the congregation assembles for worship? Why do you call it that?

Chapter Eight

UPLIFTING THE WORD

The continuing tradition of the Christian Churches/Churches of Christ is one of reverence for and adherence to the Scriptures as the sole book or guideline for both personal Christian living and the oversight of the congregations. No other book, manual, or creed has been used by the churches in even a quasi-official way. This perspective dates back to the early days of the nineteenth century when the first congregations of this fellowship were organized as part of what would come to be called the Restoration Movement. Thomas Campbell, one of the initial voices of this movement, while possessing many books of a religious nature was only observed by his colleagues to read the Bible. Walter Scott, pioneer evangelist extraordinaire, was also a stalwart advocate of the efforts for the restoration of the New Testament church. He urged that the leadership of the churches follow the practice of the memorization of a chapter a day of the New Testament until the entire book was committed to memory. Other men among the founding fathers voiced similar statements regarding the exaltation of the Bible as the only rule for the church. Leaders of the churches hastened to summarize the cardinal principles of the Restoration Movement in short, poignant slogans—and the slogans reflected this solitary emphasis on the Scriptures. "Where the Scriptures speak, we speak; where the Scriptures are silent, we are silent" became a self-accepted mandate for the congregations. While the denominations of the day were differentiated by carefully-worded, often confusing creedal positions, the slogan, "No creed but Christ, no book but the Bible," was hoisted as the Restorationists' response. Always the focus was on the Bible and especially on the New Testament writings. "People of the Book" was a cherished description of the membership and "True to the Bible" was a self-chosen description of the publications of their leaders.

However, this historic background to the contrary, a survey of existing practices of these congregations in the midwest today (see Chapter Two) indicates that it is in the area of the utilization of the Scriptures that these people evidence perhaps their greatest weakness or shortcoming in the area of worship. Their attention to the Scriptures alone as the guiding principle has not waivered nor has it been altered but their attention to such in actual perform-ance in corporate worship is sometimes alarmingly neglected. The people voice a loyalty to the Word but an examination of their services of worship indicates a frequent minimizing if not an occasional total oversight of the use of the Scriptures. It is imperative that adherence to the old paths be re-estab-lished and maintained! If the people are to be faithful to the time-honored standards of the Restoration Movement—and more important, if they are to be practicing Christians after the New Testament model—they must again be truly a "People of the Book."

The Example of the Historic Church

Faithful people of God have ever been committed to the reading of the Scriptures in public assembly. Where these people have gathered the Word has been recited. This is the stated testimony of the Bible itself. Extra-biblical historic records substantiate the practice. But more than that, atten-tion has been purposively given by far-sighted leaders through the centuries of Bible history to a balanced selection of those Scriptures for public presentation. That is, care was taken that every section of the biblical account would be read in due time in the public assembly. The synagogues of the

121

pre-Christian era, for example, carefully provided for public readings from both the Law and the Prophets. In this manner a twofold or double-edged approach to public reading was established. The moral element which the Law might overlook was strikingly stated in the Prophets, and the foundational formulations which the Prophets might simply presuppose were didactically set forth from the books of the Law.

The early church evidently followed the theory of this practice, varying it slightly as their leaders read from the Prophets (that they might establish the messiahship of the Christ) and from the Epistles of the New Testament just as readily as these writings came into the hands of the congregations. Later in the history of the church other variations or patterns arose—as readings from the Gospels and from the Epistles—but still the twofold distribution remained. Not only were the Scriptures to be read but a carefully balanced ration was to be provided for spiritual nourishment. Sometimes the distribution was that of an Old Testament reading and a New Testament reading. On occasion even a third reading was added to the liturgy and the selections became the Old Testament, the Epistles, and the Gospels.

Further it is to be noted that the importance of this reading was apparent to the early church. Among the most interesting and insightful of the early extra-biblical writings are those of Justin. Justin (known in history as the Martyr— a monumental testimony in itself to the man) is one of the first writers to give a rather concise descriptive account concerning that which took place in the corporate worship assemblies of the church in his day. It is significant to our study to recognize that Justin wrote in the mid-second century, within five decades of the period of the first century which is designated rightly as the apostolic church. It is Justin's testimony that readings from the Gospels ("Memoirs of the Apostles," to use his words) took place "as long as time permits." How grand this is, "as long as time permits." Read from the Word just as long as the schedule of worship and the necessities facing the worshipers will permit. (Remember that in the second century, as in the first, Sunday was not an official holiday for worship and these Christians had to be about the labors of the day thus relegating corporate worship activities to the pre-dawn or after-sunset hours. How meaningful therefore, the words, "as long as time permits.") If this was the case in Justin's day (we date this particular writing at about A.D. 150) we may well speculate that this was the custom of the congregations at an even earlier time, surely during that of the first century church. Such an assumption seems to be corroborated by the account of Paul's unique experience at Troas (Acts 20:7-12).

The primary, traditional worship service of the Roman Catholic Church was and is the Mass. A careful examination of the Mass as it was observed by the church during the medieval period of history indicates that it was replete with many, many selections from the Scriptures. These were read or quoted by various officiants in the service. Selections were taken from both testaments of the Bible. Unfortunately with the passing of the centuries the Latin language (in which these services were conducted) had become a lost language to the great majority of worshipers. The inevitable result was realized that there was almost no communication whatsoever of factual material to the average worshiper. Even so, in one sense the reading of the Scriptures and the unintelligible hearing of the recitation continued to be an emotional act of worship though certainly not an edificatory

123

act. (Incidentally it is only within the last several years that the Mass has been restored to the national languages of the churches.)

Pressing onward in our cursory review of church history, in the initial decades of the Protestant Reformation we see a most pronounced emphasis on the use of the Scriptures in public worship. It was in the diligent study of the sacred texts that the Reformation had its birth and it was in the vibrant proclamation of those texts that it had its early, phenomenal growth. Thus it is generally recognized that this attention to the Scriptures was one of the major contributions to the very success and permanency of the Reformation. No reformer was more insistent in this emphasis than Martin Luther. It was in fact his assessment that the power of the Reformation in Germany resided solely in the Word and not in his efforts nor in those of his able assistant, Philip Melanchthon. Many if not most of the early, principal reformers followed suit. The Word was read, the Word was preached, the Word was sung—but most important the Word was elevated to its most deserved place of prominence!

It was the gradual erosion during the seventeenth and eighteenth centuries of this emphasis that contributed to the set of circumstances out of which the Restoration Movement arose. Denominational clergy had come to substitute carefully defined doctrinal statements for the simple words of the Scriptures. While it is true that the Bible had not been removed from the setting of Protestant worship it is equally true that the Bible no longer was held in the same significant perspective that it had been by the first generation of Reformers. It was the labors of the Campbells, Barton Stone, Walter Scott, Isaac Errett, John W. McGarvey, and a host of other Restorationist stalwarts that re-established recognition of the inherent power of the proclaimed Word!

124

Commitment to a Position

If the Scriptures are to possess and hold their rightful place in the worship of the congregations then the leadership of these congregations must be committed to such an attitude. Nothing less will suffice. Elders must insist that the services be structured around the recitation and proclamation of the Word as the focal point of witness. No amount of clever contests, flamboyant leadership, or electronic gadgetry can conceivably substitute for faithful proclamation. Ministers too must realize that strong worship correlates directly to strong attention to public proclamation of the Word. Where the Word is minimized vibrant, relevant worship is dissipated.

(It may well be that some ministers will have to be convinced that their sermons must be shortened ten minutes so that five minutes can be designated to public reading of the Bible. And that probably, in eternal perspective, would be more than a fair exchange!) Surely no professional ego is so inflated as to cause the preacher to count seriously his own prepared message to be of superior value to an equal number of carefully selected sentences from the Holy Writ!

That the leadership of the congregation has such an attitude toward the exaltation of the Word must be communicated to the congregation. And it can be if certain conditions are met. The minister must commit himself without reservation to biblical preaching. This preaching may follow one or more of several homiletical styles but biblical preaching it must always be. (At any rate people who at some previous point have had exposure to such preaching will readily note the absence of it in a given situation. People truly want to know, "Is there any word from the Lord?") Those responsible for selecting the music must look to hymns with strong biblical themes. Such hymns may range from a song like, "I Know Whom I Have Believed," where the Scriptures are quoted, to songs like "A Mighty Fortress" where a powerful theme is presented. This is not to suggest that this is the only kind of songs that can be utilized in the worship service but it must be the basis of music selection nonetheless.

The manner of approach to the public reading of the Scriptures is important. Proper attitude can at least in part be engendered by having the congregation stand for the reading of the Scriptures. A simple announcement to that effect is made, either by the one reading or by a statement in the printed order of worship. In consideration of the physical needs of some of the worshipers a lengthy passage from the Bible would not be selected. A word of caution is in order: such a practice must be introduced prudently and with due explanation to a congregation not accustomed to it. (Some people will exhibit a reluctance to participate; some for physical reasons, others because of emotional reservations.) A certain bit of consistency should be followed. Have the congregation stand for the major reading on every occasion or only when the New Testament is read; do however select a standard of practice, explain it, and be consistent with it. (The practice of the historic church is to stand for the reading of the words of Jesus, that is, the Gospels, and only for these. The reason was that one stands in honor of Him whose words they are.) The idea of standing to express honor to another ought not seem strange in this land of ours. I recall vividly being advised by my attorney to rise when the judge entered, even though only three of us—the attorney, a stenographer, and I—were present in a cavernous courtroom for a simple procedure of settling an estate.

Achievement of the Objective

There is little value to be gained from the presence in the hands of worshipers of unread Bibles. It may be an impressive sight indeed, all the scholars carrying their Bibles into the house of worship, but there is no communication of the living Word involved in such an act. The desired objective then is to get the Scriptures before the congregation assembled for worship. Many things can be done to accomplish this but first there must be proper attitude. If the personnel to whom worship direction is entrusted are committed to this then the objective can be achieved.

Attention must be given to the number of times that the Scriptures are read in the course of the service. Often we simply assume that something is occurring when in reality it is not. Therefore it is not enough just to take it for granted that the Scriptures are read at adequate intervals; rather observation must be made—and the results may be startling! Let us consider therefore at what places in the order the Word may be read. For example a verse may be read as the Call to Worship. (Habakkuk 2:20 would be a suitable choice: "The Lord is in his holy temple: let all the earth keep silence before him.") There is of course the Morning Scripture Lesson, and as suggested above two complementary passages may be read at this time. At yet another point an appropriate passage of the Bible may be read in preparation for the observance of the Lord's Supper. The familiar words of I Corinthians 11:23-26 could be used. A single verse as an Offertory Sentence may be read, accompanied by a brief

127

prayer, either immediately prior to or after the reception of the offering. Another scriptural passage, perhaps distinct from the Morning Lesson, can be read as a basis for the Sermon. (Hopefully a number of passages from the Bible will be quoted or read during the Sermon.) Finally, the Benediction—if it follows a biblical model—is a verse of the Scriptures, as, "The Lord bless thee, and keep thee: The Lord make his face shine upon thee, and be gracious unto thee: The Lord lift up his countenance upon thee, and give thee peace" (Num. 6:24-26). The sequence as thus suggested here calls for six separate instances of the reading of the Scriptures—seven if the twofold reading of the Morning Lesson is counted as two.

(The reader may think that too much emphasis is being placed on the reading of the Scriptures in the public assembly. For two reasons, I think not. First, surely the reading of God's inspired Word is superior to the declaration of a comparable number of words from mortal composition. Cf. Neh. 8:1-8. And second, on more than one occasion students have commented to me that they had recently attended Sunday services where their own purposive observation revealed that not a single verse of the Scriptures was read during the entire duration of the public assembly. I am not suggesting that this is a frequent instance for assuredly it is not. I cannot, however, conceive of a people who are dedicated to the restoration of the biblical model of the church even once committing so grievous an oversight!)

The Morning Scripture Lesson should be one of the true high-points of the worship hour. It clearly was for those earlier Christians nurtured in the heritage of the synagogue. Here the Word of God breaks over us! Here the centuries pass away and we find ourselves on the shores of Galilee at the feet of the Master! Here indeed the Word becomes a lamp unto our feet and a light unto our path!

Thus the passages read for the Morning Lesson should be selected wisely with a view to the needs of the total congregation. (For this reason I often select a passage relating to a theme different from that of the sermon.) In the pastorate that I serve I often choose to read the account from the Old Testament of some incident from the life of one of the heroes of the faith and then the summarization of that individual as recorded in the eleventh chapter of Hebrews in the New Testament. Another option I sometimes choose is to read a passage on a theme in the Old Testament (as perhaps, love of neighbor) and then a passage containing Jesus' amplification of the theme. Yet again, I might cover in a series of readings over several consecutive Sundays the Sermon on the Mount or one of the shorter New Testament epistles.

Public prayers can be offered that contain verses of the Scriptures or excerpts of verses. We may pray, for example, "Lord, grant courage to those of us who walk through the valley of the shadow of death." We might confess once again, "God be merciful to me a sinner." While many such examples could be cited it is enough to acknowledge that it is most appropriate to offer again the prayers of old while in the same instance giving a second hearing to the Word. To utilize scriptural excerpts in prayer is not to demand that such prayers be written out in advance but merely that one should give thought aforetime even to extemporaneous prayer.

Some congregations are finding great opportunity of expression in a practice called Singing the Scriptures. This can be done at the morning worship hour or for that matter on almost any occasion when the congregation assembles. Words of a familiar (or sometimes not so familiar) passage of the Bible are introduced to the people along with the support of a simple, easy-to-follow melody. The song is repeated once or twice until the congregation is familiarized with it. It may be necessary to use large, printed charts or perhaps over-head projection as these songs are not commonly found in the traditional hymnals. Some of the Scriptures that I have noted that have been set beautifully to music are: Deuteronomy 6:4-5; Psalm 32:11; Psalm 91:14-16; Psalm 103:1; Isaiah 40:31; and Philippians 4:13. There are literally hundreds more available and these can be obtained in printed songbooks from selected music publishers. A trained arranger of music could of course prepare such songs using existing melodies. Incidentally, inasmuch as lengthy portions of the Old Testament text were used in worship in a fashion similar to this centuries prior to the birth of our Lord we are indeed being faithful to a biblical model of worship when we today sing the Scriptures!

Responsive reading of the Scriptures is a centuries old practice of the church—and is antedated even more by the antiphonal recitation of the Jewish worshipers. The poetic literature of the Old Testament intentionally lends itself to this. The Psalms present the finest of materials for such a public recitation. While it is true that some people have difficulty mastering the art of responsive reading the act itself is something that could be rehearsed by small groups at such occasions as choir practice or youth meetings. Any good church hymnal includes an ample selection of responsive readings that can be used by the congregation. These same readings can be read in unison by the congregation as well as responsively. This also produces a striking verbal effect.

130

There are yet other ways to lift the Bible before the eyes and the ears of the assembled worshipers. For example many congregations have purchased Bibles for general distribution along with the hymnals in the racks on the backs of the pews. (Two suggestions: these must be printed in an easy-to-read type, as economy is not the only criterion for selection; and the worship leader must allow ample time for the reader to locate the proper passage.) One congregation that I visited used the technique of rear-screen projection to transmit selected appropriate words of the Bible on a large screen forming the rear wall of the baptistry. (How much more suitable and artistic is this than some of the baptistry paintings that I have observed!) Some congregations have brief, primary phrases from the Scriptures painted in gold-leaf script on the wall of the worship auditorium. (In this instance the most careful attention to selection is necessitated.) Lincoln Christian College has each year at the front of the college chapel auditorium a large walnut-stained plank bearing in white script a phrase from the Bible as the motto for the year. (Presently the words are, "Thy Kingdom Come.") Some churches display artistically-crafted felt banners bearing similar words—perhaps fashioned by the youth of the congregation. I find it desirable to print the words of Scripture in the worship bulletin to complement a particular act of worship, as an Offertory Sentence at the time of the Offering. A particular service might call for a printed Benediction in this manner. If the congregation does not read these words vocally following direction from the pulpit they at least will do so silently. (The selection of a typewriter with elite type as over one with pica will accommodate approximately twenty percent more words on a printed page of the bulletin.) The mandate is a simple one:

raise the Scriptures often before the eyes of the congregation assembled for worship!

The Utilization of the Psalms

No better example can be cited as an illustration of the way that the Word has been uplifted before the body of believers in public worship than that of the historic utilization of the Psalms. A careful consideration of such proclamation will be profitable for us at this point in our study.

Hebrew poetry is a unique vehicle of language that is capable of recording most of life's experiences—and the Psalms are exactly that, the finest Hebrew poetry! John Calvin declared that there was no human emotion that was not mirrored in the Psalms. Martin Luther stated it even more picturesquely when he observed that to examine the Psalms was to look into the hearts of all the saints as one might look at a beautiful garden of flowers, the flowers radiating the mercy of God. (Our word "psalm" is simply a transliteration of the Greek *psalmos*, "a song that is sung to the accompaniment of a stringed instrument." The Hebrew word *tehillim* may be translated, "praises.")

When one recognizes that the Psalms are such a magnificent reflection of the emotions of the human soul it is no wonder that portions of the Psalms are quoted almost one hundred times within the pages of the New Testament writings. Consider Jesus in the agony of the cross as He cries out, "My God, my God, why hast thou forsaken me?" (Matt. 27:46, compare to Ps. 22:1), and His final utterance, "Father, into thy hands I commend my spirit" (Luke 23:46, compare to Ps. 31:5). One might consider other citations by Jesus as Psalm 8:2 (compare with Matt. 21:16), Psalm 110:1 (compare with Matt. 22:41-45, Mark 12:36-37, and

Luke 20:42-44), and Psalm 118:22-23 (compare with Matt. 21:42, Mark 12:10-11, and Luke 20:17).

The Psalms have served believers well as an instrument of worship. They have been referred to as the "hymn-book" of the Jewish church as well as of the early Christian church. The singing of the Psalms constituted a significant part— perhaps even the greater part—of the worship of the early church. Paul wrote to Christians at both Ephesus and Colossae urging them to sing psalms (Eph. 5:19 and Col. 3:16). Surviving documents from the community that produced the Dead Sea Scrolls attest to the popularity there of the Psalms. Writing in the fourth century Chrysostom observed that in the worship of the church the singing of the Psalms occurred at the first, in the middle, and at the last. Augustine, great theologian of the church, reflected that it was the reading of the Psalms that kindled a flame within him toward God. The first book to be printed in North America (Cambridge, 1640) was the Bay Psalm Book—a book to be used by the Puritans in worship. The continuing historic popularity of the Psalms is indicative of the way that they represent a unique blend of doctrine, worship, and daily experience.

It is therefore part of the purposeful plan of God that His mighty works should be both rehearsed and praised through the singing of psalms in worship. Consider these words of proclamation:

> O Give thanks unto the Lord; call upon his name: make known his deeds among the people.
> Sing unto him, sing psalms unto him: talk ye of all his wondrous works.
> Glory ye in his holy name: let the heart of them rejoice that seek the Lord.
> Seek the Lord, and his strength: seek his face evermore.

133

Remember his marvellous works that he hath done; his wonders, and the judgments of his mouth. (Psalm 105:1-5)

With these preliminary thoughts in mind what then can be done to utilize in a significant way the Psalms in the corporate worship service? Some ideas and suggestions will be presented here. Hopefully the reader will be a life-long student of worship and will continue to be observant in respect to adapting means and methods that will make worship more meaningful.

It is obvious by now in our study that the Psalms were used initially—and for that matter for centuries afterward—as musical expressions of praise. Christian Churches/Churches of Christ have forfeited a beautiful part of the heritage of worship when they have so frequently reduced the public rendition of the Psalms to a non-musical status. But this misfortune can in part be corrected by the simple expedient of singing the Psalms! There are many beautiful hymns available that are formulated on the Psalms. For example, Isaac Watts wrote the great hymn, "O God, Our Help in Ages Past," as his interpretation of Psalm 90. He also composed "The Heavens Declare Thy Glory, Lord," based on Psalm 19, and "I'll Praise My Maker While I've Breath," based on Psalm 146. His familiar Christmas hymn, "Joy to the World! the Lord is Come," has its basis in Psalm 98. Other traditional hymns include, "O Worship the King" (Ps. 104), "Be Still My Soul" (46), "Jesus Shall Reign" (72), "All People that on Earth Do Dwell" (100), "Lift Up Your Heads, Ye Mighty Gates" (24), and "Praise the Lord! Ye Heavens, Adore Him" (148). There are of course many musical versions of the ever-popular twenty-third Psalm. They need to be selected, if necessary presented for instruction and rehearsal, and used! Members of the worshiping congregation if duly apprised as to the purpose of this change in the musical format will surely be appreciative. Mention has been made previously in this chapter of the practice of singing the Scriptures. Surely no more beautiful nor appropriate selections can be found than those of the Psalms. Suitable music must be secured to complement these words—but this is readily available from a number of music publishers.

Furthermore the Psalms can be used without music to good advantage and in keeping with biblical precedent if they are read responsively by the participants in the worshiping congregation. (A variation of this on occasion would be to have a divided choir, seated in separate areas of the worship room, read the words of a psalm responsively.) The hymnal serves as the worship manual for this endeavor. (Surely no music committee would seriously consider selecting a hymnal that does not have a generous selection of responsive readings contained therein.) If pew Bibles are available to the congregation then worshipers could refer directly to the Psalms rather than using the source to be found in the hymnals.

To capture more nearly the beauty of the poetry of the original Hebrew text of the Psalms one must however use a different method of responsive reading. The essence of such poetry is that the second half of the verse repeats the thought of the first part. For example, in the first verse of the sixth psalm, the second phrase, "Neither chasten me in thy hot displeasure," echoes the message of the first phrase, "O Lord, rebuke me not in thine anger." Observe carefully then the sixth psalm in this poetic fashion:

O Lord, rebuke me not in thine anger,
   neither chasten me in thy hot displeasure.

135

Have mercy upon me, O Lord; for I am weak:
  O Lord, heal me; for my bones are vexed.
My soul is also sore vexed:
  but thou, O Lord, how long?
Return, O Lord, deliver my soul:
  oh save me for thy mercies' sake.
For in death there is no remembrance of thee:
  in the grave who shall give thee thanks?
(Etc.)

Thus the familiar twenty-third psalm might be used in worship as a responsive reading in this fashion:

LEADER: The Lord is my shepherd;
RESPONSE: I shall not want.
L: He maketh me to lie down in green pastures.
R: He leadeth me beside the still waters.
L: He restoreth my soul:
R: He leadeth me in the paths of righteousness for his name's sake.
L: Yea, though I walk through the valley of the shadow of death, I will fear no evil: for thou art with me;
R: Thy rod and thy staff they comfort me.
L: Thou preparest a table before me in the presence of mine enemies: thou anointest my head with oil;
R: My cup runneth over.
L: Surely goodness and mercy shall follow me all the days of my life:
R: And I will dwell in the house of the Lord for ever.

A word of caution to the reader: mastering this type of responsive reading will not be easy. Realize also that many of the Psalms do not lend themselves to this type of format. Even with those psalms that are selected it will be necessary to work with a carefully prepared copy. The text that the congregation uses may be printed as a bulletin insert or perhaps thrown on a screen from an overhead projector or other type of visual equipment.

One of my professors in seminary fashioned a small booklet containing slightly more than fifty selections from the Psalms. These were carefully arranged in a prepared text so that they might be used as responsive readings. The material was printed and then distributed in the hymnal racks on the backs of the pews. (I observed that the booklets were also used as a meditational guide by those arriving early at the services of worship.)

The early Jewish worshipers routinely used certain psalms on particular days or on specific occasions. For example, Psalms 113 through 118 were sung at the time of the gathering of the family (or other small group) at the Feast of the Passover. (Matthew 26:30 alludes to such a celebration in song by Jesus and His inner band of disciples.) Psalm 30 was used at the Temple dedication. Psalm 100 was used for thank-offerings. Psalm 92 was sung on the Sabbath. The other days of the week were afforded psalms as well: Sunday, 24; Monday, 48; Tuesday, 82; Wednesday, 94; Thursday, 81; and Friday, 93. While this type of arrangement might be correct enough in today's worship services it would be unacceptable to most of the congregations of the Christian Churches/Churches of Christ because it is so similar to the lectionaries used by those churches that are liturgically oriented.

(While the subject of this book is that of a study of public worship I would like to urge the reader to make the fullest use of the Psalms in private worship as well. Read from the Psalms daily. Read them from varying translations so as to gain the utmost in both beauty and clarity of meaning. Purchase those copies of the New Testament that include the

Psalms as an additional feature. Secure separate copies of the Psalms and distribute them to your friends and class members—they can be purchased individually from the American Bible Society for less than the price of a cup of coffee!)

The Psalms continue to be the hymnbook of the church. Use them, sing them! "Lift up, lift up your voices now."

Technique of Communication

There is no great advantage to the public reading of the Scriptures if they cannot be comprehended. For this reason careful attention must be given to the selection of a translation for a particular text. One of the spiritual blessings of the present day is that so many excellent translations are readily available—this in sharp contrast to the situation as it was even thirty years ago! The worship leader well in advance of the hour of worship pores over the available translations selecting the one (of course true to the meaning) that best communicates the message in modern English to the listener. One may or may not inform the listeners as to what translation is being used. On many occasions I have used three or four different translations on a particular Sunday morning, going to the extra labor of typing out the various passages on a single page if it appears that otherwise a juggling act will be necessary! I commonly do my preparatory work with an indispensable book before me that contains in parallel columns the texts of four acceptable translations of the New Testament.

Much that we have considered about the uplifting of the Word is of no avail if the reader cannot be heard. Insistence must be made—and if necessary, subtle reminders given— that the reader speak distinctly and with sufficient strength.

Voice amplification equipment may be needed. Rehearse the reading ahead of time, recording it on a convenient cassette recorder; play it back—and repeat the process until one is satisfied with the delivery. The leadership of worship can no more be conducted without study, preparation, and rehearsal than can the delivery of the sermon.

Yes, there is a word from the Lord! The Word of God is as fresh and as relevant as this morning's newspaper. It must be communicated in vital, motivational language!

Questions and Projects

1. Explore some books about Martin Luther (such as Roland Bainton's *Here I Stand*) to discover that reformer's concept of the power of the Word.
2. Make a list of verses from the Bible that would be appropriate to use as Calls to Worship. Do the same for Benedictions.
3. Are the members of your congregation encouraged to follow along in their own Bibles with the readings from the Scriptures that are used in the worship service?
4. What are the advantages of comparing a passage of the Bible in several English translations prior to reading it in public worship?
5. With the cooperation of your family (or Bible school class) experiment with using selected Psalms as responsive readings.
6. Why is it that the members of some congregations stand for the reading of the Scriptures?
7. Make a list of the ways that the use of the Scriptures could be strengthened in the worship services of your congregation.

Chapter Nine

GATHERING AROUND THE TABLE

One of the elders of the small rural church where I worship shares with me the pleasant memories of his boyhood in the same congregation. One delightful memory is of how the women of the church—his mother included—took turns baking the communion bread each Sunday morning that it might be fresh for its appearance on the Lord's Table. The aroma of baking bread on Sunday morning! The excitement of small children! The sense of family stewardship and responsibility in this simple act of preparation! I also recall as a boy gathering grapes from the arbor that spanned the walk to our country home. Other memories return—my marveling at the number of varieties of grapes that grew there, the innumerable ants that seemingly made their home on the clinging vines, the cool breezes that fanned the growing grapes! Some of the grapes that I picked went to the kitchen and there I watched my mother prepare juice from them that would be carefully canned in fruit jars and taken to the church to provide part of the supply that furnished weekly the cups on the Lord's Table. Again, the coolness of the arbor, the pungent odor of cooking grapes, the hot kitchen associated with the canning process—but always the sense of stewardship. The worship of the congregation depends at least in part on what we the worshipers do and the preparations we make.

The churches of the first century possessed something of this same sense of stewardship in connection with their observance of the Lord's Supper. Many of those earliest Christians were lowly in economic status—at best servants in their master's household. What could such a Christian be expected to bring to the church as an offering of stewardship? What could that humble Christian provide as a contribution to the fellowship meal in which all shared? Perhaps nothing more than a few left over morsels from the master's table—mere food scraps otherwise to be disposed. These the Christian brought to the congregation assembled around another table (a table of fellowship) and cheerfully gave as an act of stewardship. Some of these morsels—the appropriate ones of bread and wine—appeared on the Lord's Table and were consumed by all those present in remembrance of Him! What a meaningful act! Responsibility, stewardship, community, fellowship!

What a contrast there is in this act of preparation between the church of the first century (or the one of our childhood) and the church of today. For presently the church secures from a religious supply house the bread in sealed boxes containing several months' supply and purchases grape juice in large quantities (perhaps even at wholesale prices) from the local supermarket. And in the process the congregation has lost something both meaningful and vital!

The Restoration Heritage

Several aspects of the communion service as observed by the pioneers have eroded away. While none of these aspects are pertinent to our observance of the Lord's Supper today it is significant to our study to see what they were.

One of the early customs of the frontier churches was to use a single large cup or chalice for the observance of the Communion. Each communicant (not every worshiper then as now partakes of the memorial meal) shared from this one cup. This cup was passed from one member to another in succession or might be carried from one to another by a deacon. (On occasion there might be two such cups, one for either side of the meeting room, the men's side and the

141

women's, as it were—another striking, early custom!) By the beginning of the twentieth century most congregations adopted for hygenic purposes the use of small individual cups which could be washed after the service. (A Hoosier elder told me that the ladies' group initiated the change locally when they could no longer tolerate the idea of sharing the same cup with an old, mustachioed gentleman!) Quite commonly now practical-minded, economy-conscious congregations use plastic communion cups that can be disposed of after the service. A number of the beautiful, old chalices—crafted of polished silver or cut glass—are yet to be seen in museums or on special niches in the vestibules of the houses of worship. (It is to be noted that some quite conservative congregations of the Restorationist heritage still cling to the use of the single cup and more than a few congregations insist that such usage be made a test of fellowship. While such a demand may seem unrealistic to most heirs of the Campbellian legacy it is a reminder of the extreme consequences that sometimes derive from a tenacious adherence to a Restorationist position.)

Another custom of the pioneer churches was the regular use of sacramental wine (one wonders what was it called on Monday?) in the observance of the Lord's Supper. While this may be a startling bit of information to those of us accustomed to a strong temperance position yet one must realize that any other practice would have been surprising indeed. The process of making unfermented grape juice was only beginning to be popularized by mid-nineteenth century. By the last half of the century—with a great assist from the temperance movement—the use of unfermented juice was widely accepted and adopted.

A further variation from present practice was that in the early years of the nineteenth century of "close communion." "Close communion" was just that—only members of one's own fellowship of churches were permitted to share with the local congregation in the observance of the Lord's Supper. (Those readers knowledgeable in the history of the Restoration Movement will recall the incident in the early ministry of Thomas Campbell when he stepped across the barriers of "close communion," leading to a series of events that precipitated in the formation of the Christian Association of Washington and the writing of the *Declaration and Address*.) Members of other communions or denominations might (or might not) be regarded as Christians but they were not permitted to participate in the ordinance as observed by the local congregation.

By the time of the Civil War most of the churches of the Restoration heritage had come to the alternative position of "open communion." The Lord's Table was spread weekly, the ordinance was observed—and any attendant at the service could choose to commune. A slogan was unofficially adopted by the congregations to publish their stance on the matter—"We neither invite nor debar." That is, the decision to commune or not was the worshiper's, and not that of the officiants or the congregation. At this same time in history (late-nineteenth, early twentieth centuries) battle lines were being formed between conservative and liberal churches over a highly volatile issue, that of "open membership" (the admission by transfer to full membership status of unimmersed believers). It seemed, for more than twenty years, rather inconsistent to me that the conservative churches with which I was associated could at the same time practice "close membership" and "open communion,"

143

that is, on the one hand recognizing only immersed believers as members and on the other hand communing as
it might be with the unimmersed as fellow Christians. I now
see however, in comprehending at last the truth of th.ə
principle, "We neither invite nor debar," the realism of the
situation as our leaders first conceived it. It is indeed the
Lord's Table and it is indeed *His* prerogative—not ours—to
invite or to debar. What a grand practice this, open communion, to declare in public worship that the "church of
Christ upon earth is essentially, intentionally, and constitutionally one"—and to witness to the same by gathering
around a communion table with all our fellow Christians!

A Consistent Appraisal

Few issues have proven more troublesome to all of Christendom in two millennia than that of the nature of the Lord's
Supper. This issue more than any other kept the sixteenth
century Protestant forces from fully uniting and in fact almost
brought their demise before the Catholic Counter-reformation.
Many perspectives (or theologies) have arisen in attempted
explanation of what transpires when Christians gather in
remembrance of Him. One of the earliest views of the
church was that it was a time of *eucharistia* ("thanksgiving,"
hence the word, "eucharist"—a word that we seldom use
but nonetheless a good word and one that conveys a very
important, basic biblical concept). Also early Christians
viewed the Lord's Supper as their gift to God—and in a
sense it literally was as they brought, as we elsewhere have
noted, the two basic ingredients of the feast as an act of
stewardship. Only later did they view the ordinance as
God's gift to them. Out of this came the theory that it was

God's sacrifice for them—and from this, unfortunately but inevitably, came the idea that God's eternal sacrifice was arrested at each observance of the Lord's Supper (hence the rudimentary theology of the Mass). Sixteenth century Protestant heralds in departure from this theology in turn argued over the nature of the Lord in the elements. They queried among themselves, Is He really there, substantially there, symbolically there, or is the meal only a memorial? Their inability to come to any sort of mutually acceptable formula or compromise effectively curtailed any opportunity for the Protestant Reformation to engulf western Europe and the British Isles.

The position of the Christian Churches/Churches of Christ in respect to these issues is in no way defined nor need it be. Perhaps this is the one unrecognized (and at least for later generations, unintentional) stroke of genius for the Restoration Movement. Rather the attention of Restoration leaders has been to the regularity of the observance. As the early church observed the Supper regularly, weekly, so must we. When the body of believers assembles to read the Scriptures and to give praise, the additional proclamation is made by the body united in fellowship around a Table that testifies both to the sacrifice and the resurrection of the Lord whose Table it is! So committed to this are the churches that Sunday evening services usually offer the Communion for those absent from the morning service and visitors to the shut-ins take the elements to them that the Communion may be observed there also. (Justin Martyr, writing in A.D. 150, testified clearly of this latter practice existing in the congregations, *Apology,* I, 67.)

Further, and significantly, for Christian Churches/Churches of Christ the Communion has been a service of the people—

prepared by the people, administered by the people (or at least by duly-selected laymen) and received by the people. (If all this sounds familiarly like the words of Abraham Lincoln, why not? Lincoln was a product of the frontier, his dates coincide precisely with the productive years of Alexander Campbell, 1809-1865/66, and Lincoln too was a life-long student of the Bible.) There is no vestige of sacerdotalism. No officiant stands between the worshiper and the Lord. The minister may share in the service with a prayer, a scriptural reading, or even a devotional meditation, but it is clearly the service of the people.

A Strong Witness

I believe that it may be correctly stated that it is in the area of the observance of the Lord's Supper that knowledgeable leaders of the modern ecumenical movement look with greatest appreciation to the contributions of the Restoration Movement. Regardless of whatever merit that statement may hold for the reader I do think it imperative if we are to be faithful to our very heritage from the Campbells and Stone that we do make a bold witness to the religious world at large. If others look to us at this point then let us make it a strong witness.

At the same time, and from a totally different point of view, a faithful observance of the Lord's Supper may just be one of the strongest evangelistic witnesses that the church makes (and this certainly is not to suggest that this is the basic purpose of the observance). It was certainly so however in the early history of the church. If it is a witness then let it be made a powerful witness. Let the Lord be proclaimed from His Table as well as from the pulpit. Let us consider here some suggestions or procedures how that strong witness may be accomplished.

The location of the Communion in the order of the service is significant. The study reported in Chapter Two indicates that the practice of the churches is not uniform as to whether the Communion service comes before or after the Sermon. The important truth (as it relates to the very nature of local autonomy) is that the practice need not be uniform. Congregations are free to have the Communion before or after the Sermon. I believe that either practice can be followed satisfactorily but I do insist that the elders and the worship leader have a strong rationale for what they do. It is true that our actions speak louder than our words, and that truth is applicable here. How we arrange the order of the service carries its own message of priorities.

Careful attention should be given to the reading of scriptural passages at the observance of the Communion. The passages selected should be appropriate to the occasion. (For example, the biblical accounts of Jesus breaking bread by the sea are not in the context of the Lord's Supper.) Read the passages in a manner that indicates the solemnity, the magnitude, and yet the joyfulness of what is being shared! Use modern English translations and speak clearly, warmly. Do not be dependent upon the same text week after week no matter how appropriate it is (as for example, I Cor. 11:23-26). Refer to a concordance, a topical Bible, indexes in hymnals, and worship manuals for listings of passages that are suitable for use in this portion of the service.

Urge those who pray to focus their prayers on the single, splendid occasion at hand. (Urge them tactfully of course but urge them no less. Perhaps a few well-chosen words of suggestion delivered infrequently at some other opportunity,

as a discussion at a board meeting of the elders' responsibilities, will suffice.) These prayers are not the time to offer
petitions and praises for the mainstream of congregational
activities (that is the purpose of the Pastoral Prayer). Themes
for prayer suitable here are those relating to sacrifice, atonement, redemption, grace, love, fellowship, and thanksgiving (that is, as circumscribed by Christ's act at Calvary).
The possibilities for this prayer are limitless; there is no need
for the frequent repetition of a memorized prayer. (Again
my childhood memories include recollections of the efforts
of small boys to recite meticulously the rote prayers of
certain elders.)

In a similar vein care must be given to the selection of
the hymns (or other special music) that are used in connection with the Lord's Supper. Some of the songs that are
used simply do not carry the correct doctrinal message, and
the mood or tempo of others may prove to be distractful to
the high occasion. Nor is this the proper occasion to attempt
to learn a new hymn. An adequate number of good hymns
are available. Again, check the topical index of the hymnal.
It is my personal practice to keep a specially-indexed copy
of the hymnal conveniently accessible—a copy catalogued
to songs suitable for the Communion (and also for the
Opening Hymn and the Invitation). If a particular, familiar
hymn is desired and yet not included in the hymnal it can
still be used if the words are printed in the service bulletin.

It is my studied observation that Christian Churches/
Churches of Christ are among just a few churches that do
not emphasize the Fraction, the act of breaking of the bread.
And it is surprising that they do not in light of the Restorationist position. Some elders have been observed attempting
to do this, struggling almost futilely with the tiny particles

in their hands. In other instances large sections of the bread have been intentionally supplied that the elders may more readily perform this act. However in many congregations the bread is simply distributed with no attention given to the visible act of breaking the bread. Such an absence is certainly proper. Yet the Fraction is a symbolic act of the historic church—and it is important that in every way, the Fraction included, the continuity of the observance of the Communion be emphasized as a source of unity (and Restorationist churches are committed to unity!) Think about the implications of it! Somewhere on earth every single week since Pentecost Christians have gathered to break bread in remembrance of Him—and they will continue to do so until He comes again! Truly, "the church of Christ upon earth is essentially, intentionally, and constitutionally one."

For the Reader's Consideration

There are a number of things that can be done to make the observance of the Lord's Supper a more meaningful act of worship. Several suggestions will be mentioned here. The reader should be ever alert to new ideas and should make a serious effort both to record and utilize these ideas. (We require of our ministerial majors at Lincoln Christian College that they maintain file folders designated "worship," "prayer," "preaching," etc., and show evidence of systematically adding collected materials to these files.)

My dean in seminary once commented that on occasion in an earlier pastorate he placed a single red rose on the white cloth covering the elements on the Table. This was a means of immediately attracting the attention of the entering worshipers to one of the central purposes for the assembly

149

of the congregation. A spotlight might accomplish the same purpose.

The observance of the meal must never become routine. Do not shy away from the use of variations of the service, but of course only after the proposals have been discussed fully with and approved by the elders and the Worship Committee. "It has always been done this way," is a familiar cry to most of us. It need not, however, always be done that way in the future. Introduce innovations, and be prepared to support them with an adequate rationale for the change and with a full set of instructions for the new procedure. Certainly one would not expect to introduce at frequent intervals variations in the service, as the average worshiper cannot or will not accommodate such interruptions to the established way.

As examples of variation one might consider these. Have the congregation come a pew at a time to the Table rather than distributing the elements to the worshipers where they are seated. The elders or the deacons would then serve them at the Table. In similar fashion have families come forward to be served, two or three families coming at a time if the numbers are small. One minister has the worshipers depart from this position at the Table directly to their homes without returning to their pews. A benediction is printed in the bulletin for their personal recitation as they leave.

Mention was made at the beginning of this chapter of the experience of the first century Christians as they brought the elements of bread and wine from their homes to place on the Table. This could be dramatically and effectively duplicated today. Designated couples of the congregation could carry the elements to the front of the auditorium in the same sequence of actions when the deacons return the offering plates. Due explanation, perhaps in the form of a sermon, should accompany this procedure, otherwise the congregation will merely think that certain folk have been derelict in the performance of their obligations. Again, such a service would not be attempted without prior consultation with the elders and the Worship Committee.

Instructions for the observance of any service of the Lord's Supper should be presented clearly to the congregation, especially for the benefit of perplexed visitors. (Have we not all found ourselves at some time in that hapless position?) Concise, explicit instructions in the worship bulletin can contribute to the accomplishment of this. Ushers should be advised to seat guests in such strategic places as where they can observe the procedure of accustomed worshipers.

Realize that there is no biblical mandate that calls for elders (two of them) to officiate at the Table and for deacons to distribute the elements to the congregation. Others could be used as the occasion or the nature of the service demands. However one must remember that long-established traditions are difficult to overcome.

Several quite impressive services of Communion come to mind and though it might not be practical or advisable for use at the Sunday morning worship hour they do merit our consideration. I have conducted annually for almost twenty years a service of Communion that must be judged as popularly received in view of the comments that I receive. The service comes on Thursday evening before Good Friday and Easter. I request that the worshipers sit in family groups and refrain from all vocal communication whatsoever except for what is necessary to participate in the service. In a short devotional message I recount something of both the initial Passover Feast and of the institution of the Lord's Supper in the immediate context of the last Passover in the upper room. There are a few songs and reading of the Scriptures and then the congregation comes forward by families to receive the Communion from one of the elders and me. The major emphasis of the service is one that I clearly state— that we are purposely attempting to duplicate precisely the service each year even as the Passover was so repeated for a millennium and that the institution of the Lord's Supper in this perspective draws upon the point of continuity.

A number of congregations present a service of Communion annually, usually immediately prior to Easter, when costumed men portray the apostles and Jesus in a real-life reproduction of the famous paintings of the Last Supper. The portrayal may be still-life or animated. The entire service has a profound effect upon the worshipers.

A variation of the above service is that of a Catacomb Service where an attempt is made to portray both the suffering and the spiritual strength of the early Christians as they gathered in hidden places to break bread in remembrance of their Master. Costuming—and explanation—are important. One or several of the rooms of the educational facility of the church are usually more appropriate for decoration than the auditorium of the building.

It would be wise to apprise the congregation occasionally that the opportunity to share in the Communion is afforded to the ill and to the shut-ins. A brief page of instructions could be printed for those participating as callers in this program, suggesting ways to make the service both appropriate and meaningful. This planned activity contributes to establishing identity and continuity of the entire family of believers.

Questions and Projects

1. Why is the Lord's Supper sometimes called the Eucharist?
2. Why is it that elders of Christian Churches/Churches of Christ "neither invite nor debar" visitors (as well as members) to participate in the Lord's Supper?
3. What is unique about the fact that in the worship of Christian Churches/Churches of Christ laymen officiate at the observance of the Lord's Supper?
4. Define the word sacerdotalism.
5. Prepare a simple worship service that might be used when taking communion to the shut-ins.
6. Make a list of passages from the Bible that would be appropriate for reading at the observance of the Lord's Supper.
7. Make a list of some ways that the observance of the Lord's Supper could be made a more meaningful act in the worship of your congregation.

Chapter Ten

GIVING VOICE TO THE CONGREGATION

The minister of Shady Street Christian Church in Maple-ville, USA, is determined to enlist more of the leadership of the congregation in productive activity. One aspect of his overall plan, with the full approval of the Worship Com-mittee, is to recruit a different elder or deacon to serve each Sunday as the worship leader at the morning service. The plan is an ambitious one and apparently works well until that particular Sunday looms ahead when Clifford is sched-uled to preside. Now Clifford is a committed Christian, a faithful attendant, a good steward, and for some years a responsible worker on the church board. The problem is that Clifford, to say the least, is not very nimble of speech. Past performance indicates that he will stumble over the simplest of words, stammer when confronted with the extem-poraneous event, and in deep-rooted embarrassment gen-erally soften his speech so as to be almost inaudible to a large number of the assembled worshipers.

The minister is confronted with an unavoidable problem. He knows he must make a basic decision and yet gracefully handle a difficult situation. Should he tactfully set aside, he queries of himself, the entire program of the utilization of worship leaders and simply assume once again that role himself? Is it not better, he asks, to communicate effectively the Word of the Lord than to entrust it to an incapable assistant who no matter how conscientiously he tries simply falls short of effective communication? Surely he as a pro-fessional with his seminary training in oral communication (all those hours spent rehearsing before tape and video recorders) can perform the needed role more adequately. For that matter, he muses, perhaps all congregational par-ticipation should be minimized. He has noticed that many

154

folk have difficulty with the responsive readings and several who lead in public prayer do so rather awkwardly. Perhaps he, as the minister, should assume more and more of the responsibility of being the people's spokesman before God. He continues to ponder the problem—and then reaches for the morning's mail and the coffee pot.

The Importance of Congregational Participation

While perhaps many worship planners have let their minds wander momentarily along lines delineated by our minister from Mapleville one must remember that there is a vital principle at stake to which every responsible leader of the church must be loyal. Christian Churches/Churches of Christ are committed to the restoration of the essential practices of the churches of the first century era. Knowledgeable leaders of this Restorationist movement, from the earliest days of the Campbells to the present, have asserted that the first century ministry was a non-sacerdotal ministry and essentially a lay ministry at that. Thus the query of the Mapleville minister is answered. While the church will certainly not slip into oblivion if lay involvement is not widely utilized yet it is nonetheless imperative, to be both faithful to scriptural precedent and responsive to sound psychological procedure, that the fullest congregational participation be realized.

We have noted above (see Chapter Three) both that lay ministry was a basic feature of the synagogue worship and that in many ways (this function of lay ministry included) the worship of the first century Christian congregations followed the historic precedents of the synagogues. While the New Testament itself gives limited—but nonetheless adequate—instruction in this matter, the insights gained

155

from the writings of Justin Martyr in A.D. 150 substantiate the principle that the ministry of the first century Christian congregation was significantly a lay ministry. Of this there can be no reasonable doubt. Further—and equally relevant to this—is the observation that in the worship of the synagogue, the worship of the first century church, and the worship of Justin's time full congregational participation was an important aspect of the total worship experience. (At a later period in history a virtually illiterate people of the medieval church came to depend upon the priesthood for communication of the Scriptures and the ministration of worship. This only served to strengthen a developing sacerdotal view of ministry. Restoration leaders of the nineteenth century, along with many other erstwhile reformers, stressed the return to lay leadership. Increased opportunities for education provided for adequate training for these leaders and this significant contribution correlated directly to church growth.)

Knowing all this the worship leader—a busy individual with many important matters weighing heavily upon the daily schedule—simple decides that it is both easier and quicker to perform personally a given task in worship (a prayer, a scripture reading, a devotional meditation) than it is to recruit someone else to do it. Cannot we all identify with this? Are not most of us servants of scheduling, attempting to accomplish a given task in the quickest fashion?

Nonetheless it is important that any task for the Kingdom be done properly and legitimately. In this particular instance the task is the total worship experience—and for that worship to be a valid experience of total congregational confrontation with God all the congregation must be involved. Nothing less adequately fulfills the definition of congregational worship! Total involvement comes as the congregation shares together in the reading of the Scriptures and the offering of prayers as well as in the singing of hymns. Furthermore congregational involvement in worship leadership demands representation by all the leadership—or ministry, if you please—of the congregation, the elders, deacons, and teachers, as well as the evangelist (or pastor/minister). Similarly congregational involvement in general worship demands all classifications of the congregation, young and old, male and female, single and married.

Psychologically congregational involvement is sound. A wise Hoosier elder in my first full-time pastorate suggested to me that the more people we could enlist in the activities of the church the stronger the congregation would be. Experience proved him correct. This alone, of course, is not an adequate justification for congregational involvement but it is valid and it does complement the total rationale for congregational participation.

Areas of Participation

The most obvious as well as traditional way that the congregation participates in worship is through the singing of hymns. Most people like music (the content of popular radio programming attests to that) and most people like to sing. On several occasions I have heard folk comment with pride, "But you know, ours is a *singing* church." Therefore I would call the reader's attention to the fact that hymnology is a significant study in itself (and a subject well worthy of pursuit by the worship leader). Suffice it to say here however that hymns or songs must be carefully selected as to doctrinal message, the needs of the various ages and/or social levels of the congregation, and the tempo and style of the music itself. The most important resource for the worship leader beyond that of the Bible itself is an excellent church hymnal. Such a hymnal should always be of immediate access during the course of worship preparation.

The reading of the Scriptures provides for congregational participation. Biblical passages can be read responsively from the selections in the hymnal or from the Bible itself if pew Bibles in the same translation are available to all worshipers. Scriptural texts could be inserted in the worship bulletin at appropriate points. For example, some churches make very effective use of the people reading a printed benediction (as Ps. 19:14 or Num. 6:24-26) together. Individuals could be called upon (from where they are seated in the pews) to recite their favorite passages (experience will quickly indicate if this is a practical procedure in a given situation).

The survey of churches in the midwestern states of Illinois and Indiana (see Chapter Two) indicates that congregational prayer time is one of the real strengths of the church at worship. Here is an excellent opportunity for meaningful congregational participation. Specific prayer requests can be received prior to or during the worship hour. Individual sentence prayers can be solicited at the moment of prayer (no matter that two or more may speak out at the same time). Another approach to congregational participation is to make a specific prayer request and then to designate a person to pray for that particular need. An opportunity can be provided for people to offer "praises" (we are thinking of something slightly different from "prayer requests"). Too often we dwell on the pessimistic in our prayers ("Lord, bless those who are ill") when we ought also give praise for the glad tidings ("Lord, we praise you for all those who are not ill!"). Perhaps the most beneficial time of prayer is that of silent prayer. Suggest requests, needs, and praises—and then allow adequate time for silent response.

The offering is a time for participation by all. The child's gift of small coins is just as much an act of worship—perhaps more so—as the largest annual pledge. The act of steward-ship is a most solemn act of worship and it should be treated as such. This is no time for light-hearted humor. The author has been dismayed by some of the remarks that he has heard over the years, about making this a "silent offering," "may we have six strong men come forward," etc. Consider rather that the occasion when a new Christian places a twenty dollar bill in the offering plate for the first time is one of the highest acts of worship of that individual's life—and it is absolutely no time for frivolous humor. Frequently one of the deacons is asked to pray at this time. The doxology is sung. Appropriate offertory sentences (scriptural verses) can be printed in the bulletin and read responsively by the congregation.

A processional—the elders, deacons, minister, and choir marching in together—might be a quite dramatic introduction to the worship hour. Marching itself is historically an activity of worship, and the processional, if carried out strategically (as coming from the rear of the auditorium), can be a repre-sentative act on behalf of all the congregation.

Some sort of greeting exchanged between worshipers is appropriate—and certainly an act with long historic precedent. For well more than two millennia worshipers have exchanged the "Kiss of Peace" (though an actual kiss has usually been replaced by a warm embrace). Perhaps more appropriate to the situation of the Christian Churches/Churches of Christ would be a hearty handclasp. (The author however feels quite ill at ease in those services when this routine takes on the spirit of a welcoming committee of the local chamber of commerce!)

Vocal response to the sermon is possible. This may be accomplished by what is called "dialogue preaching." For example, the minister questions from the pulpit, "Jim, what does *faith* mean to you?" and Jim responds. (Jim, of course, is forewarned—and not all preachers are capable of adequately making dialogue.) Another form of response is to have directed small group discussion sessions immediately following the service. (Technically, this might not actually be a part of the worship service.)

A number of congregations give opportunity for members to provide flowers as memorials to loved ones on appropriate occasions. The flowers are displayed unobtrusively in the area of the pulpit or communion table and suitable mention is recorded in the bulletin. Participation is minimal but nonetheless meaningful.

Selected individuals can be significantly involved in the capacities of ushering and assisting with the reception of new members at the time of the invitation as well as at the baptismal services. These roles are crucial ones and special training is required. Only a limited number of people can be involved in the worship service in this fashion but the responsibilities can be distributed over several months until a number of people are involved.

Young People Have a Place

The older reader will recall when "seen but not heard" was an accepted working principle in respect to young people. Now all of that is reversed! (The author has often had the uncomfortable feeling that he grew up in a day when adults were in charge and reached maturity at a time when the youth had taken over!) It must be recognized now however that young people are not the church of tomorrow; they are in fact a part of the church today!

In many instances among the churches today a "junior worship" or "children's church" is conducted in another part of the building simultaneously with the worship of the adults and older youth. Responsible elders—with the input of skilled professionals—will have to determine if in a given congregation the advantages outweigh the disadvantages of such a procedure.

Assuming that the very young are in the same worship area as the older youth and adults there are ways that they can participate in the service. The youth minister can have a role in the worship service and the very young recognize him and thereby identify in some small way with the worship service. Further, the minister can deliver a brief "children's sermon" of three to five minutes to the youngsters who for the brief interval assemble in a prominent area near the pulpit. This procedure has worked well in numerous congregations. (The author has observed that adults are a very attentive audience to these "children's sermons" as well.) Parents should be carefully instructed, at times other than during the worship hour, on how to coach their own children to receive the maximum benefit from the entire worship service.

Music for the congregation at worship must be selected with the youth in mind. If there is any one thing that characterizes our present day as unique in history it is the strong expression of the desire for freedom and acceptance that the youth have—and it is especially evident in their music selection. (For youth to have preferences differing from adults is not unusual; for them to express their desires so emphatically is.) It is not easy to select music that is acceptable to all age groups. (Such a song as "Amazing Grace" is perhaps an exception to the rule.) However the difficulty must not and cannot be ignored. (Some larger congregations have confronted the problem by having simultaneous worship services in different parts of the building, one for young adults and another for the older folk.)

Young people can assume leadership roles in the local congregation. Nothing is to prohibit a young man from serving where a deacon (and perhaps an elder) normally would. (The customs of the churches almost inevitably preclude a young lady from such a role.) Reading the Scripture Lesson or leading in public prayer is not limited to the adult membership. (We have noted that even in the Jewish synagogue provision was made for an adequately prepared youth to participate in this way.) Extreme caution must be exercised however when youth do serve to eliminate any intimation that the youth are imitating their seniors (or in any way "playing church")—they are worship leaders in their own right.

There are other innovative ways that young people can serve in the worship service. Some can be selected to hand out bulletins. Others can see that hymnals are equally distributed among the pews and that silent-roll call cards are in the racks. One or more responsible youth can be appointed as "lighting technicians." It goes without saying that the performance of all these tasks requires careful coaching and supervision. It might appear to the reader that we are simply providing responsibilities for the youth irrespective of contribution to worship. Recall however our discussion of one of the words for "worship," *latreus*, and the implications that word has for service activity in worship.

Youth can be involved more directly in the traditional aspects of worship. Youth choirs render a remarkable contribution to the worship hour. Speciality groups such as bell choirs are another possibility if the opportunities for training are available.

The experienced worship leader will be alert to ever-developing occasions when the interests and energies of youth can be enlisted in the worship hour. One minister used young people to light candles as a prelude to worship. While that practice would draw criticism from some of our churches it does have historic precedent and might be acceptable on some occasions today. And yet another example: the treasurer of the small rural church where I worship has endeared himself to at least one generation of children by letting them place the offering in the canvas bags that the bank provides—"service," indeed!

Things to Consider

When changes are to be made in some aspect of the worship service go over these changes carefully with all participants. Go through the order of the service step by step with the organist, pianist, and song leader. If a new pattern for the distribution of the communion is proposed for the deacons, take those men into the worship auditorium after the board meeting and literally walk through the new routine. Post diagrams in inconspicuous places—even as a football coach might sketch out a new play.

If it is difficult for the congregation to hear the prayers of its leaders, provide voice amplification equipment. (The author is familiar with a congregation that installed an amplification system at the pulpit costing some five thousand pre-inflationary dollars and yet nary a nickel for additional microphones for the elders.) Perhaps the one who prays could do so from a different location in the worship area so as to insure audibility.

In various instructional settings give guidelines and suggestions for the content and presentation of public prayers. This can be accomplished tactfully in the Bible school classroom or at a board meeting or committee meeting.

If a call for silent prayer is made provide ample time for response to those prayers. The author on one typical occasion heard a worship leader state a number of requests and then proceed to provide a total of seventeen seconds to respond to those needs. While admittedly the author should have been praying rather than eyeing the second hand of his watch, it is obvious that a serious weakness exists. A very simple corrective for the problem is for the worship leader to pray silently for each of the requests and then add a few additional silent prayers in case someone else's prayers were prolonged!

It is well that the worship leader, early in the performance of that role, determine the favorite hymns of the congregation. This must be done to insure congregational participation. The information can be acquired through some sort of poll or balloting. The worship leader ought not be confined to the results of this poll but it certainly provides a proper perspective from which to view congregational singing.

Having difficulty in recruiting folk to play the instruments, read the lessons, or lead in prayer? Attempt first to enlist them to fulfill the same responsibility before a small group within the church family. This assists in establishing self-confidence and prepares for performance at other occasions.

The worship leader will quite probably observe that congregational participation in the worship service correlates directly to the strength of the worship service. Measurable evidence of this will be that people speak less frequently of "the church" or "our church" and more often of "my church." It is at this point that worship as a reality intensifies—and it is one point at which worship contributes significantly to church growth!

Questions and Projects

1. Prepare an outline of worship suitable for use in a children's worship service at the Sunday morning hour.
2. Conduct a poll of the members of your congregation to determine their favorite worship songs.
3. What are the names of some worship songs that seem to appeal to all age levels?
4. Make a list of biblical selections that would be appropriate for reading at the time of the offering.
5. Begin the practice (if you do not already do so) of asking for sentence prayers in your Bible school class.
6. Is it necessary for a person to be an elder or a deacon to serve at the observance of the Lord's Supper?
7. Make a list of ways that more people could be involved in leadership capacities in the morning worship service.

Chapter Eleven

PUTTING TOGETHER AN ORDER

A significant number of Puritan leaders and their congregations came to the rugged shores of North America in the early seventeenth century. They came seeking not religious freedom but rather freedom to worship freely—along lines, incidentally, that they thought were consistent with the model of New Testament Christianity. (They also were a restorationist group of sorts.) One of their principal reactions was against the official, prescribed liturgy of the state church of England. They spoke critically of English clergy who read prayers and sermons as "bare readers" and "dumb [silent] dogs." Rather they said the prayers should be extemporaneous and the sermons delivered in a vigorous, yet learned manner. (Such a presentation of the Word they likened to a "fire stirred" to give "more heat.") Especially did they object to the prescribed liturgy of the state church, prepared as it were by a national council. Their argument was a simple one, If God had desired that His people follow such an order He would have clearly stated such a demand within the pages of the Holy Scriptures. While, in their opinion, there was nothing inherently wrong with the contents of such a liturgy the error was that it was wrong to insist that every congregation (or for that matter even any congregation) be compelled to follow the order. Their reaction was based on the recognition that such liturgies are clearly prepared by man and not by God. They argued that there must be freedom within which the Holy Spirit could act. (One might ask in response, Is not the Holy Spirit sufficiently strong so as to act from within a prescribed liturgy?) Make no mistake, the leaders of a local congregation of these Puritans could and did prepare a liturgy for their own people (and for all purposes that liturgy became

166

official). But the point is these congregations (like Christian Churches/Churches of Christ) were strong practitioners of local autonomy—it was a liturgy *their* leaders had prepared. Within it, they believed, the Holy Spirit could guide the people as to what to say. Therefore for these Puritan congregations the Bible was the only book allowed in worship. (These people even seriously debated if it was proper to use in worship any hymns other than those expressly composed by divine inspiration, for example, the Psalms of the Old Testament.)

Commitment to an Ideal

Because of certain obvious similarities between the American Puritans and the nineteenth century efforts of the Campbells, Stone, and Scott, some historians have attempted to identify the latter movement as one directly related to the former. While admittedly the Campbells and their co-laborers were influenced to some extent by other English Congregationalists, the Glasites, Sandemanians, and Haldaneans, this is an inaccurate identification. The nineteenth century Restoration Movement simply was not derived from the earlier New England Puritans. There were certain principles in common, however, and most important was the fact that both groups appealed to the Holy Scriptures as the sole source for authority and direction!

We have noted in Chapter One that the significant early nineteenth century Restoration leaders shared a common position in their belief that the New Testament contained no liturgy. They did recognize that there were certain essential factors (as the elements cited in Acts 2:42) that had to be present. (Recall, for example, that Thomas Campbell admonished that there could be no New Testament worship

167

without the observance of the Lord's Supper.) But these men deemed that there was seen to be no inspired guideline for an order of worship; only was there a general guideline that all be done decently and in order (I Cor. 14:40).

Leaders of these churches hold the same position today. There are no official structures for us—not from the Bible and certainly not from the Restoration fathers. There is nonetheless a principle to be followed: Not only are we to embody the essential elements of the first century church in our day, we are also to attempt to discern and adhere to the mood and spirit of that early worship. If in the course of our biblical investigations we should discern that there is a variance between the mood and spirit of first century worship and that of the twentieth century (or even nineteenth century) church then it is imperative we evaluate the former (i.e. the first century) set of circumstances as preferable to the latter. Even so tactfulness demands that we move slowly in the accommodation of our worship designs for the "sake of the weaker brethren" who may not conceive of worship in terms comparable to those presented here.

(In all fairness I must add this postscript: While to say that the twentieth century church must emulate the practices of the first century church is theoretically sound it is not that easy to realize in actual practice. I believe that it is a correct assessment to say that while the various heirs of the nineteenth century Restoration Movement—the Disciples of Christ, the non-instrumental churches of Christ, and the Christian Churches/Churches of Christ—at one point agreed on the validity of the premise it is obvious that in actual practice they did not interpret the premise from the same philosophical perspective. Nonetheless these are the principles we have elected to follow—and follow them we must!)

Selection of a Model

Where does the worship leader begin in preparing an order of worship? One correctly begins with that with which the people are familiar and to which they have grown accustomed. There is little legitimate value in changing simply for change's sake. If for no other reason, there is the historic continuity of the local congregation to consider as well as the significance to them of continuing tradition. "It has always been done this way" is ample justification for proceeding with caution in suggesting changes in the area of worship.

But even as the worship leader begins with the people where they are, one still weighs carefully the value of a given order of the service. Certain questions need to be asked. What are the objectives and priorities of this congregation in worship? Are they legitimate from a biblical perspective? How well does the present structure of this service contribute to the achievement of these objectives and priorities? Is the present service true to the description of biblical worship that we have attempted to discern (see Chapter Four)? Are the basic elements of biblical worship to be found in this service? Is this particular service of worship sufficiently consistent with the heritage of Christian Churches/Churches of Christ so as not to confuse people expecting it to be thus?

It is the belief of the author (if the reader has not already so deduced) that many congregations could indeed sharpen the focus of their services of worship so as to make them more in keeping with the biblical model. Such an alignment will call for a greater attention to a strong, repeated presentation of the Word, a more careful consideration of our objectives in music (especially in respect to

169

congregational singing), and the development of a conscious philosophy for the proper placement of the Lord's Supper and the sermon in the service in respect to one another. An awareness will be established that the folksy, public-relations-oriented, "Is everybody having a good time?" approach so frequently observed is probably inconsistent with a biblically-based orientation of ultimate values in public worship. Truly, the church of Christ upon earth is not a community-service organization and its worship should not be conducted as though it were!

With these reflections in mind we shall consider one outline (or order, if you please) of worship that bridges the gap between where we ought to be and where perhaps we are. (It is certainly not to be intimated that this is the only model that will serve the purpose—for such a presupposition would be totally self-defeating and again untrue to the biblical perspective. It is simply one model, selected from many, to which much thought has been given and whose general outline and rationale has been established by actual practice in the author's personal experience. Other models, equally good, could be presented that contribute to the achieving of the same desired objectives.)

One will note in the following model that the sequence of the service is divided into four sections or phases. These phases intentionally parallel the fundamental movements of worship, as considered in Chapter Four. The subheadings (An Attitude of Awareness, An Act of Confession, A Time of Renewal, A Spirit of Commitment) clearly describe these natural transitions. They are stated in the printed bulletin as an educational aid to the development of a sound understanding of good worship principles. The selected scriptural passages (as for example, Hab. 2:20,

A MODEL ORDER OF WORSHIP

An Attitude of Awareness

"The Lord is in his holy temple: let all the earth keep silence before him."   Habakkuk 2:20

*PRELUDE

CALL TO WORSHIP

HYMN, "Holy, Holy, Holy"
   (all verses)

An Act of Confession

"God be merciful to me a sinner."   Luke 18:13b

SCRIPTURE [or perhaps a Responsive Reading]

BIDDING PRAYER

SOLO [or perhaps a Hymn]

A Time of Renewal

"For God so loved the world that he gave his only Son, that whoever believes in him should not perish but have eternal life."   John 3:16

SCRIPTURE READING

PASTORAL PRAYER

CHORAL RESPONSE

SERMON, "The Redemptive Message of the Cross"

*HYMN OF DECISION   No. 43

A Spirit of Commitment

"They were all filled with the Holy Spirit and spoke the word of God with boldness."   Acts 4:31b

COMMUNION HYMN   No. 452
   (first verse)

PRESENTATION OF TITHES AND OFFERINGS

*DOXOLOGY

WORDS OF INSTITUTION, 1 Corinthians 11:23-26

COMMUNION PRAYERS

DISTRIBUTION OF THE CUP AND LOAF
   (partake in unison)

COMMUNION HYMN
   (last verse)

*BENEDICTION

(*worshipers stand)

etc.) carefully support them. The passages may be read audibly from the pulpit, in unison by the congregation, or more commonly they may be read silently by all. (Other passages from the Bible could be chosen and at regular intervals should be.) It would be helpful if on infrequent occasion the worship leader from the pulpit (and in the classroom) would make both reference to and explanation of these movements. The regular, unannounced appearance of these subheadings in the printed bulletin however will contribute to a deepening awareness of fundamental worship principles. Further, the proper selection of music for each transition of the service is quite significant. It would be totally inappropriate, for example, to sing "Onward, Christian Soldiers" (as grand as that song may be) at a time when one is attempting to establish dramatically a sense of the awareness of the presence of God! Each good song makes its proper contribution in its proper place; it is the responsibility of the worship leader to see that this principle is observed.

The reader will note that nine distinct quotations from the Scriptures occur in the model service—if one uses a scriptural benediction (as for example II Cor. 13:14). Additional verses will be read and cited in the Sermon and snatches of biblical passages may appear in the words of the hymns. At various times in the service the entire congregation is enlisted in the reading of these selections from the Scriptures, both audibly and visually. It is a service strong in the Word! Perhaps this is the most powerful feature of this particular model.

Ample opportunity is provided for prayer. The survey of Illinois-Indiana churches (Chapter Two) determined that the possibilities for prayer was one of the forceful features of

172

these churches at worship. An examination of the model indicates at least five varying opportunities for prayer. One may feel uncomfortable with the term "Bidding Prayer" in the model—so call it what you wish! (The English Churches of Christ call it the "Prayers.") What the author makes reference to is that type of prayer where the worship leader says something like, "May we pray for the leaders of nations as they search for peace" (more traditionally, "I bid you pray . . ."), and then pauses for a sufficient period of time that each worshiper can offer a silent, appropriate prayer response before continuing with the next prayer concern. (It is the author's observation that with the exception of those ego-inflating comments about the sermon, he has received perhaps more comment about this aspect of the service than another.) In contrast with the Bidding Prayer in the order is the Pastoral Prayer. This is the prayer (probably delivered by the minister but not necessarily so) of the pastor for the flock. The needs of the congregation are rightly raised here (and not in the Communion Prayers!) It is usually regarded as the principal prayer of the service. The Communion Prayers (it could be singular as both elders need not pray) are just that—prayers focusing on one or more of those themes central to the communion observance.

In this particular model the observance of Communion follows the Sermon. However the Communion could precede the Sermon—as in reality occurs in the majority of these churches—and the same four-point transition of worship movement yet be justified. Whichever follows the other, those responsible for the development of the worship service must have a clearly defined rationale for their determination. Note that the first verse of the Communion Hymn is used to "open" this part of the service and the last verse is used to "close" it. This serves to focus attention on this high act of worship. Not appearing in the model is the Fraction—the act by the elders (or other ministrants) of breaking the bread. While this act is common to the worship of most mainline churches it is omitted here because it is an unfamiliar routine to Christian Churches/Churches of Christ. The author feels that the observance of Communion would be a more effective witness if signal attention were given to the actual breaking of the loaf, whether or not that act is stated in the printed bulletin. Instructions given in the model suggest that the worshipers "partake in unison." Other directions could just as well be followed: "partake when served," "partake after appropriate, silent meditation," "return cup to rack on pew." It is important that the worshipers—especially visitors—are duly instructed as to proper procedures.

It has been determined that the Presentation of the Offering follows the observance of Communion in approximately two-thirds of these churches. The author however would prefer to have the Offering received first that the act of Communion might indeed be the climax of the service.

Most worship leaders would prefer to conclude the entire service of worship with a Closing Chorus. The author believes that a scriptural Benediction is the appropriate final act. Note also that at various places throughout the order the worshipers are directed to stand. This serves not only to relieve physical discomfiture but also, as in the Prelude and the Doxology, as an act of worship in itself.

Coordination of the Service

Few things are more disheartening to this student of sound worship practices than to observe the song leader and the pianist hurriedly selecting a roster of songs just moments before the service is to begin. (Admittedly one thing is worse and that is the song leader making the query— reflecting total lack of preparation—"Who has a favorite song?") What does such a practice say to the congregation about the importance of worship, let alone contribute anything to the presentation of a magnificent public worship of God!

The worship leader, the minister, the song leader, the musicians at the instruments, and the chief participants among the elders and deacons should consult in advance on the procedure of the service. If this entire group does not confer weekly (and they probably will not) they must in reference to any significant changes in the order—and certainly the principal leaders of the service should confer at least briefly every week.

It is certainly wise and expedient that occasional variations in the order of the service take place and that even major changes sometimes be made. It is not wise that a worship leader who is a relative newcomer to the congregation be hasty in the attempt to initiate change. In any event the approval of the elders must be secured for any significant change in the format of the service. This procedure is both scripturally and administratively sound. Ministerial prerogative does not alter this fact. Any changes in the service should be both clarified for and rehearsed with those who are closely involved in the performance of the acts being changed. For example, when the deacons have been confronted with a new procedure for the distribution of the communion or the reception of the offering, I have gone with those gentlemen to the auditorium to rehearse their steps. Also explicit instructions should be made from the pulpit and/or printed in the worship bulletin. Even in consideration of all this it is still not wise to change the order frequently. It is important that the worshipers feel at ease. The author's mother, a regular attendant at worship for over eighty years, nonetheless expressed apprehension in an uncritical fashion when the changes in order came too frequently.

A Reservoir of Materials

Where does the worship leader gain awareness of new, illuminating approaches to worship? One must read, listen, observe, and inquire! There are good books available and occasional articles in the periodicals. Workshops and booths at the conventions offer a wealth of material. One-day seminars are frequently presented at the Bible college alumni homecomings. Cassette tape rental libraries (for example, the Lincoln Christian College Media Center) have numerous items for use. Sister congregations may make a contribution.

Every worship leader should create a private resource library with readily accessible material. Such a library would contain a variety of Bible translations, a complete concordance, as many worship manuals as can be secured (for example, James DeForest Murch, *Christian Minister's Manual,* Standard Publishing Company), and a basic selection of good hymnals (of necessity including the ones that the congregation uses). The worship leader should constantly be alert to collecting worship bulletins from other churches and should ask vacationing friends to assist in this task. (This might be an excellent summer project for one or more Bible school classes.) These bulletins, especially those pertaining to special occasions, should be catalogued in such a way as to be readily retrievable. A complete set of bulletins of the local congregation should be maintained, either filed or bound for future reference. (The author keeps two such sets, one for his own personal use and another to be left in the office of the church in the event of a change of pastorates.)

It may be that the worship leader can strengthen congregational participation in certain aspects of the service, specifically those of the reading of the Scriptures and prayer, by the use of carefully-selected collects, introits, and litanies. The introduction of such (with appropriate approval) should be made carefully and with adequate explanation as most congregations of the Christian Churches/Churches of Christ look with suspicion on that with which they are unfamiliar. Yet it is the author's firm belief that these forms (or at least variations thereof) were used by the first century church and could be used profitably today. In the event these particular forms are on occasion used, special attention will need to be given to adding such material to the worship leader's resource collection as these forms are not commonly available among these congregations.

The worship leader should begin to prepare now. The preparation and the ministry of worship is an exciting one. There are almost no limits on the possibilities that can be utilized. Remember that we are motivated by the knowledge that we are preparing people now for that which they shall do for all eternity!

Questions and Projects

1. What questions need to be asked as the worship leader confronts the preparation of a particular worship service?

2. What are the fundamental movements of worship?
3. Experiment with the use of a "Bidding Prayer" in your Bible school class or other small group.
4. Does the worship bulletin of your congregation provide adequate instruction that visitors to the service might feel comfortable?
5. Collect and analyze worship bulletins from other congregations. Ask yourself, What do these churches do and why do they do it?
6. What do we mean by the expression, "local autonomy"?
7. In preparing a service of worship how does one respond to the premise, "It has always been done this way"?
8. What person or group of people in a local congregation has the final authority in authorizing a new order of worship for the congregation's use?

Chapter Twelve

UTILIZING EVERY AVENUE

When the author was attending seminary he elected at frequent intervals, as students so often do, to go off campus for the purpose of dining. In traveling to one of the popular restaurants he drove past a thriving Christian Church. The building itself was designed in modified Gothic architecture. Immediately adjacent to the major structure was a small prayer chapel of similar design. There was convenient, off-street parking and a friend, familiar with the purpose of the small building, suggested that a stop be made. While the building was used for small weddings it also served as an open chapel for prayer and meditation for the week-day passer-by. The interior was furnished appropriately with several short pews, an organ, a cross, and a lectern bearing a Bible. Recorded organ music began to play softly, the recorder activated by the act of turning on the light switch that illuminated the interior. The walls of the chapel, constructed of the same Indiana limestone as the main building, muted the sound of passing traffic on the street just a few yards away. The entire setting provided a marvelous atmosphere for solitude and meditation.

Here was a congregation in a teeming city attempting to extend its worship opportunities beyond the periphery of Sunday morning. Here was a congregation reaching out to its neighborhood. And here was a growing church. Surely every congregation has numerous, often untried means of developing its worship possibilities.

Special Services

Leaders of a concerned congregation will confront every service, every gathering, every activity with the question,

What are our priorities for this occasion? This is equally true of a midweek Bible study, a meeting of the Official Board of the church, or an outing for the youth. Now while the first priority of each occasion may be respectively, study of the Scriptures, conducting the business of the congregation, or fun and fellowship for the youth, it is inconceivable that a secondary (if not ultimate) priority ought not to be personal confrontation with God, hence, worship! After all is said and done, the church must be the church! Therefore leaders must pose the question constantly, What are our priorities for this occasion?

When church leaders are accustomed to raising this query it will become readily apparent that a baptismal service is much more than a highly significant act of receiving redemption and initiation into the kingdom. When they regularly ask this question it will be obvious that a wedding is more than a civil (or even, church) ceremony celebrating the union of two people as one. When this question is made a perpetual principle of procedure it will be apparent that a funeral is more than the family's final, public expression of love. Rather each instance, the baptism, the wedding, the funeral, is also a confrontation with God—an act of worship. And, as an act of worship the occasion should be carefully viewed from that perspective in which worship is ordered.

Is it too much to ask that a baptismal service be considered as an act of worship? Is it not recognized as an ordinance even as is the observance of communion, and have we not recognized the celebration of communion as one of the highest acts of worship? Thus the same careful preparation must be given to the readiness for the observance of baptism as for any other high act of worship. Every step of the procedure is carefully explained to the candidates that undue anxiety on their part may be alleviated. (It is helpful to talk with them about such things as water temperature, water depth, buoyancy, and duration of time in the baptismal waters.) Those giving assistance are carefully instructed (for example, as to precise timing in pulling curtains open and close—if curtains are to be pulled). Assignments are made far in advance of the moment of the service. Appropriate readings of the Scriptures and suitable hymns are selected in advance and people are designated to assume leadership in these activities. The candidates are carefully aided in entering and exiting the baptistry. The act of baptism itself is performed gracefully so as not to solicit a subdued titter from the congregation. (Some ministers actually practice this act, immersing their wife or some other willing assistant.) The baptismal service may be planned as an integral part of the morning worship service or it can be added in a complementary way at the close of the regular worship hour. The baptismal service can of course be planned as an independent and yet meaningful act of worship to be observed on any day of the week. A post-baptismal communion service, involving the candidates, their immediate family members, the minister, and selected elders, can be an extremely meaningful experience for the participants.

Marriage in the long tradition of the historic church has been considered an act of worship, though admittedly the trend is presently in another direction. Perhaps the continuing celebration of marriage in a manner reflective of solemn, awe-provoking reverence would go far in speaking of the permanency of marriage in a divorce-prone society! The entire wedding ceremony—especially the words, "What therefore God hath joined together, let no man put asunder" (Mark 10:9)—should strike a resounding note of the reality

181

of the seriousness of this new life-relationship. The minister who presides can set the stage for a proper approach of reverence by letting it be clearly known to all in the wedding party that while there may be a time for joviality later this is a moment of solemn covenant before the presence of Almighty God! Nothing should deter him from this tack. The selection of vocal music, the decorum of the wedding party, the total prohibition of the evidence of the use of alcoholic beverages by members of the wedding party, everything, is to coordinate with this high principle. The officiating minister is completely free to function on his own terms; he does not have to condescend in the slightest to the public image of marriage. The elders of the church by official action should give their fullest support to this stance.

(In recent months I have initiated two changes in the ceremony that I use. (1) I now go to the pulpit to make my initial statement to the party and the congregation; I feel that this desk gives the added authority to my brief message that I desire. (2) I now request of the congregation that they also audibly state their intention to offer support to the couple in years to come.)

The funeral should be an act of worship—and must be if it is to bring lasting assistance to the bereaved. There are of course many different and unique situations that present themselves at the time of death. The service for a non-Christian held in a funeral home in no way parallels that held for the godly saint within the confines of the church building that the deceased so dearly loved. At any rate the funeral service is for the living—and for the living it can be an act of worship. Select the biblical readings, outline meditational thoughts, and choose music that will point to the One who is the Lord of Life. Nothing can be done for the deceased but the living remain with us! Through the years in officiating at many services I have observed it to be helpful to the family when the Scriptures are read at greater length and my message shortened proportionately.

The occasions and locations for special activities of worship are almost as endless as the ventures of life. I have conducted Easter sunrise services on a golf course, community Thanksgiving services in a richly liturgical setting, and World Day of Prayer services in a humble rural church. I have led Boy Scouts in worship in the open woods and week-end Nimrod campers in a cow barn. I have worshiped with airmen in a hangar, athletes in a locker room, and students in a dormitory hallway. I have directed worship in a nursing home and also with youth in a public school, P. M. M. (Pre-Madalyn-Murray). I have worshiped with my family in a motel room—and shared a final communion with my father in a hospital room!

The possibilities for special services of worship like these are endless. Search them out! Make the best of them! Capitalize on the opportunities before you! One of the things unique about such special services is that they provide more freedom for adaptation than do the custom-decreed Sunday morning services. The folk are certainly not as tradition-conscious when it comes to worshiping in these special situations. New ideas can be adapted; experimentation with worship can be conducted (within reasonable limits, of course). The initiative rests with you the worship leader. Be innovative! Venture along new, expressive ways of worship of our Lord!

Creativity and Worship

Many church buildings were designed and erected with things other than worship in mind. Some were built primarily for purposes of preaching, others for effective education, and yet others as auditoriums acoustically engineered for excellence in music appreciation. (While it is true, as certain of my colleagues remind me, that one can worship almost anywhere, yet my own actual experience forcefully indicates that certain facilities are much more conducive to me for worship.) It is not likely in terms of cost-justification that an existing building can be radically altered to suit our needs for worship, so other approaches may be taken.

Significant functional changes can be made however. Perhaps the pulpit can be moved—or elevated. A divided chancel (the use of both a pulpit for preaching and a lectern for reading) might be the answer in some situations—or a divided chancel might be redesigned with a single, centrally located pulpit in others. The communion table can be re-located; an elevated, more visually evident location could be the choice—or perhaps a location more nearly in the midst of the worshiping congregation.

The organ may be moved if the acoustical and mechanical specifications permit. The choir may be placed in a different location. I have observed on occasion the choir to be placed in a rear balcony, in the vestibule (narthex), or in the first rows of the general seating area of the worship auditorium— all to good advantage. I worshiped with one congregation where the choir was seated in the raised area back of the pulpit but out of the visual range of the congregation—and the musical effect was quite striking. If the worship area is designed on the cruciform plan the traditional place for the choir is in either transept.

Additional lighting fixtures can be used to create dramatic effects. Many buildings seem to be under-illuminated in the worship area so spotlights can be installed to focus attention on those areas where high points of the worship service transpire, as the communion table, the pulpit, and the baptistry. In some instances a rheostatic control is used to good advantage with the lighting of the baptistry; the intensity of the light is raised and lowered at the proper time in respect to the position of the candidate for baptism. A variation of this is to switch from red to white illumination as the candidate emerges from the baptismal waters. (Every available tactic should be utilized to make the worship act of baptism a dramatic sermon in itself.) A number of congregations have installed exterior doors of plate glass so that even the passer-by is at least momentarily attracted to worship when one's gaze through the transparent doorway is attracted and arrested by a spot-lighted pulpit. Stained-glass windows can be illuminated from the interior so as to present a similar summons to worship to the passing traffic—as might a spot-lighted steeple.

Art work can be used to significant advantage—but worship leader, be careful; it is much easier to introduce a work of art than it is to remove it! Under no circumstance should a piece of art be accepted for permanent installation without the approval of a committee designated by the elders for that purpose. Yet art work is rich in worship symbolism and the well-read worship leader can use it wisely.

If at all possible in this age of energy conservation, rising energy costs, and government regulation, the temperature range of the worship facility should be maintained at a comfortable temperature. It is difficult to worship under the adversity of the extremes of temperature range.

The psychology of the selection of color of paint for interior areas is a critical one. Some colors and some shades are simply not conducive to a proper setting for worship. (The author once served in a pastorate where by actual count seventeen rooms bore the same shade of green! To this day his son has an aversion to the color green.) Consult a professional when selecting the color of paint.

One of the true blessings of the modern day is the focus of attention that has been given to the meeting of the needs of the physically handicapped. Those confined to wheel chairs are properly provided with adequate parking facilities, inclined ramps, and if necessary, electric lifts to circumvent impossible steps. Headphones are provided for those who have hearing difficulties. (I shall never forget one of our dearest ladies, when first using a headphone, blurting out, "Why, I can hear the preacher!") If necessary, provision should be made to sign the services to those needing this level of assistance. Other needs may be met in ways unique to the situation.

The Worship Committee

The responsibility for the direction of holy worship should never rest on the shoulders of one individual alone. Every congregation should have a Worship Committee, carefully selected across lines of age and professional status so as to be truly representative of the congregation. At least one elder will serve on the committee and the committee in turn is responsible to the eldership. The committee should meet at regular intervals and will always meet prior to significant changes in the worship format. It will be the further responsibility of the committee to insure a respectable continuity with the past as well as to provide a creative adaptability to the present. The committee must see that the worship needs of every age and social grouping within the congregation are recognized and in some measure met. The committee will have at hand a selection of excellent hymnals and books on worship as well as access to the collection of old worship bulletins that provides an important link to the heritage of the congregation. Yet while maintaining a heritage, committee members also must be open to new ideas.

The task of ushering will come under the direction of the Worship Committee. This is indeed an important task as the proper seating of worshipers relates directly to effective growth in both worship appreciation and evangelism. Ushers must be selected who are warm and genial and yet very conscious that they are welcoming guests into the presence of God. The ushers should be trained and a number of resource books are available to be utilized in this area. It certainly helps if the ushers are able to identify newcomers and to remember names.

Worship and the World

The cry of our day (and rightly so) is for church growth! It is the author's cherished conviction that one of the significant elements contributing to church growth is that of the evidence of a congregation caught up in transforming worship experience. The growth will be twofold (and genuine church growth must always be twofold): (1) those who are already believers will have their spiritual faculties extended and at the same time (2) the congregation will be expanded numerically as others are attracted to the body of believers who have seen the Lord in His Temple and like Isaiah cry to be sent! It is only a secondary function of worship but the worshiping church will nonetheless serve as a magnetic force to draw others to the Source of Power!

And there is worship experience to be considered beyond the periphery of one's own immediate congregation. Christian

Churches/Churches of Christ, especially those in smaller cities, will frequently have the opportunity to share in community worship services with other churches. What a grand opportunity to share one's biblical worship! (Perhaps one can learn something from the experience as well.) This indeed calls for careful study and reflection on that which constitutes meaningful worship experience. Care must be exercised to focus honestly on the first century church and not simply on the nineteenth century Restoration heritage.

The ground level of worship is the personal worship experience. This is where it all begins. Many of the principles of worship considered in our study are immediately adaptable to both personal worship and family worship. And they should be adapted! Personal worship is so important. Without it there will soon be no corporate worship. Indeed the growth of congregational worship correlates directly to personal worship growth!

A Summons to Worship

"Praise ye the Lord. Praise the Lord, O my soul. While I live I will praise the Lord: I will sing praises unto my God while I have any being" (Ps. 146.1-2). The Psalms have been characterized as the mirror of the worship of the Hebrew people, a people who poured out their deepest emotions of praise, thanksgiving, and petition to God through music and song. Truly the dominant note—the grand test—of real religion is its quality of praise!

Worship is inherent to our relationship to God. The psalmist observed, "The heavens declare the glory of God; and the firmament sheweth his handiwork" (Ps. 19:1). The Scriptures record that when the people praised Jesus at the Triumphal Entry, certain sour-faced people challenged the Master to rebuke them, and He replied, "I tell you that, if these should hold their peace, the stones would immediately cry out" (Luke 19:40). The grand act of worship is the very purpose for which humankind was originally created, and this is the purposive result to which all redemption points. The giants of the Protestant Reformation would praise God even if they knew beyond a doubt that they would be lost. Calvin thought of the whole of creation as a vast orchestration of praise. Too often we feel that the spotlight of God's special interest must follow us wherever we move across the stage of human experience, when actually, by the very nature of reality, the spotlight is reversed. God alone is worthy of praise, for He is faithful, loving, and the keeper of covenant with His people.

Worship is imperative to our own total well-being. The act of giving praise is one of the greatest healers of the soul as it is also of the whole mental and physical perspective of life. It provides the balance that the tension of living demands. There is far more truth than cheap sentimentality in the expression, "The family that prays together stays together." The act of giving praise lifts us from the diminutive, frustrating hovel of our existence to the very presence of the Holy Throne where we may truly say in regard to our personal anxieties that Christ is the victor!

Worship is obligatory to our witness to our peers. It is recorded of that great missionary figure, Francis Xavier, that his co-workers when saddened would but look at their leader to become gladdened again. It is recorded of those early martyrs of the faith, John Huss and Jerome of Prague, that they went to their death reciting Psalm 31: "In thee, O Lord, do I put my trust; let me never be ashamed: deliver

189

me in thy righteousness. . . . O love the Lord, all ye his saints: for the Lord preserveth the faithful, and plentifully rewardeth the proud doer. Be of good courage, and he shall strengthen your heart, all ye that hope in the Lord" (Ps. 31:1, 23-24). Christian worship has the unique quality of being contagious!

Thus the imperative of worship is clearly upon us. We must submit to an introspective examination to determine the level of prominence to which we have accorded worship, in our life, in our circle of intimate fellowship, and in the gathered body of believers. We must always seek to develop the quality of and to extend the periphery of our worship. We must develop a well-rounded life of worship so that we can sincerely praise God for the bitter experiences as well as the sweet.

And now may we conclude, as did the Psalmist, "Let every thing that hath breath praise the Lord. Praise ye the Lord" (Ps. 150:6).

Questions and Projects

1. Prepare a brief order of worship for a baptismal service, including a list of appropriate songs and scriptural readings.
2. What can be done to make a funeral more of an act of worship?
3. What can be done to make a wedding more of an act of worship?
4. What might well be on the agenda for the regular meeting of a worship committee?
5. List some physical ways that the church building could be minimally altered so as to make public worship more intimate, purposeful, and dynamic.

190

6. Write a brief statement on how strong biblical worship complements the evangelistic witness of the local congregation.
7. To what extent are the principles that govern public worship applicable to private and/or family worship?

Special Study

ALEXANDER CAMPBELL AND THE HYMNBOOK*

by Alger M. Fitch

Chapter One

A CONSPICUOUS SILENCE

Two facts become quickly apparent to readers seeking to learn more about the religious leader Alexander Campbell (1788-1866). The first is the strange silence of many church historians regarding this church-reformer. To thumb through a lengthy index of an extensive history of American Christianity may give the reader but a few lines on this man, if it lists him at all. An example may be found in *American Christianity* (New York: Scribner, 1960), an historical interpretation with representative documents, by H. Shelton Smith, Robert T. Handy, and Lefferts A. Loetscher. In the 615-page first volume, covering the years 1607-1820, Alexander Campbell is mentioned once and shares half a paragraph with his father. In the 634-page second volume, covering the years 1820-1960, the name Campbell does not appear in the index and "Campbellite" appears once.

That Mr. Campbell must have been an impressive person is evidenced when, today, nearly four million Christians— a general estimate combining memberships of Christian churches and churches of Christ, "leftist," "rightist," and "centrist"—affirm the principles he espoused. In his day

*Printed by Standard Publishing Company, 8121 Hamilton Avenue, Cincinnati, OH 45231 in the *Christian Standard* as a series of articles from June 26, 1965 to October 30, 1965.

almost everywhere in America the name "Alexander Campbell" was a common topic of conversation by friends and foes.

Campbell has been called the "multivocationed Scot."

As farmer and manager of an extensive acreage at what is now Bethany, West Virginia, he was successful enough so that he never accepted remuneration for his extensive labors as a preacher. He was editor of a monthly publication of vast influence for forty years—the *Christian Baptist,* 1823-1830, and the *Millennial Harbinger,* 1830-1863. He was a debater, pressing his views of Scriptural Christianity in discussion with noted secularists, Universalists, Roman Catholics, and paedobaptists. He was an educator, founding (1840) and presiding for twenty years over what is now Bethany College.

He dared to mix religion and politics, being elected in 1829 as a delegate to the Virginia Constitutional Convention. He did not just vote but gave significant speeches regarding each major social and political issue. His ninety-six colleagues included such men as James Monroe (1758-1831), James Madison (1751-1836), and John Tyler (1790-1862). If freedom and democracy, a high court and a congress of nations, the threat of "communism" and racial inequality, Roman Catholicism, and Christian unity appear to be twentieth-century issues, then Alexander Campbell is more relevant to our day than present historiography suggests by its near omission.

Debates and Proceedings of the Constitutional Convention Virginia includes evidence that as early as 1820 Mr. Campbell was opposing slavery. In 1829 he faced in debate the English socialist, Robert Owen (1771-1858), who was advocating the redemption of society by the elimination of private property, marriage, and religion.

Hymnbook Little Noted

A second noticeable silence is that of "Campbellite" historians regarding the hymnal their patriarch edited.

Robert Richardson, in his 1225-page *Memoirs of Alexander Campbell,* gives only eighteen and one-half lines to the hymnbook, and seven of these are relegated to the footnotes. Louis Cochran, after searching both modern and older historical works on Campbell for material to be used in his novel, *The Fool of God,* refers to it, as they do, only in a side remark: "The hymnbook was off the press; William Llewellyn had done a good job" (p. 238). James DeForest Murch, in his 392-page *Christians Only,* devotes only one paragraph to hymnody, and in that paragraph makes no mention of Mr. Campbell or his hymnal.

To fill the gap in the general field of hymnology and music amongst Disciples of Christ five theses and one dissertation are known to have been written between 1943 and the present time. A letter from Claude E. Spencer, curator for the Disciples of Christ Historical Society, Nashville, Tennessee, to the author posted October 30, 1963, lists these as follow:

Bellville, Miriam Priscilla, "Trends in Hymnody in the Disciples of Christ, 1828-1941"; unpublished M.S.M. thesis, Union Theological Seminary, 1943.

Hanson, Kenneth Christian, "The Hymnology and the Hymnals of the Restoration Movement"; unpublished B.D. thesis, Christian Theological Seminary, 1951.

Hanson, Kenneth Christian, "A Theological Study of the Hymns of the Restoration Movement"; unpublished M.A. thesis, Butler University, 1958.

Heaton, Charles Huddleston, "The Disciples of Christ and Sacred Music"; unpublished D.S.M. dissertation, Union Theological Seminary, 1956.

Teague, Kenneth Pat, "A Study of the Development of Hymnals in the Restoration Movement"; unpublished M.A. thesis, Harding College, 1959.

Tichenor, Gerald Wesley, "Protestant Church Music with Emphasis upon the Disciple of Christ Churches"; unpublished M.A. thesis, Butler University, 1958.

There may, of course, be other such studies not known to Mr. Spencer, who did a prolegomenous work of eleven pages, "The Campbell Hymn Book; A Bibliographical Study," which appeared in the Society's publication, *Discipliana* in January, 1950.

Deserves More Attention

That serious attention should be given to Alexander Campbell as the editor of *Psalms, Hymns, and Spiritual Songs* is seen when one observes the importance he attached to it, and also how much time and attention he gave to the improvement of psalmody in the churches.

Next to the Bible the hymnbook was the most popular reading material of the Christian. What was not sung was read. Much of a hymnal was stored in the memory and most of its hymns were imbedded in the heart. Campbell said:

> The Christian Hymn Book, next to the Bible, moreover, wields the largest and mightiest formative influence upon the young and old, upon saint and sinner, and of any other book in the world. Poetry . . . partakes so much of the spirit of its author, that it insinuates itself into the soul with more subtlety and power than any other language of mortals. . . . Permit me, I also say, to dispense the psalmody of a community, and I care not who dictates its creed or writes its

195

catechism. If the hymn book is daily sung in the family, and in the social meetings of the brethren, it must imbue their souls with its sentiments more than all the other labors of the pulpit or of the press.[1]

He declared that the hymnal of any people is "the best substitute in the world for what is usually called a confession of faith." It was "the doctrinal embodiment and exponent"[2] of a community's faith, hope, and love. In the October, 1851, issue of the *Millennial Harbinger,* this key statement is made:

Were I, indeed, obliged or Providentially called upon, to publish what is usually called a confession of my faith—a full exhibit of my attainments in Christian knowledge—I would rather present to the world a copy of my Christian Psalmody —the psalms, hymns and spiritual songs which I adopt and use, than any other documentary evidence which I could offer; not only of my faith and hope in God through the Lord Jesus, but also of my measure of knowledge in the mystery of God, and of Christ, and of man's redemption (p. 576).

Using this, as if it were a sermon text, I propose in forthcoming chapters to look at the man through his hymnal and then endeavor to see the hymnbook in the light of that man. The first section will treat Alexander Campbell as hymn editor, hymn writer, hymn singer (or worshiper), and

---

1. "Introduction," *Psalms, Hymns, and Spiritual Songs,* compiled by A. Campbell, W. Scott, B. W. Stone, and J. T. Johnson (2d ed., Bethany, Virginia: Printed and published by A. Campbell, 1853), pp. 13, 14. Pierre Jean de Beranger (1780-1857), the French lyricist, is one who originally said: "Let me make the songs of the people, and I care not who makes their laws."
2. "Psalmody—No. I," *Millennial Harbinger* (October, 1851), p. 6.

as music critic. Part two will study the hymnal for an awareness of its history, sources, theology, and arrangement with a final word relating to its norm (ideal) and influence.

Chapter Two

CAMPBELL AS A REFORMER

What was the dream that fired the heart and challenged the mind of Thomas Campbell and his son Alexander? It was the holy vision of a Christian world, a united church, and a pure gospel, replacing the nightmare of scandalous division which had blighted the name of Christ and His church.

Restoring the "Ancient Order"

The movement of which Alexander was a part, and of which he was the most classic expression, is sometimes called a unity movement, sometimes an evangelistic movement, and at other times the Restoration movement. It was all three, with the world's conversion the ultimate goal. The high-priestly prayer of our Lord, recorded in the Gospel of John, chapter seventeen, had implied that the world would not be won to Christ until the disciples were one in Christ. Alexander Campbell regarded the union of all Christians to be an immediate objective if the final goal of world evangelization were not to be thwarted.

> We might as reasonably expect that Indian corn will grow in the open field in the midst of the frost and snows of winter as that pagan nations can be converted to Jesus Christ till Christians are united through the belief of the apostles' testimony. We may force corn to grow by artificial means in the depths of winter but it is not like the corn of August. So may a few disciples be made in pagan lands by such means in the moral empire as those by which corn is made to grow in winter in the natural empire but they are not like the disciples of primitive times before sectarian creeds came into being. It is enough to say on this topic that the Saviour

198

made the unity of the disciples essential to the conviction of the world and he that attempts it independent of this essential sets himself against the wisdom and plans of heaven and aims at overruling the dominion and government of the great king (*Christian Baptist*, March 5, 1927).

Jesus' prayer to the Father had been for those that would believe on Him through the apostolic witness. Campbell's plea to the church became, therefore, a call to return to apostolic faith and practice. The restoration of the New Testament church or of the "ancient order of things" became the quickest means to the imperative end of immediate Christian unity for an ultimate world redemption. "Original Christianity in faith and practice, in letter and in spirit" (*Millennial Harbinger*, September, 1847) became the battle song of those who called themselves "reformers." "The plea" to unite was accompanied by the program or method for obtaining the objective. Iconoclastic as it may seem, much of the conventional and established had to fall before the purer religion could rise. Not "orthodoxy" but "apostolicity" was to be the measuring rod. Judgment would begin at the house of God with the clergy and the creeds first in line for measurement by the New Testament rule.

The hallowed creeds of the ancient church were counted as causes of division. The former Old Light Anti-Burgher Seceder Presbyterian was even rejoicing that the "quaint scholastic diction of Geneva, anglicised and covenanted in Scotland" was passing away; and Campbell's last words for this old loyalty were: "The sooner its requiem shall be sung, the better for Christianity and for the human race" (*Millennial Harbinger*, September, 1853).

Words from Foreign Sources

Christians had drawn verbal swords against each other in religious controversy over "words of foreign importation"—"the barbarous words and phrases of scholastic divinity"—words such as:

> The Holy Trinity—Three persons of one substance, power, and eternity—Co-essential, co-substantial, co-equal—The Son eternally begotten of the Father—An eternal Son—Humanity and divinity of Christ—The Holy Ghost eternally proceeding from the Father and the Son—God's eternal decrees—Conditional and unconditional election and reprobation—God out of Christ—Free will—Liberty a necessity—Original sin—Total depravity—Covenant of grace—Effectual calling—Free grace—General and particular atonement—Satisfy divine justice—Reconciled God—Active and passive obedience of Christ—Common and special operations of the Holy Ghost—Imputed righteousness—Inherent righteousness—Progressive sanctification—Justifying and saving faith—Historic and temporary faith—The direct and reflex acts of faith—The faith of assurance and the assurance of faith—Legal repentance—Evangelical repentance—Perseverance of the saints, and falling from grace—Visible and invisible church—Infant membership—Sacraments—Eucharist—Consubstantiation—Church government—The power of the keys &c. &c. &c. (*Millennial Harbinger*, August, 1835).

Such speculations and phraseology were beyond what is written. Hence, being unscriptural, unauthorized, and schismatical they did not demand acceptance or disproof. Generating "folios of the most verbose controversy, without converting a single sinner to God, or comforting the heart of any saint" they were to be abandoned for the sacred oracles. The essential word of the Lord to the church went forth not from Sinai, from Rome, nor from Westminster, but from Jerusalem. The Christian ought to be satisfied with "Bible names for Bible things."

This was the first principle listed in a "Synopsis of Reformation Principles and Objects" for recent readers of the *Millennial Harbinger*. Restoration of a pure speech was called "a sovereign cure and preventative of Protestant partyism" (*Millennial Harbinger*, November, 1837). To heal division and prevent debate among believers the language of Canaan was to be used and the speech of Ashdod avoided.

> For example: Instead of "sacraments," we prefer *ordinances*; for "the Eucharist," *the Lord's Supper*; for "covenant of works," the *law*; for "covenant of grace," *the gospel*; for "testament," *institution* or *covenant*; for "Trinity," *Godhead*; for *"first, second and third person," The Father, the Son, and the Holy Spirit*; for "eternal Son," *The Son of God*; for "original sin," *the fall, or the offence*; for "Christian Sabbath," *Lord's Day* or *First Day*; for "effectual calling," *calling* or *obedience*; for "merits of Christ," *righteousness* or *sacrifice of Christ*; for "general atonement," *ransom for all;* for *"free* grace," *grace*; for "free will," *will* &c. &c. (*Millennial Harbinger*, September, 1847).

Ideas Foreign, Also

Observation taught that if a word was not in the Scripture, the idea was not likely there either. Permanent union among Christians would have to be a union in truth. The new scholastic nomenclature, rather than being an improvement, was judged to issue "in a new class of ideas, rather than in a new class of names for old ideas" (*Millennial Harbinger*, November, 1837). Thomas Campbell had declared, "Where the Scriptures speak; we speak." His son could have echoed, "*As* the Scriptures speak; we speak," for he does testify that "*this unity never can be obtained while any other creed than the sacred writings is known or regarded*" (*Christian Baptist*, August 7, 1826).

Writing on Bible terminology in his monthly, Campbell spoke:

> It is said that if the English language be divided into *one hundred parts*, *sixty* parts would be Saxon; *thirty* would be Latin, including French; *five* would be Greek, and the remaining *five* from the other languages of the world.
>
> We presume to think and to say, that if the ecclesiastico-heretical terminology, or nomenclature, of modern Christendom, were evangelically analyzed, or repudiated in wholesale, and the apostolic diction, suggested by the Holy Spirit and consecrated by the prime ministers, or apostles of Jesus Christ, were substituted for it, more would be achieved to the cause of Christianity; to the union, harmony, and cooperation of Christians, and to the progress of the reign of the Lord Messiah throughout the earth, than has been effected since the Lutheran Reformation, by all the schisms and schismatical leaders that have figured on the pages of ecclesiastical history during the last three centuries (*Millennial Harbinger*, March, 1856).

The writings of many years show the sage of Bethany constantly arguing the importance of Biblical phraseology as an aid to union. Logic he combined with illustration. The nineteenth-century reformation as a vine dresser was to lop off the immense exuberance of fruitless boughs of scholastic words and phrases, "which in addition to their own sterility, so shade and obscure the fruitful branches as greatly to depreciate and diminish the vintage" (*Millennial Harbinger*, August, 1835). As typical of a multitude of others, here is one early (1826) illustration:

But how shall we all speak the same things relating to the Christian religion? Never, indeed, while we add to, or subtract from the words which the Holy Spirit teaches. . . . Now every human creed in Christendom, . . . is a new mound of doctrine, and into whatever mould metal is cast, when moulded it must assume the size and impress thereof. Let silver be cast into a French, Spanish, English, or American mould of the same size, but differently constructed; and although it is all the same metal, and of equal size, each crown, whether French, English, or Spanish, assumes a different stamp. . . . Now does not reason and experience teach us that if ten thousand pieces of coin were cast into the same mould they would bear the same impress. We have but one apostolic mould in the world, and all the sons of man cannot construct a mould of doctrine like it. A human conscience cast into the mould of the Episcopalian, Presbyterial, Methodistic, Baptist, and Apostolic coin, not only wear a different date, but a different image and superscription. . . . Not only is the *Anno Domini* different, but the image or head is different on each. . . . They are not one, and therefore cannot pass current in another country. Let them, however, be tried with fire, and melted down, and all cast into the apostolic mould, and they will come out with a new image and superscription, and pass current through all the empire of that head which is stamped upon them (*Christian Baptist,* August 7, 1826).

Testimony of Results

Did the program of unity by restoration work? From the field came letters to the editor at Bethany, Virginia. These he printed under the caption "Progress of Reform." Many were testimonies from various parts of the frontier concerning local unity found on apostolic ground. For example, in a letter from Petete John River, Crawford County, in the

Arkansas Territory, dated June 11, 1834, Thomas Wood, a Christian minister, and Benjamin Clark, a Baptist preacher, extol the happy harmony that resulted from the following agreement:

> *First* — Not to investigate anything merely speculative in public; but preach the word as it would stand on a fair translation, as needing no explanation.
>
> *Second* — That we use no words or phrases in which all Christians could not heartily agree; but as much as possible to use New Testament language in singing, praying, preaching, and all our administration (*Millennial Harbinger*, August, 1834).

The note claims that in a few weeks this prescription produced a whole congregation speaking "in all parts of worship as though they had been raised in one school."

Chapter Three

CAMPBELL AS AN EDITOR

A reformer who believes that the desired reformation will come only by a restoration of "pure speech," consistently can edit hymns (sermons in song), religious magazines (sermons in prose), and even a translation of the Bible itself. While the hymnbook is the theme of this series, the other works must be mentioned, for they are parts of one editorial ministry.

The New Version

Alexander Campbell produced a modern-speech version of the New Testament which in the view of P. M. Simms (*The Bible in America;* New York: Wilson-Erickson, 1936, p. 249) was "unquestionably the best New Testament in use at that time." *The Sacred Writings of the Apostles and Evangelists of Jesus Christ, Commonly Styled the New Testament* is still sold today under the title *The Living Oracles.*

In this edition Campbell had revised the earlier translations of three men. In 1778, in Edinburgh, George Campbell had published the four Gospels. In London, Philip Doddridge's New Testament (1765) and James MacKnight's Epistles (1795) had come from the press. Alexander Campbell, wishing to expunge the terms in the Authorized Version "which had taken on a distinctive theological cast," presented in revision the Gospels by George Campbell, the Epistles by MacKnight and the Acts and Revelation by Doddridge. These he gave to the world in 1826, two years before his first hymnbook.

The emendations, and their intention, were given in the prefaces and appendix by Campbell. *Angel* became "messenger"; *repent*—"reform"; *Christ*—"Messiah"; *grace*—

205

"favor"; *church*—"congregation." *Holy Ghost* was never used to apply to the Spirit; *immerse* always stood in the place of baptism, and *basileia theou* was sometimes "reign of God" and in other instances "kingdom of God."

The Periodicals

In Alexander Campbell's mind, July 4 held a highly significant place as it called to mind two providential revolutions—one political, one religious. According to *Millennial Harbinger* reports, that day called for Christian gatherings of festivity, song, and exhortation. Not without significance, then, is the fact that the apology for initiating the new venture of a monthly periodical dedicated to this revolution or reformation in Christendom was written and dated "Buffaloe, July 4, 1823."

The first issue of the *Christian Baptist*, a monthly periodical for the defense of primitive, apostolic Christianity, came from the press at his home in Bethany bearing the date August, 1823. At this period of his life the editor-preacher was in fellowship with Baptist churches in his area. Thomas Grafton labeled Campbell "a veritable John the Baptist in religious journalism," stating that the magazine's "continuous message was a call to repentance to erring ecclesiastics." Awareness of a mellowing change in attitude or approach in his later years of writing was noted by Campbell himself. Irritated by the hymnbook of S. W. Leonard, the *Christian Psalmist*, and its "speculations and lubrications on theology, morality, and psalmody," he wrote:

> The spirit of the *Christian Baptist* has been groaning within me, for some months past. It cannot be suppressed much longer, unless there appear a spirit of reformation (*Millennial Harbinger*, April, 1849, p. 228).

206

When the relationship with the Baptist churches ended in 1830, the publication changed its name to *Millennial Harbinger*. The tenor of the paper also became slightly different, tending more toward restoration than reformation. The religious parties had been unexpectedly indifferent to the reformers, leaving the advocates to reform with little alternative but to draw around their principles "Christians from the churches, as well as sinners from the world." The *Millennial Harbinger* served the emerging communion with its only real guidance, until, four years after Campbell's death in 1866, it also announced in October its own chosen demise for the close of the year 1870.

The same presses that gave us the seven volumes of the *Christian Baptist* and the forty years of the *Millennial Harbinger,* presented to the world six volumes of its owner's published debates and doctrinal works such as the *Christian System* of 1835 and *Christian Baptism—Its Antecedents and Consequents* of 1852.

The Hymnal

The editor's logic was that if what is preached from the pulpit should be the unadulterated, ancient gospel; then, what is sung from the pew when Christians speak "to one another in psalms and hymns and spiritual songs," should be true to the same standard.

Religious poetry and music impress the memory and sway the heart as prose never can. Aware of this force, Campbell was driven to harness it for service in the coming reformation. Magazines could be read and then set aside. Not so easily could the hymns be forgotten. Hymnbooks were in fact often attached to the sacred Word by more than the

207

bookbinder's skill. The words of song ran through the mind at time of devotion, places of inspiration, experiences of sorrow, and moments of meditation.

Existing hymnbooks had been "contaminated," as had every part of Christian worship, by "sectarianism and speculative philosophy." Campbell wrote:

> Some are on improper subjects—such as odes in praise of principles, abstract views, and favorite words ("Christian Psalmody—No. 111," *Millennial Harbinger*, July 1844, p. 290).
>
> Our Christian psalters are in general a collection of everything preached in the range of the systems of the people who adopt them. In other words, they are our creeds in metre, while it appears in the prose form in our confessions.
>
> This, we presume to say, is founded upon an idea that we are to praise God by singing our *opinions* and our *controversies, as well as the works, and wonders, and excellencies* of the Lord our God (*Psalms, Hymns, and Spiritual Songs,* 1853 ed., Introduction, p. 9).
>
> The world is full of hymn-books, psalm-books, sacred melodies, psalters, &c. &c., but where is the volume free from servile imitation of the corrupt speech of a captivated Christianity, or pure from speculative theory of a sectarian profession! ("Christian Psalmody—No. I," *Millennial Harbinger*, May, 1842, p. 231).

Samples of such comment can be found throughout Campbell's writings from beginning to end. The year before Campbell died, Isaac Errett accused the Protestant secretary of designing to *sing* the peculiarities of his creed into people's hearts "with better success than he found arguing them into their heads" ("Protestant Hymnology," *Millennial Harbinger*, September, 1865, p. 396).

Theology in Tune

A. M. Toplady (1740-1788), sought to put the Church of England in the Calvinist camp and produced a hymnbook advocating the "five points" of Calvinism by such titles as "Original Sin," "Election Unchangeable," "Electing Grace," "Efficacious Grace," "Imputed Righteousness," "Preserving Grace," "Assurance of Faith," *etc.* David Denham arranged his collection of 1837, *The Saint's Melody,* around the "Five Points"; and Edward Mote, the year before, made "spirituality" and "Calvinism" inseparable terms in *A New Selection of Gospel Hymns, containing all the excellencies of our spiritual poets, and many originals. For the use of all spiritual worshipers.*

Campbell was disturbed that a preacher who was teaching his flock that the time and place of their conversion was decreed from all eternity, would then call upon the congregation

> —out of complaisance to the preacher . . .
> (to) *praise* the Lord by singing—
>
> 'Twas fix'd in God's eternal mind
> When his dear sons should mercy find:
> From everlasting he decreed
> When every good should be conveyed.
>
> Determin'd was the manner how
> We should be brought the Lord to know,
> Yea, he decreed the very place
> Where he would call us by his grace.
> ("A Restoration of the Ancient Order of Things—No. XXI," *Christian Baptist, August 6, 1827, p. 396).*

Methodist sermons were also accompanied by Arminian songs. *Wiatt's Impartial Selection of Hymns and Spiritual*

Songs did not sound "impartial" to all who heard its song entitled "Against the Calvinian Doctrine" (Louis F. Benson, *The English Hymn, Its Development and Use in Worship*; London; Hodder and Stoughton, 1915, p. 295). A nineteenth-century partisan cry at many a camp-meeting was:

> The devil, Calvin and Tom Paine
> May hate the Methodists in vain;
> Their doctrines shall be downward hurled . . .
> The Methodists shall take the world.

William Warren Sweet (*Religion in the Development of American Culture* 1765-1840; New York: Scribner, 1952, p. 159) quotes this as typical Methodist hymnody in the opinion of *The Calvinist Magazine* (December, 1829) and he lists many further versions and verses such as the following from Stith Mead's *Hymns and Spiritual Songs* (Number 107):

> I'm bound to march in endless bliss,
> And die a shouting methodis (*sic*) . . .

An article, "Aspects of Methodism from the Inner Temple, No. IV" from the London *Christian Remembrancer* denied that the Wesleyans were "men of one book" except it were "the hymnbook." It then gave seven verses from the *Englishman's Magazine*, every one of which contained the party name. The last two stanzas rang:

> A better church cannot be found,
> Their doctrine is so pure and sound;
> One reason I will give for this—
> The Devil hates the Methodists.

> When that happy day shall come,
> When all the Christians are brought home,
> We'll shout with high enraptur'd bliss
> Amongst the blood wash'd Methodists.

210

Isaac Errett relates through the pages of the *Millennial Harbinger* (September, 1865, p. 404) the hymn sung by a Baptist preacher after a "delightful union meeting . . . in which they first unite to make converts, and then scramble for the spoils." Three stanzas ran:

> I had rather be a Baptist,
>   And have a shining face,
> Than to be a Methodist
>   And always fall from grace.
>
> I had rather be a Baptist
>   And despised every hour,
> Than a Presbyterian
>   And never have the power.
>
> If sprinkling is convenient
>   It has no claim to truth,
> It may be good for babies,
>   But will not do for youth.

Andrew Broadus, a popular Baptist preacher, produced in 1805 *Hymns and Spiritual Songs* in which the preface revealed that the Episcopal Methodist Church in the United States had told their people to buy only hymnbooks signed by their bishops and had enjoined them to sing only hymns imposed by their group.

Pure Speech in Worship

While Alexander Campbell could join the wail of Broadus against unbrotherly conditions, he felt that Baptist hymnody was short itself of Biblical terminology. He subjected the *Psalmist*, an 1843 Baptist collection by Baron Stow and S. F. Smith, to his canons of criticism. That thirteen out of the book's fourteen doxologies should follow "papistical innovations" and Athanasius' "extreme orthodoxy in praising

211

the Trinity, rather than 'him that sitteth on the throne and the Lamb'" as the Bible does, was castigated for going beyond what was written.

It troubled Campbell that twenty-six out of thirty-five hymns under the heading, "the Holy Spirit," were addressed *to* the Spirit. This brought the rebuke of being unscriptural, since, neither Old Testament nor New Testament example could be found where a believer prayed *to* rather than *for* the Spirit. After several examples of what he considered "bad taste," the further specimen was given:

> Come thou eternal Spirit, come
> From heaven, thy glorious dwelling place;
> O make my sinful heart thy home,
> And consecrate it by thy grace.

He concluded:

> To ask the Holy Spirit to leave his glorious dwelling place, and to make "my sinful heart his home," is superlatively incongruous. Rather sing with David, "Lord, create in me a new heart, and renew within me a right spirit." . . . ("Christian Psalmody—No. III"; *Millennial Harbinger*, July, 1844, p. 294).

With the sensed danger of false doctrine being "unconsciously absorbed through the medium of hymnology," Campbell set out to select some songs, and reword others. This he proposed to do by editing according to the norm of "apostollic Christianity" rather than the later norms of creedal orthodoxy. He urged the use of Christ-centered; Scripturally-phrased songs in which all Christendom could join.

Psalms, Hymns, and Spiritual Songs: Adapted to the Christian Religion: Selected by Alexander Campbell, published in Bethany, Brooke County, Virginia, in 1828, sought to be a book of praise for all disciples of Jesus.

212

Chapter Four

CAMPBELL AS HYMNWRITER

The Christian religion has inspired half a million hymns, according to Paul W. Dear, in his thesis, *Christology as Expressed in Protestant Hymns.*

Cotton Mather was not alone in noting that when the kingdom of God was making any new appearance, "a mighty zeal for the singing of psalms has attended and assisted it." The Bohemian Brethren, followers of John Hus (1369-1415), published a hymnbook in 1505 and paved the way for Luther, Calvin, Wesley, and their successors. Congregational singing—and that in the tongue of the people—was a child of the Protestant Reformation.

Luther (1483-1546)

In Roman Catholic practice every essential in worship was performed by the clergy for the communicant. Luther, on the other hand, understood the substance of worship to be Christ's speaking to the Christian in word and sacrament, with each worshiper, in return, talking with Him in prayers and songs.

Like Campbell's hymns, those from Luther's pen were almost unnoticed when compared with the vast output of his other writings. However, unlike Campbell's hymns, some are still known and sung by millions today. Luther created thirty-seven hymns—or rather thirty-six hymns and one poem ("In Praise of Music as the Gift of God")—to Campbell's five. The former was a musician, who played both lute and flute, and sang well from boyhood days; the latter never claimed any accomplishments in music. Both, however, regarded music highly for its creative and inspiring power, and both wanted evangelical content for their

213

songs. Luther wrote to Spalatin: "What I wish is to make German hymns for the people, that the Word of God may dwell in their hearts by means of song also." The words of the hymns of each reveal confident faith, strength, simplicity, reverence, and the optimistic note of joy.

James Moffatt honored Luther by saying, "With the hymns he gave them on their lips, the German people sang themselves into the Reformation." Cardinal Cajetan (1469-1534) cursed him, saying, "By his songs he has conquered us." No such testimonies could ever be given for Campbell's hymns, and fellow-Disciples (myself not included) generally might join with Royal Humbert:

> Fortunate for the hymn singers of posterity, Alexander's folly in attempted verse succumbed to a natural and inevitable death. The permanent contributions of Alexander Campbell to hymnology are not in the field of hymn writing but rather in his work as an editor and as a critical and appreciative student of a "Christian Psalmody" worthy of a place in the hymnal and the sanctuary ("Alexander Campbell Edits a Hymnal," in *The Christian-Evangelist*, Dec. 31, 1936).

Calvin (1509-1564)

At age twenty-one Alexander Campbell had moved from Scotland to America, as he was beginning to move religiously from traditional Presbyterianism to a new world of religious thought. Musically speaking, had he traveled far from John Calvin?

Like Calvin and Zwingli (1484-1531), he opposed organ and other instrumental music in the worship of God. Zwingli went even further, opposing vocal as well as instrumental music in public worship, though he himself played well the horn, clarinet, lute, flute, viol, and harp. Campbell, like Calvin, frowned upon trained choirs which performed for, or gave entertainment to, the flock of God, and, urging the "priesthood of all believers," they called for congregational singing in which all the church participated.

Calvin, the sixteenth-century reformer, divided the whole service of worship into prayer, preaching, and singing. Campbell, the nineteenth-century restorer, gave "conspicuous part" in public assemblies to the apostolic admonition to sing "psalms, hymns, and spiritual songs."

At Strasbourg in 1539 a small book was published, entitled *Aulcuns pseaulmes et cantiques mys en chant*. This work, which marked the beginning of Calvinistic psalmody, contained metrical versions of six psalms sometimes attributed to Calvin. Campbell's *Psalms, Hymns and Spiritual Songs* in later editions (but not originally) presented to the community five songs from his own pen. If another parallel is sought between the two men, it can be said that the *Genevan Psalter*, like the *Strasbourg Psalter*, reached its artistic zenith during the lifetime of its compilers. Campbell's book, which provided words alone, joined its Calvinistic predecessor in a stark contrast to the songs from Luther, which flowered into the famous Lutheran chorale and the music of Johann Sebastian Bach (1685-1750).

Here the Calvin-Campbell comparison ends and contrast begins. In leaving the elaborate ritual of the Latin church for the simpler praise of the primitive church, Calvin preferred Davidic psalmody to Lutheran hymnody for the reason that purely human compositions could never improve upon songs of inspiration. Campbell loved the metrical psalms he had known since childhood. His hymnbook, however, was clearly for a Christian church and not for a

Jewish synagogue. It contained the New Testament gospel rather than the Old Testament psalms in paraphrase.

The song of one was designed to be true to "the Bible alone"; the song of the other was by design centered in "Christ alone."

Calvin did not deny the church's right to make her own hymns, but with Augustine he believed that we have nothing as worthy to sing to God as that which we have received from Him.

Wesley (1703-1791)

The religious reform of John Wesley, that failed to conquer his own Church of England, brought forth a large denomination in which hymn singing was a characteristic note. He had been affected by a new type of fervid song learned from the Moravians, and he had created "a new type of spiritual experience . . . that clothed the whole man with a mental and emotional mood, exalted, affectionate, ecstatic, tinged by mystical suggestion, lit by an aroused imagination" (Louis F. Benson, *The Hymnody of the Christian Church*, p. 78).

Campbell's emotional makeup was different from that of Samuel and Susanna Wesley's famous sons. John and Charles Wesley had composed hundreds of hymns. The whole body of Wesleyan hymns was published in 1872 and filled thirteen volumes—six thousand pages. Charles Wesley, the composer of "Come Thou Almighty King," "Hark! the Herald Angels Sing," and "Christ the Lord Is Risen Today," was head and shoulders above John Wesley in hymn production, and John stood tall above Campbell. But the reformers are more alike in their sensed need for hymnal production.

John Wesley's first hymnbook was called *Collection of Psalms and Hymns.* This was published in Charleston, South Carolina, in 1737. While in England the next year, he produced, anonymously as before, a second volume. This is in contrast to all Campbell's volumes, which bear his name on the flyleaf.

Along with their collection of songs, both the eighteenth and nineteenth-century reformers thought it expedient to attach instructions for worshipers. Campbell's first hymnbook was prefaced with an article on singing and concluded with one on prayer; "Wesley attached his "Directions for Singing" to his book, so that it would be "more acceptable to God" and "more profitable to singer and hearer." The seven rules for Methodists at song are:

> Learn these tunes before any others; sing them exactly as printed; sing all of them; sing lustily; sing modestly; sing in time; above all sing spiritually, with an eye to God in every word (Quoted by Louise F. Benson, *The English Hymn*, p. 241).

Campbell's monthlies and Wesley's *Journals* show continuing interest in the improvement of psalmody amongst their followers. What marked "improvement," however, was not the same in each mind. Christ and His acts are Campbell's major theme. The Christian's experience was Wesley's. Campbell arranged the songs topically and used the major headings of (1) Psalms, (2) Hymns, and (3) Spiritual Songs. Wesley divided his work into the three sections of (1) Psalms and Hymns for Sunday (i.e. general worship), (2) Songs for Wednesday and Friday (i.e. songs on confession and humiliation), and (3) Hymns for Saturday (i.e. praising God).

No historian has said or could say of early Disciples, as of early Methodists:

> . . . With their hymns and their singing (they) burst like heralds of new life. Crowds were drawn to their services simply by the irresistible charm of the music (H. C. Macdougall, *Early New England Psalmody;* Brattleboro: Stephen Daye Press, 1940).

Yet we have already taken note of Alexander Campbell's importance as a reformer, through hymn editing; and we are now to view the significance of his own hymns as a reflection of his faith.

Alexander Campbell's Hymns

Selina Huntington Campbell, in the *Home Life of Alexander Campbell,* informs us that her husband was the source of "several hymns" in this hymnbook. She names them by first lines in this order:

> "On Tabor's Top the Saviour Stood"; "'Tis Darkness Here, But Jesus Smiles"; "Upon the Banks of Jordan Stood"; "Come, Let Us Sing the Coming Fate"; "Jesus Has Gone Above the Skies" (*Home Life of Alexander Campbell;* St. Louis: John Burns, 1882, p. 335).

Whether there is any significance in this sequence or not, it is notable that all but the last appear for the first time in the 1834 edition. "Jesus Is Gone Above the Skies" is added in the edition of 1843, possibly suggesting that it was written last; and, also, possibly implying that Mrs. Campbell's list is an attempt at chronology.

"Come, Let Us Sing"

At Cincinnati, in the year 1836, the Roman Catholic Church had allowed its Bishop (later Archbishop) John

Baptist Purcell (1800-1883) to meet a Protestant in a public discussion of its religious convictions. The opponent, representing all Protestantism, had been the champion of all Christianity in the debate of 1829 with Robert Owen (1771-1858) at the same city in Ohio. The Protestant was Alexander Campbell.

Campbell challenged Rome's claim to be the one, holy, apostolic, catholic church, and affirmed that it was neither one, nor holy, nor apostolic, nor catholic in the true meaning of the words. He had always pled for the separation of church and state. He feared the loss of cherished freedom, if this church's hierarchy achieved its supposed goals for America. Like many interpreters of Bible "prophecy," such as William Miller (1782-1849), Campbell identified the church of Rome with the harlot and the beast spoken of in the Apocalypse. To the "fall" of this spiritual system Campbell looked when he wrote:

> Come, let us sing the coming fate
> Of mystic Babylon the Great—
>   Her doom is drawing near:
> Jesus now comes on earth to reign,
> His cause and people to maintain—
>   For them he'll soon appear.
>
> Before him flows a fiery stream,
> The heav'ns above with lightnings gleam,
>   A thousand thunders roar:
> A heav'nly host with him descends,
> His voice to all the earth extends,
>   His saints now grieve no more.
>
> Eclips'd by glory so divine,
> Sun, moon, and stars refuse to shine,
>   The spheres now cease to roll:

219

Earth, wrapt in darkness deep as night,
With horror stricken at the sight
　　Now quakes from pole to pole.

Angels of light, at his command,
Ten thousand times ten thousand, stand
　　Waiting his voice to hear:
The fiery cherubs spread their wings,
The heav'n with loud hosannas ring,
　　While all his saints draw near.

The day of recompense has come,
His people all are gath'ring home,
　　With joy they hear his voice:
The promis'd curse, the threaten'd woes
Combin'd now fall upon his foes,
　　The martyrs all rejoice.

She who the Twelve Apostles griev'd,
And by her sorceries deceiv'd
　　All nations of the world,
Now looks with anguish at their bliss,
Then sinks into the vast abyss,
　　To endless ruin hurl'd.

The living saint, and all the dead,
Now gather round their glorious head,
　　And reign with him below,
And endless age of perfect peace,
Of love, and joy, and righteousness,
　　Exempt from ev'ry woe.

Then let us keep the end in view,
And ever on our way pursue,
　　The crown is yet before:
A few short days the conflict's done,
The battle's fought, the prize is won,
　　And we shall toil no more
(*Psalms, Hymns, and Spiritual Songs*,
pp. 482, 483 in 1853 edition).

The song appeared in 1834 admidst the third division of Campbell's hymnal as a "Spiritual Song." Its cadence was marked as 8's and 6's and a suggested tune was "Harmony." It continued with Campbell's other songs until the American Christian Missionary Society replaced its president as editor of the hymnbook in 1865.

Chapter Five

TEACHING THROUGH HYMNS

Four of the five hymns written by Alexander Campbell and included in various editions of his *Psalms, Hymns, and Spiritual Songs* were definitely related to incidents in Scripture, usually in connection with Christ. Thus they supported his insistence that Christian hymnody should declare the Christian gospel. The one exception we have already noted in the apocalyptic and polemic view of papal Rome's ultimate destruction: "Come Let Us Sing the Coming Fate." We turn now to the others.

"Jesus Is Gone Above the Skies"

That this Communion hymn should appear in 1843, and not with the other four in earlier editions of Mr. Campbell's hymnbook, would be explained if it could be found to have been written later than the rest. The same explanation would account for its being in Part II of the 1843 hymnal when the others are in Part I. Churches "after the ancient order" would have more need for Communion hymns than would religious bodies that observed the Lord's Supper quarterly or monthly.

The Lord's Supper had always had a focal place in Campbell's mind. His flame for Christian unity had been fanned when Presbyterians of other groups than his own Seceder Presbyterian church had been excluded from the Communion service in Glasgow. His pen and voice often had taught the benefits and wisdom of this feast as a vital part of the normative Christian praise practiced by the primitive and ancient church.

The six stanzas of "Jesus Is Gone Above the Skies" guide the mind to look back through these "kind memorials" to "his own flesh and dying blood"; forward to the hope of "our returning Lord"; inward, to our personal need, since "wand'ring hearts we have"; and upward, in prayerful communion, for "Jesus is gone above the skies." The whole hymn reads:

Jesus is gone above the skies,
　　Where our weak senses reach him not;
And carnal objects court our eyes
　　To thrust our Saviour from our thought.

He knows what wand'ring hearts we have,
　　Apt to forget his lovely face,
And to refresh our minds he gave
　　These kind memorials of his grace.

The Lord of life, his table spread
　　With his own flesh and dying blood;
We on the rich provision feed,
　　We taste the wine and bless our God.

Let sinful sweets be all forgot,
　　And earth grow less in our esteem;
Christ and his life fill ev'ry thought,
　　And faith and hope he fix'd on him.

While he is absent from our sight,
　　'Tis to prepare for us a place;
That we may dwell in heav'nly light,
　　And live for ever near his face.

Our eyes look upward to the hills,
　　Whence our returning Lord shall come;
We wait his chariot's awful wheels
　　To fetch our longing spirits home
(*Psalms, Hymns, and Spiritual Songs*, pp. 228, 229 in 1853 edition).

A book of *Christian Hymns*, compiled in Columbus, Ohio, in 1858, contains this single hymn of Campbell. The work acknowledges the "Hughes' Collection" as source for the hymn and changes the fifth stanza's second line to read "'Tis to prepare our souls a place."

"On Tabor's Top the Saviour Stood"

The first in Mrs. Selina Campbell's list of songs by her husband is a psalm on the transfiguration of Christ. It is to be sung in common meter to such a tune as Pleasant Hill. Its importance lies in reflecting Campbell's exegesis, in addition to reflecting his ability to make a metrical psalm out of a New Testament passage in the way his Scottish ancestors had done with the Old Testament Psalter.

> On Tabor's top the Saviour stood
>   With Peter, James, and John;
> And while he talk'd of Calv'ry there,
>   His face resplendent shone.
>
> While on his suff'rings he convers'd,
>   And spoke of griefs to come,
> His countenance assum'd a light
>   Much brighter than the sun.
>
> In dazzling brightness all array'd
>   Jesus transfigur'd stands,
> From Heav'n descends the man who gave
>   To Israel God's commands.
>
> Elijah, too, of burning zeal
>   Who did that law restore,
> Appear'd with Moses on this mount
>   And talk'd his suff'rings o'er.

Transported with this glorious scene,
    The witnesses exclaim,
'Tis good, Lord, with such guests to dwell:
    Here let us still remain.

Three tents with joyful hands we'll raise,
    And place them side by side,
For these celestials, and for thee,
    And here let us abide.

While thus they spoke, a cloud descends
    And takes them from their sight;
But Jesus yet remains with them,
    The Father's chief delight.

This is my Son, his voice declares,
    Hear him in all he says,
Not Moses nor Elijah now
    Shall guide you in my ways.

With joy this more illustrious guide
    Henceforth we'll glad obey,
Till we behold the glorious light
    Of an eternal day
(pp. 48, 49 in 1853 edition).

Correct hermeneutical principles for correct Biblical understanding required the reader to ask not only who is speaking and to whom he is speaking, but under what dispensation. Campbell knew that to "rightly divide the word of truth," the student must be conscious of the different covenants and the progressive revelation that moved from the starlight of the patriarchal age, through the moonlight of the Mosaic period when God dealt with a nation, to the full sunlight of the Christian dispensation.

This meant that questions like, "What must I do to be saved?" were not to be answered in the law (Moses) or the prophets (Elijah) of the Old Testament, but by the "more illustrious guide" (Christ) whom "henceforth we'll glad obey."

This idea of a Bible that was not all on a level led the Baptist church to purge out the Campbellites in 1830. Campbell had clearly presented this "liberal" view in the "Sermon on the Law," which he delivered at the meeting of the Redstone Association at Cross Creek, Virginia, in 1816.

"'Tis Darkness Here, but Jesus Smiles"

The prison setting of this spiritual song is given in the hymnal as "Paul and Silas in the Philippian Jail."

Singing to an old "Scotch Air" in long meter, disciples relived the story of Acts 16. By affirming the faith of Paul and Silas, they shared their confidence that the cause of right, in which they believed themselves engaged, could not be ultimately defeated. No matter what opposition came, man could "not keep the world in night, For God has said, 'Let there be light.'"

> 'Tis darkness here, but Jesus smiles,
> His presence ev'ry pain beguiles;
> He has the wine that cheers the soul,
> The oil that makes the wounded whole.
>
> While silence reigns as in the tomb,
> And midnight spreads her deepest gloom;
> Come, let our tongues an anthem raise,
> And sing our great Physician's praise.
>
> Though fast our feet within these stocks,
> Our hands secur'd with num'rous locks,
> No iron chains our thoughts can bind,
> There are no fetters for the mind.

226

Though we are bound, the word is free,
The truth cannot imprison'd be;
The word shall visit ev'ry land,
Though kings and people all withstand.

The word of life which Jesus sent,
Jails, chains, and swords cannot prevent;
Man cannot keep the world in night,
For God has said, Let there be light.

To Jesus let our praise ascend,
His care for us shall never end;
He felt our griefs, he bore our pains,
His blood has wash'd us from our stains.

No—'tis our choice to bear his cross;
For him all things we count but loss;
Our joy, for him to suffer shame;
Our honor, still to bear his name.

One smile from him all pain repays,
One word of peace all grief allays;
With him in glory to appear
Will compensate our suff'rings here.

His presence now this prison cheers,
Relieves our pains, dispels our fears;
His presence, then, our heads will crown
With endless glory and renown
(p. 221 in 1844 edition).

"Upon the Banks of Jordan Stood"

Campbell and "Campbellites" were known to stress the book of Acts as a rediscovered record of conversion experiences, the Lord's Supper as of central importance, and baptism as the culminating step in the gospel plan of salvation. Pedobaptist John Walker, of the Secession Presbyterian Church, crossed verbal swords with Campbell at Mount Pleasant, Ohio, in 1820 over this issue.

227

Two years later in Washington, Kentucky, the battle on "Christian Baptism" continued with William McCalla, the champion on infant sprinkling.

An eighteen-day contest centering on "The Action, Subject, Design, and Administration of Christian Baptism" at Lexington, Kentucky, in 1843, showed the steel of Dr. N. L. Rice and the moderating skills of Henry Clay. If one attending the last debate had gone to church with the "Christians only" in Lexington, he might have heard them sing, to the tune of Mount Nebo, Song 149 from that year's edition of *Psalms, Hymns and Spiritual Songs:*

> Upon the banks of Jordan stood
>   The great reformer, John
> And pointed to the Lamb of God,
>   The long-expected one.
>
> He loud proclaim'd the coming reign,
>   And told them to reform,
> If they God's favor would obtain,
>   And shun the gath'ring storm.
>
> He bade all those who did repent,
>   Forthwith to be immers'd,
> Assuring them that God had sent
>   The message he rehears'd.
>
> Forsake your sins, the Baptist said,
>   That you may be forgiv'n;
> Forsake them now, and be immers'd,
>   For near's the Reign of heav'n.
>
> Thus did the man of God prepare
>   A people for the Lord;
> To him did all the Jews repair,
>   Who trusted in his word.

But now the reign of God has come,
  That reign of grace below,
And Jesus reigns upon God's throne,
  Remission to bestow.

He bids all nations look to him,
  As Prince of Life and Peace;
And offers pardon to all them
  Who now accept his grace.

If the time of this song had not been the common meter (C.M.) of 8,6,8,6, excluding a word of three syllables at that point, John would not have been a "baptist" in the fourth stanza, but rather the "immerser," as he is in the *Living Oracles*. He is the "great reformer" in verse one and in Reformer Campbell's thoughts. The anglicized Greek term *baptized* is in the two instances translated "immers'd"; and, as if echoing the favorite text of Acts 2:38, we hear "reform" or "repent" and "be immers'd." The obedience of the hearer is expected because of divine authority: "God had sent the message."

Preachers who read the *Millennial Harbinger* and the *Christian System* learned to talk of the kingdom of God as the "reign of heav'n." They could find with ease those Gospel passages that promised the kingdom even before the passing of all Jesus' contemporaries (Mark 9:1). In their understanding no Davidic kingdom was to be established at the second coming of Christ, for since that Pentecost when the church was established "Jesus reigns upon God's throne" as David's successor. "Thy kingdom come" was believed to be a prayer that had been answered.

The Hymns Disappear

Locke Miller has written a thirty-one page manuscript titled, "The Hymns of Alexander Campbell," in which he fails in his attempt to prove that many of the hymns without author-accreditization in the 1865 printing of *The Christian Hymn Book* were written by Mr. Campbell. That edition rather was the first to *drop* Campbell's known hymns, much to the disappointment of Mrs. Campbell as sensed in her words:

> The hymns he wrote are contained in the edition published previous to his donating his interest in the Hymnbook to the "American Christian Missionary Society" (*Home Life of Alexander Campbell,* pp. 335, 336).

Campbell, himself, had noted early in life "the law of human action" regarding the selecting of a few favorite songs and neglecting the many.

> Amidst all the varieties of animal sustenance, and the almost incalculable aliments provided for our common wants, but a few of them are universally or even generally acceptable. . . . Man can live on many things on which he desires not to live; and even of the desirables but a few are of high relish and esteem. So is it of authors and their works. Few are universally pleasing; few are even generally acceptable ("Christian Psalmody—No. II," *Millennial Harbinger,* June, 1842, p. 277).

He would have been more concerned that his ideas live than his hymns—that the Messiah be praised, than that his words be used in that praise.

Chapter Six

PRIVATE FAMILY, CONGREGATIONAL WORSHIP

The first interest in hymnody on Campbell's part was not as an editor nor as a writer of songs, but as a worshiper. The hymns of Zion were a part of his life—a life consisting of prayer and praise in the secret closet, in the family circle, and in the social hall.

Like covers to the hymnbook were Campbell's introduction on psalmody and his concluding essay on prayer. Each day of praise was enclosed in morning and evening prayer. He believed that the regenerated man was not

> . . . pious by fits and starts . . . religious or devout on one day of the week, or for one hour of the day. It is the whole bent of his soul—it is the beginning, middle, and end of every day ("Regeneration," *Millennial Harbinger,* August 5, 1833, p. 367).

He expected his hymnbook to be used in private, family, and congregational worship.

Private Worship

Regarding private prayer, we ask if he practiced what he preached. He taught:

> There is no school under the heavens in which the *art of prayer* can be so easily acquired—in which the spirit of prayer can be so fully possessed, and in which the language of prayer can be so fully and perfectly attained—as in the closet, in the fields, or forests, where no human ear can hear, and where no human eye can see us. Besides, no prayers have so much influence upon ourselves as those which are offered up in secret to God ("On Prayer," *Millennial Harbinger,* November, 1831, p. 198).

In his "Sermons on Christian Practice" he calls for a Bible reading where "the soul pants for this reading as a thirsty roe pants for the brooks of water" (*Millennial Harbinger*, August, 1839, p. 343).

We hear his sermons; and, whether they are addressed to student bodies or societies in assembly, it is his custom to intersperse his remarks and to conclude them with the words of some appropriate hymn.

We read his articles; again, the hymnbook proves to be the source of that clinching verse which climaxes an argument and imbeds a truth in the memory. Just before the signature *A. C.,* or the word *Editor,* or some pen name like *Christianos* or *Daniel,* you characteristically will see one stanza from a throbbing hymn.

Especially in the time of a death the words of song memorized in private made themselves public. Campbell received for the obituary column of his periodical many notices of departed loved ones in the church. A goodly number of these contained stanzas of comfort, and others told how the deceased had expired while with his last breath he spoke the victorious words of a song. When death struck his own family, the natural expression of Campbell's thoughts found poetry more fitting than prose. As the *Millennial Harbinger* of March, 1866, reported the "Death of Alexander Campbell," W. K. Pendleton, the new editor of the journal, described his father-in-law's last hours:

> A few days before his death, upon some allusion to the creation, he quoted the first verse of the first chapter of Genesis in Hebrew, and then, the first verse of the first chapter of John in the Greek.
>
> The sublime words of the Psalms were constantly in his mind—and he quoted with remarkable accuracy and propriety from the old metrical version of the Scotch Psalmody, which he memorized in his youth, such as spoke the comfort he needed or the praise he felt.

232

Times of disappointment, sickness, or danger; and seasons of evangelism, thanksgiving, and moments of private correspondence were further occasions to draw from the hymnbook. Brethren providing this journal with news of victories in the field, echoed with songs of conquest.

If Campbell often raised his voice to sing from his hymnal, "My God, My Heart With Love Inflame," the prayer was not unheard:

> My God, my heart with love inflame,
> That I may in thy holy name
> Aloud in songs of praise rejoice,
> While I have breath to raise my voice.
>
> No more let my ungrateful heart
> One moment from thy praise depart;
> But live and sing, in sweet accord,
> The glories of my so'reign Lord
> (*Psalms, Hymns, and Spiritual Songs,*
> pp. 213, 214 in 1844 edition).

Family Worship

Conversion marked "a real change" in family life as well as private affairs, wrote the *Harbinger's* editor in 1840. A man of God dresses differently; his children act differently and study a different kind of music; his house ceases to be a place of gossip and noisy merriment to become "a Bethel —a house where prayer was wont to be made and hymns to be sung."

In harmony with exhortations that from patriarchal days "the service of the altar belonged first to the father of the family," Campbell took his rightful place in the home at Bethany. Fourteen children were born to him. To those who lived, he was "father" both in the physical and spiritual sense.

Robert Richardson (*Memoirs of Alexander Campbell*, p. 300) speaks of evenings being given over to the social and religious improvement of children and domestic servants alike. Describing the gatherings in the large parlor of the Campbell mansion, he tells of each individual's participation with recitations of hymns and Scriptures; and records that the head of the house commented on these and asked questions. Then the mother, "who had a good voice," led out in singing. The time of worship was concluded as, on their knees, the family was led "before the throne" by father Campbell. Details were varied and the period consciously kept from becoming "mere routine."

Those who lived at Bethany, claimed him to be "the most persistent man in the religious instruction of his family" that they ever knew. They speak of Scriptures and hymns as "regular as morning and evening" at his home.

It was as natural as breathing for the Campbell family to "speak to one another in psalms, hymns, and spiritual songs." When writing to his sister Alicia in her last illness, or to his daughter Clarinda from his travels in Europe, Alexander might quote a hymn in passing! Similarly his wife would write some member of the family and refer to hymns sung and prayer made.

In various series, running in the monthly, Campbell would teach by creating the scene of a family circle. Within such a setting he would allow the different members of the family involved to raise questions for the father to discuss. In the descriptions of life at the "Carlton House," at "Mr. Fowler's," or "Mr. Reed's," we see a typical Christian home by Campbellian definition (*Millennial Harbinger,* January, 1841; May, 1849; February, 1851; February, 1834; July, 1834).

Congregational Worship

To Campbell the Christian, each home was a church (building); and each church (congregation) was a part of God's family; and each worship gathering was a foretaste of heaven, where all the redeemed joined in praise to Him who sat on the throne, and to the Lamb. The music of earth was to be patterned after the singing in heaven.

Campbell worshiped in many places and with many groups during his travels in America and abroad. What in corporate worship appealed to him, and what was repulsive to him? This is a key question, since Campbell's hymnal and his hymns were meant to assist reform at this point.

When meeting with "the sons of Abraham according to the flesh" in Baltimore, Campbell was undecided whether the style of praying, chanting, and reading he had observed in this synagogue was "designed as a satire upon the Jewish worship, or an expression of respect" (*Millennial Harbinger*, January 1834, p. 16).

Open-air protracted meetings, where emotionalism got the upper hand, disturbed him above all. His paper received and published a critical analysis of Methodist and Baptist gatherings, decrying the shouts of "Glory! Glory!" accompanied by jumping and clapping and "altar" calls. This rebuke received Campbell's "Amen!" By contrast, the proper attitude for a solemn assembly should be that of "serious cheerfulness, equidistant from the morose austerity of Pharisaic sanctity and the thoughtless gaity of Sadducean levity."

One Lord's Day in Buffalo, New York, he worshiped with Baptists in the morning, with Universalists (he thought the meeting house belonged to Presbyterians) in the afternoon, and with Episcopalians at night. As to the preferred worship service, the Episcopalians readily got his vote:

They have a very neat and tasteful church, after the fashion of the olden times. The congregation was much more respectable in number and in appearance, and certainly much more reverential and devout in their worship than either of the other two. There seemed to me much more marrow and fitness in the bones of the English liturgy and various services, than in the sermon, songs, and prayers of the Baptist or Universalian worship. There are, indeed, too many forms, too many repetitions, and too indiscriminate readings and collations of sacred scripture in the whole service; yet, with all these subtractions, it has more of the substance, and form, and spirit of ancient worship, than any of the popular forms of Congregationalism, Presbyterianism, Methodism, or Baptistism ever seen by me (*Millennial Harbinger,* September, 1846, pp. 540, 541).

At this point Mr. Campbell told of literature left in the pews at the other churches which was diverting to devotion. He commended, rather, the exclusive presence of the Bible and the hymnbook for the worshiper.

Opinions and Decorum

It seemed to him only good etiquette to refrain from chewing or smoking tobacco in the house of worship. Holding the high view that he did of prayer, he felt that the time of worship was not the time to

. . . turn round, shake hands with a brother or neighbor, and speak to him of his health or worldly condition and then resume their worship of the Lord as a matter that may be interrupted at pleasure, or in courtesy to a friend or brother (*Millennial Harbinger,* April, 1836, p. 180).

His opinion was that prayer appropriately was offered while standing, or, preferably, when kneeling. The King of kings was worthy of more respect than an emperor; and Biblical precedent would discourage "sitting in prayer." He reminded his readers: "There are no sofas in the heavens for the aristocracies of the skies."

> To see a congregation of professed believers sitting in the act of prayer, gazing around them as in a theatre, or in a popular assembly, convened on some ordinary occasion, exhibiting a wandering eye and a vacant mind, is a heart-chilling, and a soul-paralyzing spectacle (*Millennial Harbinger*, January, 1858, pp. 37-39).

The opening verse of one of the hymns in his book was consistent with Campbell's view that the congregation should stand to sing hymns of thanksgiving.

> Stand up and bless the lord,
>   Ye people of his choice:
> Stand up, and bless the Lord your God,
>   With heart, and soul, and voice
> (p. 18 in 1844 edition).

Alexander Campbell took care to separate his opinions and preferences from God's revealed design. He taught that while there were divinely instituted acts of Christian worship, there were no divinely prescribed forms for their observance. (For example, the Lord's Supper was ordained, but no ordinance directed whether we stand, sit, kneel or recline in its observance.) Yet, some procedures commended themselves above others by their orderliness. Some practices, though proper at other times or places, would be in church as out of place "as snow in summer, or a plaudit in the midst of a prayer."

He pictured for his readers what he considered a model service; and he received from them reports of how worship

237

was being practiced among the reformers. While these folk gathered on the first day of the week for corporate worship, they also came together for baptisms, love feasts, ordinations, and even contests with skeptics.

At any and all assemblies where Christians were present, these would find occasion for song. But, always it was the Christian, and not the worldling, who had been given the privilege of prayer and praise. "We cannot pray *with* an unbeliever," he wrote in January, 1859, *Millennial Harbinger,* "though we may pray *for* him, nor [can we] sing hymns with him, unless he sings with us." For Masons or other fraternities to ape Christian prayer and hymns Mr. Campbell judged to be desecration of the name and worship of the heavenly Father.

Since Christians enjoyed so signal a privilege, however, they dared not let it fall into neglect:

> And will man alone be dumb,
> Till that glorious kingdom come?
> No; the church delights to raise
> Psalms, and hymns, and songs of
> praise (p. 236 in 1844 edition, *Psalms,
> Hymns, and Spiritual Songs*).

Chapter Seven

CHOIRS AND SINGING SCHOOLS

In an article dealing with Alexander Campbell's concept of worship, attention must be given to his views regarding choirs, instruments, musical scores, etc. This is true because his reasons relate, not to opinions regarding music, but to convictions regarding the genius of Christianity. It is not enough to know what he proposed and what he rejected. It is necessary, if we are to understand him, to know his reasons.

Opposed Choirs

Mr. Campbell opposed choirs for the church of Christ. He sought to preserve a positive value by this negative decision. He had an historic consciousness and was fully aware of dark ages in Christian history when the singing congregation and the priesthood of believers went together into oblivion. The gains of the Protestant Reformation were not to be lost again. The Council of Laodicea (between A.D. 343 and 381) in its thirteenth canon had decreed: "Besides the appointed singers who mount the ambo and sing from the book, others shall not sing in the church." For centuries only the voices of clergy, choirs, and monastic bodies broke the silence left by a songless laity. Then came the recovery of the doctrine of a believer's priesthood, when Lutheran hymnody and Calvinian psalmody restored, from the choirs to the congregations, the service of praise.

History, in Campbell's thinking, was repeating itself— this time in America. Between 1760 and 1780 choirs were first established in America. Congregations started listening. Louis F. Benson aptly says:

> Seated between a pulpit asserting its supremacy in everything but song and a choir loft monopolizing the song, the

239

people were no longer a band of common worshipers but merely an audience attending a performance of worship (*The Hymnody of the Christian Church:* Richmond, Virginia; John Knox Press, 1956, pp. 259, 260).

The reformation on American soil would commend to the churches music books like A. S. Hayden's *The Christian Melodian;* because, as Campbell said, the selection was

. . . not got up after the Bostonian style—for singing choirs and instrumental devotions—but for *worshipping assemblies, not by proxy,* but *in person* (*Millennial Harbinger*, May, 1849, p. 300).

In articles on "Christian Psalmody," Campbell raised the question of "importance . . . *who shall sing?*" and, then answered with the firmness of Elijah:

Shall a choir only with organs, or the whole congregation sing, are questions in doubt with some.—For my part, I vote that *every* Christian man, woman, and child—every professor that has one note of praise in his heart, one chord of music in his soul, should open his mouth and make a joyful noise unto the Rock of our Salvation. Why should I with David say, "Sun, moon, and stars—mountains, hills, and forests—seas, rivers and all fountains of water—birds, beasts, and every living thing, praise the Lord"—and yet be silent, or countenance any one in being silent while the noblest and most transporting exercise of devotion is going on? No! "Let my tongue cleave to the roof of my mouth, and my right hand forget its cunning," sooner than I acquire the habit of singing dumb while my brethren are in full chorus of praise to Him whom angels worship on their golden lyres (*Millennial Harbinger*, July, 1844, p. 289).

The possible spiritual danger in having a choir was simply the danger of religion by proxy with its consequent sickness unto death. Campbell warned:

Fill your churches, brethren, with organs—with singing choirs—and your pews with "Christian hymns and appropriate music," and you will become as cold and as fashionable as Bostonians and New Englanders, and may sing *farewell* to revivals, and Christian warmth, and Christian ardor, and everything that looks like living, zealous, active, and soul-redeeming Christianity. . . . We shall, I fear, need velvet cushions, or praying stools for our knees, and a few downy pillows for our pews, that we may take a comfortable nap during "divine service" at the chapel (*Millennial Harbinger*, December, 1848, p. 711).

There was a quantitative difference in his thinking between artistic accomplishment by a "performer" and acceptable worship by a humble disciple. Congregations sat, looked, and listened to choirs, while they themselves were "silent as the dead." Worship had degenerated into entertainment. Becoming an audience, as at a theatrical, the worshipers let substitutes take the place rightfully their own.

The choir itself could be tempted to pride with special seats apart from the rest. From the singing schools had come the village church choir, and with their special training came remuneration, first for the choir leader and then for the quartet around which amateurs assembled. Professionalism, pride, vanity, and worldly ambition drove some to seek excellence in carrying out their assignments in order to please man's ear with little concern for the ear of God.

John Calvin had allowed a choir to sing in four-part harmony, but the congregation was to sing only in unison, for the similar reason that simple worshipers could be drawn so easily from the glorification of God to the admiration of human skills.

241

In the essay that concludes the first two editions of his *Psalms, Hymns, and Spiritual Songs,* Mr. Campbell discussed public prayer. Part of what he said applies to singing as well as to prayer.

> These remarks are not offered with any desire, or with the least intention, to promote or cherish a spirit of criticism on the performance of others; but to put every one on his guard against temptations to a departure from all that is valuable in prayer—from all that is sacred in devotion—and from all that is pleasing to Him whose approbation is more to be desired than the smiles of all the universe besides (p. 177 in 1829 edition).

Opposed Musical Notes

Today it appears that certain hymn texts are so wedded to certain tunes that they cannot be put asunder. It is difficult to imagine an earlier time when these words and melodies were not joined together. In some communities tune and text often went with different partners. There was that time when hymnbooks contained only words and not music. A number of songs were sung to the same tune, and various congregations readily joined the same hymns from the same hymnal in different music.

When in 1824, Ashael Nettleton prepared a supplement to the Psalm-Hymns of Isaac Watts, he brought an innovation in church music by naming at the head of each hymn one or more tunes to which the words could be sung. As another "first" he issued with these *Village Hymns* a companion book of recommended tunes (*Zion's Harp*). This was not yet the modern hymnal with tune and words printed together; but it was the start in that direction. Not until

242

Henry Ward Beecher's *Plymouth Collection* in 1855 did America have a hymnbook with each hymn and tune printed together on the same page. In 1824 the congregation had books with words only, while the choir member was supplied a book for each hand, causing heads to bob "like shuttle-cocks" between the oblong tune-book and the hymnbook.

As a matter of course the first edition of Campbell's *Psalms, Hymns, and Spiritual Songs* in 1828 contains no musical notes; but as a matter of conviction no hymnal that bore his name was allowed to have them. He wrote:

> I would prefer to have an organ, or a fashionable choir as a means of my worship than the words of a hymn set to the notes of a tune on which to fix my eyes while engaged in the worship of God (*Millennial Harbinger*, March, 1847, p. 179).

The mind of the worshiper must not be diverted from spiritual things to the science of music itself. Worshiping is one thing; reading music at the same time is another. Calvin had opposed part-singing for the congregation; and, Anabaptists disliked any congregational singing in parts or reading the words while singing.

After Campbell's death, the editors of his periodical advertised music books, but always with qualifying comments. A. D. Fillmore of Cincinnati had readied *Harp of Zion,* a book of church music with a variety of tunes "adapted to all 1324 hymns of the new Hymn Book," and *Christian Psaltery* in which nearly 200 various meters "will be adapted to the new Hymn Book."

After highly complimentary words for Fillmore's music found in the *Harp of Zion,* the *Harbinger's* editors said:

> It has the special merit of arranging the hymns of our Hymn Book under tunes that in Bro. Fillmore's judgment,

are suited to their sentiments. We do not mean that he has printed Hymns of the Hymn Book, in his music book, but that he has taken the numbers of the Hymns and arranged them in an order with the tunes to which they should or may be tastefully sung, so that any one can readily use the two together. This is a great advantage. . . . We have the best Hymn Book in the world; let us also have the best music Book—and, what will be the crowning best—the best singing, we trust will soon follow (*Millennial Harbinger*, March, 1867, pp. 154, 155).

Opposed Singing Schools

The tune-book, the organ, the choir, and the singing school were all interrelated efforts at improving church music. Each innovation met with strong opposition. The "singing school" was an institution of early New England. Meeting in the school house or the village tavern to avoid profaning the church, the singing school had felt free to introduce pitch pipes to set the key and bass viols to support the singers. Getting used to instrumental accompaniment, and now desiring more complex and varied tunes, pupils from the new school had brought change into the worship habits and practices of each community.

In the fourth decade of the nineteenth century Silas W. Leonard of Jeffersonville, Indiana, strove to organize singing schools amongst that religious community which had been influenced by Alexander Campbell. For his classes he sought a hymnbook with appropriate music on alternate pages. He proposed that Campbell's hymnbook be the base. Strong objection came from Bethany.

It was considered bad taste, and the thoughtless desecration of Christian psalmody, to convert a hymnbook of the

244

church "into a sort of Guido Aretine *hexachord*," for the singing school. The *Millennial Harbinger* through various writers and editors reflected Campbell's basic objection. They wrote that in such schools

> . . . saints and sinners by profession, united in profaning the divine names, titles and attributes, by substituting them, occasionally, for sol, fa, la, mi (*Millennial Harbinger*, August, 1850, p. 455).

Since God will not hold guiltless those who take His name in vain; how guilty, it was thought, would be students in the singing school.

Campbell argued that:

> The name of God and the name of the Lord Messiah, should never appear in any mere musicbook, to be used for music lessons (*Millennial Harbinger*, February, 1854, p. 114).

Before Leonard sought to promote the singing school amongst Disciples, Campbell had already spoken negatively on the matter. The earliest edition of his hymnbook contained that negation in its preface and was quoted against such schools in columns of the *Christian Baptist*. The schools were said to include "many who neither fear God nor regard man," who in boisterous and mechanical ways were singing.

> . . . in the midst of jests and laughs, in the midst of every species of frivolity, the death of Christ, the day of judgment, or the glories of redemption (*Christian Baptist*, February 5, 1828, p. 165).

The "profanity" could be avoided, if schools to learn music were kept unmixed from gatherings to utter praise. Campbell had said:

> I cannot, as a Christian, approve of teaching anyone to practice for improvement upon the sacred songs which are

only to be sung in the worship of God. I have always re-monstrated against this custom as a species of profanity (*Millennial Harbinger*, March, 1847, p. 179).

Good moral poetry could displace religious words. Campbell asked:

> Are the poets of the English language so few, or so barren, as not to furnish suitable moral verses—I mean verses of good moral sentiment, adapted to our tunes, without obligating us to invade the temple of God, and sacreligiously to steal from the Christian's altar the praise of Jehovah, to adapt them to the notes of some tune-teaching syllabus, to be reverently pronounced by every gamut-earning pupil!!! (*Psalms, Hymns, and Spiritual Songs*, 1829 edition, p. 18.)

The unconverted, it was said, cannot sing meaningfully and innocently Christian praise. The disciple of Christ, while concentrating on notes and techniques of musical execution, cannot avoid speaking God's name lightly. Men of all spiritual states cannot but profane divine worship when the praises of God are set to the music of "a love song, an amorous ditty, or a bacchanalian lilt."

A worldly tune was not appropriate for an other-worldly text. Church and world were two realms to remain separate.

The art of music and the singing school had a place in a Christian's life; but no confusion was to exist between worship and all other activities.

> Christians should not go to church to learn to sing, nor to learn to spell or read—Let them have good music books and good teachers, and good schools, but let them not desecrate religious worship, or profane the Lord's house by converting it into a school room, instead of a house of prayer and praise (*Millennial Harbinger*, March, 1847, p. 179).

Chapter Eight

INSTRUMENTAL MUSIC

There was to Mr. Campbell a time and place for every good thing, including the use of instruments of music; but a worship hour was not the time, and a "house of God" was not the place. He drew clear distinction between the disapproved instrumental music in the worship of God and its accepted place in social enjoyment. It would be an error to class Bethany's sage with opponents of music.

Calvin before him had silenced the organ in Geneva (St. Peters) as Zwingli, the talented master of six instruments, did in all his churches. The Wesley's hardly faced the issue, since "in open air meetings the great volume of sound would have drowned out any accompaniment, as it often drowned out the voices of the people sent to break up the meeting" (Benson, *The English Hymn*, London, 1915; p. 243).

Appeal to Worldly Tastes

It was not, therefore, peculiar that the former Presbyterian should frown on other than vocal music in worship; especially, since the three branches of the Presbyterian church in Scotland did not officially authorize organs until the latter half of the nineteenth century. When a Christian brother who signed his correspondence "G." has argued valiantly that instrumental music would "add very much to the solemnity" of their worship, Campbell's revealing reply was:

> The argument drawn from the Psalms in favor of instrumental music, is exceedingly apposite to the Roman Catholic, English Protestant, and Scotch Presbyterian churches, and even to the Methodist communities. Their churches having all the world in them—that is, all the fleshly progeny of all

the communicants, and being founded on the Jewish pattern of things—baptism being given to all born into the world of these politico-ecclesiastic communities—I wonder not, then, that an organ, a fiddle, or a Jews-harp, should be requisite to stir up their carnal hearts, and work into ecstasy their animal souls, else "hosannahs languish on their tongues, and their devotions die." And that all persons who have no spiritual discernment, taste, or relish for their spiritual meditations, consolations and sympathies of renewed hearts, should call for such aid, is but natural. Pure water from the flinty rock has no attractions for the mere toper or wine-bibber. A little alcohol, or genuine Cognac brandy, or good old Madeira, is essential to the beverage to make it truly refreshing. So to those who have no real devotion or spirituality in them, and whose animal nature flags under the oppression of church service, I think with Mr. G., that instrumental music would be not only a desideratum, but an essential prerequisite to fire up their souls to even animal devotion. But I presume, to all spiritually-minded Christians, such aids would be as a cow bell in a concert (*Millennial Harbinger*, October, 1851, pp. 581, 582).

The apostolic ideal for the music of the "psalms, hymns, and spiritual songs" was supposed to be "of the simplest character," according to Robert Richardson's words and Alexander Campbell's publication. As Christian meeting-houses rose across the land where the primitive gospel was to be heard, disciple would remind disciple not to mistake "the genius of Chritianity and that of human nature," but to continue in that place a worship

. . . free from all those degrading ephemeral and gewgaw appendages, trappings and tinsil, by which the mind is too often diverted from the great soul and centre of every system of true religion (*Millennial Harbinger*, June, 1853, p. 332).

248

Virtue in Simplicity

The words of church music were the essential things. The trend of the century was for the emphasis upon text to give way to emphasis upon music. Campbell accredited the appeal of the revival aspects of exuberant Methodism to temperaments that required

> . . . stimulants and excitements of a higher order than can be found in a marble church, a crimsoned pulpit, cushioned sofas, gilded canopies, solemn organs, animated by an half-hour essay of well-turned periods, graceful sentences, read from golden pages, turned over by a lily hand, sparkling with its diamond ring . . . (*Millennial Harbinger*, July, 1843, p. 318).

In days when hardy men were cutting out small places for their families in a difficult wilderness it seemed incongruous to have churches matching the cathedrals of Europe, or music equaling that in the palaces of kings. Instead of being impressed favorably while in St. Peter's at blind devotion:

> . . . that can be pleased with such a satire upon him that was born in a stable and who said—"The foxes have their dens, and the birds of the air have their nests, but the Son of Man hath not where to lay his head." Had the taste of the Roman or English hierarchy been consulted, Christ would have been born in a palace and rocked in a golden cradle enamlled [sic] with diamonds of the most costly brilliancy (*Millennial Harbinger*, November, 1847, pp. 608, 609).

Perhaps a slight influence on Campbell's view came from economic consideration, since organs were costly—he named a thousand dollars as the price of one he has seen—and transportation difficult. Perchance more was due to the size of the congregations and the cultural opportunities of their memberships. Possibly he made a mental relationship between instruments and worldly indulgence—at least his wife confessed "associating dancing with fiddling" and therefore insisted that Alexander's cousin Enos do his violin playing at the farm on the hill rather than in the domicile near the public road lest passersby misinterpret the sounds in relation to activities within.

More likely, he would have pointed to father Thomas Campbell's dictum, "Where the Scriptures are silent, we are silent," and then have considered the silences of Scripture as prohibitive rather than permissive. I say "likely," for Alexander died before the sour note of division was heard amidst those calling for the harmony of all Christians. He had expressed, in 1851, his views of instruments in worship as being as fitting as "a cowbell in a concert." Had he lived when lesser lights were making the use or nonuse of instruments tests of fellowship, what would have been his stand?

Continual Discussion

The *Harbinger* allowed free discussion during the trying years. Coeditor Isaac Errett, in 1861, wrote favorably of the instrument, saying that "pride is not in the notes, the choir, nor the organ, but in the *heart.*" J. W. McGarvey, an opponent of the organ, in 1864 called on its advocates to discuss fully and finally to settle the question. By 1865 coeditor W. K. Pendleton noted "a growing heat" under the discussion but mistakenly, naïvely, and hopefully predicted:

> I do not think the organ is likely to be a syren [sic] of much mischief among us, at present (January, 1865, p. 40).

Pendleton, Campbell's son-in-law, expressed the wish that affluent churches would have better use for the funds than the purchase of "such 'wind of doctrine,' as an organ." The other editor, C. L. Loos, called attention to the fact that no lesser music critic than Mendelssohn preferred man to worship God without any artistic medium. By the fall of the year, James Challen wrote an article that sensed the trends of the future:

> Music in our churches is giving us no little trouble, and will continue to do it in the future. Some have thought it expedient to introduce instrumental music as an adjunct; and others have the matter under consideration, but are reluctant to take the step. It is easy for us to see that in process of time, what others have done before us, will be done by us, whatever of evil or of good may follow. . . . For one, I shall take no offense at good congregational music, even though aided with an instrument, as I do not think that there is any sin in musical sounds no matter where they come from. Intelligence directs the mouth, as an instrument, and so it does the organ. But I should object to either as an element of discord among us (*Millennial Harbinger*, September, 1865, p. 414).

This last sentence seemed to express the spirit then prevailing; but, could the spirit prevail when the war of words continued? Pendleton began the year of 1868 writing on "Religion Degenerating into Music," hoping music would remain the "aid, and not the essence and end" of worship.

> If the people will have an idol, music is perhaps as respectable a one as the religious development of the nineteenth century can invent. . . . 'Tis too impious. Better for the people that some stern iconoclast should rise in the holy indignation of the old prophets, and break to pieces all the senseless organs and scatter all the godless choir

251

that desecrate our fashionable cathedrals, than that this fatal tendency to substitute a musical sentimentalism for a living Christianity (*Millennial Harbinger*, January, 1868, p. 40).

J. S. Lamar ended the year asking that instruments be used (as aids) and not abused (as substitutes).

An amusing and clever satire, "Music or No Music," greeted the New Year 1869.

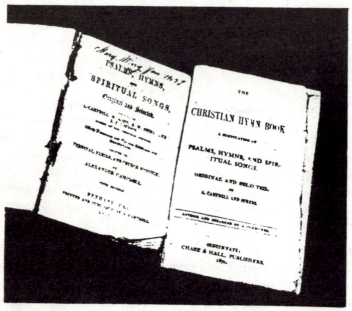

Title pages from two editions of *Psalm, Hymns, and Spiritual Songs.*

This contrasted the "instrument of man which is a melodian, with the instrument of God, which is the larynx." A letter by spring of the year bites bitterly concerning the "filthy trial of the 'mother of abominations'" seen when a "wicked hireling" grinds out music as a substitute for the worship in spirit and truth (April, 1869, p. 233). The final year of the *Millennial Harbinger* started off reminding the reader:

> It is not the air forced through either the human lungs or organ pipes, that is the praise. . . . Of all things beware of making a bond of union of this music question. I cannot call that act by any other name than wicked which would rend assunder a Church of Christ on any such issue (Article by "E," January, 1870, pp. 19, 20).

By fall the columns of the paper are announced to be closed to the "music question" which had "gone on almost ad nauseam" (p. 503).

Campbell had sought unity, and therefore became a reformer to reach that goal. The reform extended to the area of worship. While desiring to call all Christians to participate in the offering of praise, he pointed to the hurtful abrogation of that general privilege of believers, when they permitted specialists in voice or musical attainment to substitute for them. He could not have dreamed that brethren who rejected all human creeds as tests of fellowship would elevate instruments meant for harmony into occasions for division.

The purpose of this present writing is not to weep over the past, nor to propose solutions for the future, as much as both are needed; but it is to gain an appreciative understanding as to why Mr. Campbell felt as he did, and why he cared enough about improvements in worship to edit a hymnal and to write throughout his years upon the theme.

Chapter Nine

CAMPBELL AS MUSIC CRITIC

The common accusation made against the Puritans that they "hated music," or that they "at first used but five tunes for their psalmody," has been given the lie by the testimony of modern scholarship. Henry Wilder Foote (*Three Centuries of American Hymnody;* Harvard University Press, 1940) and Percy Scholes (*The Puritans and Music;* Oxford University Press, 1934) have shown that the Puritan was fond of music and did not hesitate to use stringed instruments and organs.

Approved Education in Music

Is there evidence that Alexander Campbell would be falsely judged, if we gave the verdict that he opposed music, itself, to some degree? One clue should be noted in the female schools founded by Disciples. When the music controversy got underway, James Challen attributed the demand for better music standards and hymnbooks with tunes to the following cause:

> Music is found in nearly all our families. Pianos, melodeons and cabinet organs are to be seen in almost every well-furnished parlor. Our daughters learn to play on them and sing *in all our boarding schools* (italics mine) and children of both sexes are taught music in all our common schools and Sunday Schools (*Millennial Harbinger*, September, 1865, p. 415).

Earlier Alexander Campbell had praised the academic standards of the Pleasant Hill Female Seminary. Two of his own daughters graduated from there, and he frequently visited the school and shared in the most thorough examinations he had ever seen given. We note that, beyond the

254

twenty dollars tuition per student for ten months, there was the extra charge of thirty-two dollars for piano lessons, twenty dollars for guitar lessons, twenty-five dollars for melodeon lessons, and only four dollars for the vocal music.

When commending the Henry Female College of New Castle, Kentucky, Campbell revealed his own evaluation of himself—musically speaking:

> The musical performances at this Commencement were regarded by amateurs, as admirable. Not gifted in that department, I have no confidence in my own judgment; but whatever Mrs. Campbell says on that subject, I unhesitatingly endorse (*Millennial Harbinger*, September, 1850, p. 540).

It thus appears that he favored a musical education for his wife and daughters, and recognized his own limitations in this high art. As president of Bethany College, he did not disapprove of the singing school of A. D. Fillmore and Carman (composed mostly of students of Bethany College) with its lectures on music theory and the practice of appropriate songs.

A Taste of Appropriateness

He was interested in all scholarship and had a good classical education. To read his debates or editorial writings is to see how completely at home he was in the best of Old World scholarship. While confessing an amateur status in the field of music, he still showed an interest in its history. For instance, observe his insert concerning "Old Hundred":

> The music in harmony of four parts of this venerable and deservedly popular church tune, was composed by Claude Goudimal, about the year 1544. The composer, who was a chapel-master at Lyons, France, died in 1572, a victim

of religious opinion. The harmony of his hymn has since been altered, (not for the better,) as may be seen by comparing the same as arranged in the present collection of church music with the original. It is popular musicohistorical error, that Martin Luther was the composer of this noble choral (*Millennial Harbinger*, March, 1845, p. 137).

In failing to know a C augmented chord from either a G diminished, or an F seventh, or in lacking the skill to run a chromatic scale on an instrument, Alexander Campbell did not prove himself unable to sense that which was appropriate in the realm of church music. An introduction to one of his hymnals finds him asking that attention be paid not only to the subject-matter of the hymns, but to "the style of character of the tunes employed."

The "grave sweet melody," the "joyful strains," and the mournful sounds of "harps hung upon the willow trees," ought to correspond with the meaning of the song and the occasion. To hear a joyful tune sung to the song, "Why do we mourn departed friends?" or a mournful air to the words, "Rejoice, O Earth, the Lord is King," is so unharmonious and discordant, that half the world feels the incongruity as they would frost in August, or solstitial heat in December (*Psalms, Hymns, and Spiritual Songs*, 1853 edition, p. 11).

Poetry in Millennial Harbinger

Besides Campbell's major interest in the correct doctrinal content of a hymn and the minor attention given to their appropriate melodies, he gave thought to their literary merit. In 1846 he had explained the lack of space given "to the Muses" on the ground that the *Harbinger's* purpose of reformation was the work of prose and not poetry. However, he refers to his "always resolving to give a little more poetry" (August, 1846, p. 469). A backward glance to former issues shows columns dedicated to "stanzas," "paraphrases," and "poetry." A look beyond 1846 shows poetry of equal quality and of hardly increased quantity; but a use of the art as an aid to the reformation is to be observed.

Written for the *Millennial Harbinger* by "R." (a designation for Robert Richardson, a co-editor of 1851) was an eleven-stanza "Appeal to Christians" for the unity of believers in Christ:

> If meanest insects wisely join,
> In summer hours, to gather grain,
> On which in harmony to feed,
> While chilling winds their toils impede,
> Then should not saints *united* be,
> In labors for eternity?
>
> If birds unite at break of day,
> To greet the morn with gladsome lay,
> And thus, in mild and merry glee,
> Pour forth their untaught melody,
> Should not our tongues, with one accord,
> Be tuned to praise our risen Lord?
>
> . . .
>
> If moon and stars their rays entwine,
> And joy in union thus to shine,
> And shed o'er earth their silver light,
> To cheer the dreary hours of night,
> Should we not thus in union join,
> To fill the world with light divine?
>
> . . .
>
> If holy martyrs, side by side,
> United stood, and bled, and died;
> If flames and faggots could not make,

Those holy men their union break,
Should party zeal and names divide,
The laurels for which the Saviour died?

. . .

Has God the Father and the Son,
And Spirit in sweet unison,
Put forth their energies and breath,
To rid the world of sin and death?
And now, shall those by blood made free,
Refuse to thus united be?

Did Jesus pray? Ah! yes he prayed,
In that sad night he was betrayed,
That union might his people crown—
That they on earth should be but *one*.
O! then, should we not live and love,
As angels do in realms above?

If Jesus once for *union* died,
No more let party names divide;
The middle wall was broken down,
That peace might Jew and Gentile crown;
O then! let those who love the Lord,
United be upon his word!

Say not you would, but can't be one;
The Lord commands, it must be done:
Oh let us *fast*, and *weep*, and *pray*,
Throw *party names* and *creeds* away;
And then the glorious work is done
The saints on earth *again are one*
(*Millennial Harbinger*, April, 1851,
pp. 296, 297).

Expressed Himself in Verse

From childhood our editor of Bethany had not only
memorized the proverbs and psalms of the Bible, but also

the gems of the better English poets. In maturity he could distinguish the present "rhymsters" from the true "poets." His writings and speeches showed embellishment from that acquaintance. Besides the hymns he wrote, we can place at least two poems he penned. These ought to be read for their literary quality by those interested in more than the theology of the hymns.

On boat deck one Sunday morning, while upon the Cumberland River, Campbell used poetic verse to express his heart in correspondence meant only for the eyes of his wife. The words speak volumes about his fellowship with the muses through reading, with the saints through communion, and with his wife through conversations about their heavenly hope.

> Serene the morn, and bright the sky;
>   I walked the deck alone;
> The morning-star with silvery rays
>   In all its splendor shone.
>
> Some golden streaks of brightest hue
>   Were trembling on the sky;
> The forest leaves with drops of dew
>   Gave hope that Spring was nigh.
>
> It was, indeed, the Lord's-day morn,
>   And soon my thoughts were turned
> To those bright scenes of hope and joy
>   With which our hearts have burned.
>
> How soon shall all the toils of earth
>   Give place to Heavenly rest;
> And those who live for God and Christ
>   Shall be forever blest!

Hold on thy way, my sister wife,
    In faith, and hope, and love;
And when our toils on earth are past,
    We'll meet in Heaven above.

Be this our aim, our happy choice,
    Till all our toils are o'er;
Then we shall meet among the blest,
    And part again no more.
(Quoted in *Home Life of Alexander
Campbell;* John Burns, St. Louis, Mo.,
1882).

An earlier boat trip, this time upon the sea, was the
occasion for a lengthier poem of two printed pages. Bound
for the new world, he wrote what he entitled simply, "The
Ocean," including these lines:

Ere yet, in brightness, had the radiant sun
In Eastern skies the course of day begun,
Ere yet the stars in dazzling beauty shone,
Or yet, from Chaos dark, old earth was won;
When darkness o'er the deep extended lay,
And night still reigned, unbounded yet by day;
When awful stillness filled the boundless space,
And wild confusion sat on Nature's face,
Old Ocean then in silent youth did stray,
And countless atoms on its bosom lay.
Th' Almighty spoke; its waters trembling fear'd
They yawned; and straight in haste dry land appear'd.
The land he bounds; and to the waters said,
Here, Ocean, let thy haughty waves be stayed.
They swelled; and angry at their bounds, they roar
And pour their rage against the peaceful shore.
See Ocean's varied face, its wat'ry fields;
The dreadful terrors which it constant yields;

See liquid valleys sink, and mountains rise,
Behold them, angry, tow'ring to the skies;
In pride they rear their hoary heads, and rage,
And soon they sink, like man's declining age.
See yonder azure wave, in beauteous trim,
Rise from the mighty deep, and slowly swim;
From gay green youth to hoary age it tends,
Then to the depths below it quick descends;
And where, ere while, it reared its lofty head
The spot's unknown, another's in its stead.
Next look where skies and seas converging tend;
See waters joined to waters without end;
See next thyself, borne on the mighty flood,
Supported on the floating fragile wood.
Behold thyself, the central point, and learn
The Almighty's power and goodness to discern.

. . .

When night comes on, and darkness veils the skies;
When black'ning clouds, and howling storms arise;
When dismal horror broods upon the deep,
And awful terrors wake the mind from sleep,
See, from the poles, the forked lightnings fly,
And paint in solemn glares the black'ning sky;
Then from the south, begin the dreadful blasts,
Hark! how they roar amidst the groaning masts:
See hemp and canvas to their force give way,
And through the air in shreds and fragments stray.
Lo! expectation, wit, and judgment fail,
Man's counsel and his arm no more avail,
Despair and horror fill the aching breast,
No time to think, and for the soul no rest.
But while man, trembling, waits his dreadful fate,
And thinks what unknown scenes him soon await,
At his command who bids the tempest fly,

The storm subsides, hope gladdens every eye
The clouds clear off, and tranquil calm pervades,
Save where the wat'ry mountains rear their heads;
But soon they sink when angry tempests cease,
And all is changed to gentle, joyous peace.

. . .

Thus while we wander through the mighty deep
Some foreign clime, some distant shore to seek,
These mighty scenes our wand'ring minds engage,
Too great to tell, or for th' historic page.
But let us still that Power, that Goodness love,
That rules o'er all below and all above;
Each of His creatures move at His command
In the great sea, or on the spacious land.

Line upon line, precept upon precept, here a little poetry, there a little logic, we have attempted to broaden our understanding of the man Alexander Campbell. In the mirror of hymnody we have seen his reflection as if in a glass darkly. By the further light of the hymnbook he edited we hope to make the image yet clearer, as if face to face.

Chapter Ten

PSALMS, HYMNS, AND SPIRITUAL SONGS

Alexander Campbell began editing a journal in 1823 and a hymnal in 1828. The hymnal he named *Psalms, Hymns, and Spiritual Songs* after Pauline terminology from Ephesians 5:19 and Colossians 3:16. This title it retained, until the editorship went to the American Christian Missionary Society in 1865.

It is not easy to be dogmatic about all phases of the history of this book, because of the inexact use of the words *edition, printing, etc.* There have been found between forty-five and fifty different "editions." Many of these were but reprintings. We shall follow the seven major periods of the hymnal's history pointed out originally by Claude E. Spencer of the Disciples of Christ Historical Society. These will point up the major revisions, and not the minor but innumerable alterations.

From 1828

Psalms, Hymns, and Spiritual Songs, selected and published by Alexander Campbell was an independent production. It was called forth in that May of 1828 not by church authority nor by divine authority, but by a personally felt need. Such had been the case of most hymnbooks to that time.

The poem "Elegant Extract" and 125 hymns were placed between a sermonic preface on "Psalmody" and a concluding essay on "Prayer." In all, there were two hundred pages. The songs were of Campbell's choosing and emendation, but not of his composition. By gradual growth the number of songs had increased by thirty-five in four years. To arrange the volumes of some forty years in chronological

263

order before the eye, is to register objectively the certain and steady increase in size and weight that did come during the life-span of the hymnal.

At this present decade of the twentieth century only one copy of the 1828 edition is known to have survived. This was sold through the Midland Rare Book Company of Mansfield, Ohio, in 1950. The private party owning that edition has not, as yet, allowed it to be microfilmed.

A copy of the second edition is in the Disciples of Christ Historical Society library in Nashville; one of the third edition is in the library of the Western Reserve Historical Society in Cleveland; and copies of a fourth edition are to be found in Nashville (defective) and in the Library of Congress at Washington. The twenty-five "psalms" used in 1829 had become twenty-seven in 1832. The "hymns" remained the same, but the "spiritual songs" had increased to 101 plus an additional page of choruses. By this last edition of the first period, the concluding essay on "Prayer" was omitted, but not forgotten. This appeared then in the *Millennial Harbinger* of November, 1831 (pp. 497-503).

For $3.75 per dozen, or 37-1/2¢ per copy, the original work was offered "to the wise and discerning Christians dispersed amongst all the sects of the present day" (*Christian Baptist*, April 7, 1828, p. 215). Within four months distributors were named in Maysville, Mays Lick, Lexington, Mount Sterling, Winchester, and Louisville, Kentucky; in Nashville, Tennessee; and even in Indiana. Distribution was a more serious problem to the editors of that day than was the clearing of copyrights. In the early days of the hymn-book there seems to have been no effort to note authorship. Apparently it was a sufficient editorial burden to sift the many hymns for the few that both met the Scriptural test and satisfied the heart.

The book contained words alone. At the head of each song an abbreviation marked, for the initiate in musical arts, a meter. This in turn was intended to suggest a group of suitable tunes from which to select. By 1832 *C.M., P.M., L.M., S.M.* had been written in full as "Common Metre" (four-line stanzas having eight syllables in the first and third lines, and six in the second and fourth), "Particular Metre" (a tune peculiar to the words of that hymn), "Long Metre" (four-line stanzas having eight syllables in each line), and "Short Metre" (the same as long meter except that the third line in each stanza has only six syllables). The words of song were the important thing in Protestant hymnals everywhere, and these were changed to suit each editor. To find an author's original text was very difficult since no common text existed in many instances and there were variant readings even of the emendations. The great scholar in church hymnody, Louis F. Benson, says that Roundell Palmer's *Book of Praise* in 1862 was the "first attempt to recover and restore the original text of our hymns" (*The Hymnody of the Christian Church;* Richmond, Virginia: John Knox Press, 1956, p. 218).

We find Campbell as a typical editor, using hymns without giving credit to any source and making emendations without any acknowledgment of that fact. He did index helpfully by first lines from the beginning of his editorship. All the editions of Campbell's hymnbook in this period were in hand-set type.

From 1834

It was more than the spirit of the Christmas season that brought together on January 1, 1832, the "Reformers" who looked to Alexander Campbell and the "Christians" who were led by Barton W. Stone. It was more than a lightly made New Year's resolution when these groups on that day joined forces in a program of brotherhood through exalting Christ and the Bible alone. This unity brought about the first major change in the hymnbook under our consideration.

Stone, with the help of Thomas Adams, had compiled in 1829 the hymnbook, *The Christian Hymn.* In 1832 Stone and John T. Johnson had combined their efforts in editing *The Christian Hymn Book,* which may be a possible revision of the former. The united church then had two strong leaders in Campbell and Stone, two good papers in their *Millennial Harbinger* and *Christian Messenger,* and one too many hymnbooks to suit Alexander Campbell. To assist the new union he proposed that the two hymnals be combined. The result was the 1834 enlarged edition of *Psalms, Hymns, and Spiritual Songs,* under the joint editorship of four men: Alexander Campbell, Walter Scott, Barton W. Stone, and John T. Johnson.

It is suggested as a high probability that since Scott is connected with later hymnals, he likely had produced an earlier one to contribute to this new edition. If each editor of the 1834 hymnbook did not have a book from which to contribute, he at least had a sphere of influence where the combined work would now be received. Campbell's fourth edition had sold nearly eight thousand copies and the book by Stone and Johnson had reached the three thousand mark in sales. The combined work in this period, 1834 through 1843, met the demand for five editions and several stereotyped printings. Six thousand copies of the first of these five editions came off the presses at Bethany, bearing the title *Disciple Hymn Book* before protests against the term "Disciple" by Stone and Johnson stopped production.

An 1835 edition, called the fourth edition, was printed by Scott in Carthage (now a part of Cincinnati), Ohio. This caused the present curator of the Disciples of Christ Historical Society to ask three still unanswered questions:

> Did each of the various compilers issue the book under his imprint? Were all editions so issued? Did Campbell's shop do all the printing and furnish a separate title page for each compiler? (Claude E. Spencer, *Discipliana*, April, 1949, p. 4).

We have our interrogations about what happened at Bethany, Virginia; Carthage, Ohio; and Georgetown, Kentucky; but the editors of the volume had no question that they had produced "the best collection . . . extant." Each revision, to avoid inconvenience to owners of earlier editions, kept the same songs on the same pages. All additional hymns were placed at the end of major sections, bringing the accumulating total by 1838 to thirty-three psalms, thirty-five hymns and one hundred eighty spiritual songs, with two additional pages of anthems. Thanks to the sterotype machine the greater quantity and variety of songs did not increase the cost. In fact, the new book sold for twenty-five cents. Bound with a pocket Testament, the hymnbook was only half of a dollar in Pittsburgh, provided the purchaser could pay cash.

From 1843

In 1843 the price of the hymnbook was again back to its original 37-1/2¢ per copy; and, if the gilt edges of Turkey morocco binding were desired, it would retail at $1.00. The addition of a "Part II," with 217 additional hymns and its own first-line index was the reason for the increase in cost. The two parts together contained 475 songs. Many of the new pieces were accumulated by Campbell on a tour abroad and in an examination of other hymnals and psalm books both ancient and modern. He was hesitant to increase the content of the book, but "numerous and oft-repeated requests" from the brethren forced him to yield his own judgment. This yielding, with resultant increased costs for a constantly enlarging book, was finally to defeat Campbell's desire to have only one hymnbook used in the churches.

The 1856 edition of *Psalms, Hymns, and Spiritual Songs* compared in size to *Great Songs of the Church*.

Competitive books were becoming more numerous and the whims of the purchaser had to be met, if business were to continue. James Freeman Clarke, the distinguished poet, preacher, and scholar amongst the Disciples of Boston, produced *The Disciple Hymn Book* in 1844. He was a hymn writer and the hymn editor responsible for introducing Sarah Flower Adams' "Nearer, My God, to Thee" into the American hymnal. B. W. Stone, the same year, had shared with David P. Henderson, John O'Kane, and Love H. Jameson in publishing *The Christian Hymn Book* in Dayton, Ohio.

Most irritating of all the competition was that coming from Jeffersonville, Indiana. In 1847 Silas W. Leonard, with Augustus Damon Fillmore (1823-1870), brought out *The Christian Psalmist;* and it created such a stir that in its first three months six editions were required. It ran eighteen editions in all and sold 560,000 copies. Mr. Campbell disliked both having Leonard's singing school use his hymnal and having Leonard's hymnbook, in its first edition, use his copyrighted hymns and emendations with no acknowledgement. Yet, Leonard was giving Campbell's followers the increased number of hymns they desired.

While yielding in regard to the sum of songs to be included in his book, Campbell would not be rushed into stereotyping immediately. He promised to do this only after "two or three years . . . but not before" (*Millennial Harbinger,* July, 1843, p. 340). Aware of the fact that individual tastes differ and change; and that a general committee could not "be conceived, or attained" under their present organization, Campbell proposed following a path similar to one the Presbyterians had just successfully walked. With the broader committee of J. T. Johnson, B. F. Hall, S. Church, R. Richardson, Thomas Campbell and others guiding the original edition of 1843, their best judgment would be circulated for a long enough time to register the emendations and corrections desired by the churches for which it was intended. Then the two dozen or more stereotyped editions could be produced after the more permanent form had come from the *de facto* vote of the people.

The voice of the brotherhood at large was also sought at this time for a proposal, originating in Kentucky, that "the profits resulting from such a volume should be sent back to the churches in the form of educated evangelists" (*Millennial Harbinger*, March, 1843, pp. 132, 133). The president of Bethany College was pleased with this suggestion. The 1848 edition from the Bethany press sold one hundred thousand copies and netted two thousand dollars. This publication was exclusively in Campbell's hands; and thus, by him, contributed to the education of young men for the ministry. If all brethren had paid their bills, he said, there would have been a larger amount. He suggested that if each family member had his own private hymn book, this would increase sales and thus profits.

Beyond our period 1843-1851, Mr. Campbell continued the practice of placing earnings from the hymnal into the education of Christian ministers. Brethren in conventions in eastern Virginia, Indiana, Illinois, and Ohio selected young men for whom the profits from the hymnbook would pay expenses of education, including board and laundry, for the one or two years of preacher training then demanded.

Chapter Eleven

LATER EDITIONS

We have noted the development of Alexander Campbell's *Psalms, Hymns, and Spiritual Songs* through a number of editions and reprintings in three periods from its first appearance in 1828 to the middle of the nineteenth century.

A number of variations marked the hymnbook during the next period, 1851-1864. The division into Parts I and II were eliminated; and the indexes of first lines for both sections were consolidated into one. Consecutively, now, the hymns were numbered through the book without starting from number one again for some part or section. All tune names, that had earlier appeared above the texts of songs, were omitted. The new "Preface" gave Campbell's explanation for this as the awareness of variety in taste, and the fact that most tunes were not universally known. The latter problem was a real difficulty when the hymnbook was "being used in every State of the Union, and in the British provinces."

The size had continued to expand. There were now, in 511 pages, fifty-four psalms, fifty-two hymns, and four hundred and sixty-two songs plus an additional four baptismal selections. The book retained the customary cover title, *Christian Hymn Book*, but it varied slightly in the actual reading of the sub-title. At this time it became *Psalms, Hymns, and Spiritual Songs, Original and Selected. Compiled by A. Campbell, W. Scott, B. W. Stone, and J. T. Johnson, Elders of the Christian Church; With Numerous and Various Additions and Emendations adapted to Personal Family, and Church Worship by Alexander Campbell.*

A minimum of seven editions of the hymnbook were made in this period. Although the names of the four compilers remained, Campbell was again, as in the very beginning, the sole owner.

271

The threat of competition and replacement was especially noted at this time. *Campbell's Hymns;* published by W. H. Derby & Co. of Cincinnati and printed by Morgan & Overend, was circulating in Missouri. Campbell labeled this edition of his own book "fradulent and dishonorable." As evil as the violation of copyright, in his mind, were the "clandestine movements for another hymnbook" (*Millennial Harbinger,* August, 1852, p. 474). Such action implied that his own work was behind the rapid progress of the age. The executive committee of the Ohio Christian Book Association, has argued that

> . . . a large majority of the Christians in the West have decided, that the hymnbooks in use among us are deficient, either in arrangement or variety; and, in some instances, in the sentiment contained in the hymns (*Christian Hymns Complied by the Executive Committee of the Ohio Christian Book Association;* Columbus, Ohio: John Geary & Son, 1858, p. 4).

Similar efforts in the North, South, and Southwest were referred to (but not by name) in Campbell's replies through his paper. He seemed hurt and disappointed when he wrote:

> I will cheerfully resign all connections with hymnbooks, whenever a *general convention* of our brethren, or delegates from the States in which our churches exist, shall be held (*Millennial Harbinger,* August, 1852, p. 474).

From 1865

The Civil War that raged between North and South concluded in the year 1865. Yet a cold war was going on across the country among Disciples over a "slavery," felt by some,

272

to the Campbell hymnbook. A growing revolt "especially among our preachers" was intended to free many valuable hymns for inclusion in the book from which they had formerly been excluded.

Alexander Campbell had resented and resisted what he thought were independent and private ventures into the field of hymnal production for Disciples. A general expression from the entire brotherhood, which he had desired, came in 1863. October of that year found brethren from several states in Cincinnati for an informal meeting to consider "*the book of the brotherhood*" (Isaac Errett, "The Christian Hymn Book," *Millennial Harbinger,* November, 1864, p. 520). These men appointed a committee, with Isaac Errett as chairman, to correspond with Mr. Campbell on their wishes. To their gratification he "kindly and benevolently" proposed to transfer his copyright to certain brethren in trust for the American Christian Missionary Society. His twofold stipulation was that a revision committee be mutually acceptable to the missionary society and to himself; and that all profits go into the work of the A.C.M.S. At the convention of that society in October of 1864 the plan was approved and two committees of five were appointed. The first, to arrange for the publication of a hymnbook, consisted of R. M. Bishop, C. H. Gould, W. H. Lape, O. A. Burgess, and J. B. Bowman. The second, an editing committee to concern itself with the "matter" of the hymnal, was composed of Isaac Errett, W. K. Pendleton, W. T. Moore, T. M. Allen, and A. S. Hayden. This last committee called for help from William Baxter and other men of competence in music.

The "Introduction" to the new reproduction expressed its high desire:

We hope that it may minister to the comfort, strength, and purity of the church of God; throw over many a hearthstone, and many a weary pilgrim path, the sweet radiance of heavenly song; and give fresh encouragement to the cultivation of all pious sentiments and emotions, alike in the closet, the family, the prayer-meeting, and the public assembly (Cincinnati; H. S. Bosworth, 1868).

This revision was based clearly on Campbell's hymnbook and thus belongs in a study of the original *Psalms, Hymns, and Spiritual Songs.* Although the book now contained 1,323 hymns in its 840 pages it was still the earlier hymnal with further additions. The new editors claimed that "comparatively few hymns had been expunged," and they complimented the former editor by saying:

> . . . we were more than ever convinced of the value of the labor, judgment, and taste, displayed in the compilation of the book we have so long used and cherished.

There is something strange that when "few" were expunged, the total number written by Alexander Campbell were among those dropped. Among the more than thirteen hundred songs there was room, however, for "a few original hymns prepared expressly for this work." Since the index now included authors' names after the first lines, it is easy to find the work of most of the new editors and their consulted brethren.

Amongst the changes from former times was a new classification by subject matter, and the omission of Campbell's three major classifications according to type (psalm, hymn, or spiritual song). Stanzas were numbered with the expectation that congregations would like to omit some.

The monies that were above expenses, since 1851, had gone to educate ministers at Bethany College where Campbell was president. Now they were to go to the Missionary Society of which he was also president. The fears of many, that this organization "would grow to be a great monied monopoly from the fancied proceeds of its sale," were relieved by Pendleton's assurance that the profits were nonexistant as of November, 1867. The trustees had put the A.C.M.S. second in their consideration and the needs of the churches first. Profits had been used to get out the work in every form and size that differing ages and desires requested. For the dim-eyes in old age, there was provided in 1868 a large clear-type edition that could be read by them under "tallow candles."

Even though the price inflated to 90 cents through $2.75 (sheepskin binding to Turkey morocco with gilt edge and gilt clasp), the promoters reasoned that the price for an arabesque bound hymnal in November of 1867 had dropped to 65 cents, and that was "only about five hundredths of a cent per hymn!"

The brotherhood that, in 1864, knew that the quality of the book would depend upon the committee of revision and could not be judged till the work was done, was unanimous in its praise after its completion. Glowing testimonies came from Robert Milligan, J. S. Sweeney, J. W. McGarvey, and a host of others. Amongst the champions of the 1865 edition were former competitors A. D. Fillmore, S. W. Leonard, and Dr. L. L. Pinkerton—who introduced the first melodion into a church stemming from this "Restoration movement."

After 1871

Campbell had surrendered control of the hymnal in 1864, but the hymnal published from 1865 to 1871 was

275

based on his earlier work and begun with his blessing. He passed away in 1866. We include, however, a brief report of events following 1871 because of the revised hymnal's roots in, and removals from, his influence.

The "official" hymnal of 1865 was not to be superseded by the revision of 1871. Rather, the same publication committee now provided an alternative for those who wanted musical notations printed in the hymnal. The name of Alexander Campbell is for the first time absent from this revision's title page and it is presumably for the reason that he had been opposed to musical notations in a book of praise. A. S. Hayden, who had been on the editorial committee, had produced in 1870 a *Hymn and Tune Book* with more than 130 varieties of metres; and therein provided music adapted to all the hymns of *The Christian Hymn Book* of 1865. He is, no doubt, a key figure in the Society's own *The Christian Hymnal: A Choice Collection of Hymns and Tunes for Congregational and Social Worship* (Cincinnati: Bosworth, Chase and Hall, 1875) with its musical notes. The final edition, *The Christian Hymnal: Revised* contained 748 hymns and a few chants. Because of rising costs, the expensive bindings gave place to cloth and board. Still the price could not be brought below 90 cents and compete in a market where another hymnal might be bought at only a quarter.

Chapter Twelve

EARLY INFLUENCE ON CAMPBELL

From what wells of hymnody and cisterns of psalmody did Alexander Campbell draw the hymns that were to refresh the souls of those Disciples thirsting for righteousness and hungering to praise the Messiah? Where did he turn to find the songs that met his tests of acceptable religious poetry?

As the man of today is in part the product of yesterday's heredity and environment, was Campbell's hymnbook the fruit of his parsonage upbringing, of his university training, or of some other influence of molding power? What fathered his thought and mothered his selectivity regarding the songs by which Christians ought to "admonish one another"? How important were his parents to his ideas on religious song?

Campbell's Parental Influence

Robert Richardson, biographer of Mr. A. Campbell, referred to the impact that the "domestic circle" had, and asserted that it held a "most important bearing on his future life." Richardson then quoted a tribute that the son had paid to his mother long after her death, in which he concluded:

> I can but gratefully add, that to my mother, as well as to my father, I am indebted for having memorized in early life almost all the writings of King Solomon—his Proverbs, his Ecclesiastes—and many of the Psalms of his father David. They have not only been written on the table of my memory, but incorporated with my modes of thinking and speaking (Robert Richardson, *Memoirs of Alexander Campbell*; Cincinnati: Standard Publishing Company, 1897, p. 36).

Alexander Campbell's mother was French. Like the Huguenots, she loved the psalms of David and bore that same love for them to her children. The singing of psalms in France had become an exclusively Protestant practice. When Clement Marot's *Psalms* first appeared, the thrill ran as well through Catholics; for the metrical psalm was an appealing part of the Bible in their own tongue. Catholic joined with Protestant in singing to popular airs these texts which in that day were considered not so much a hymn based on Scripture as a revised version of Scripture. When the Sorbonne suppressed Marot's *Psalms,* the Huguenots had continued alone in France as the singers of the Genevan psalm tunes. Prothero, in *The Psalms in Human Life,* described a fact that would have been equally true of Mrs. Campbell's home:

> The Psalms were identified with the everyday life of the Huguenots. Children were taught to learn them by heart; they were sung at every meal in households like that of Coligny; to chant psalms meant in the course of time and in popular language to turn Protestant (*The Psalms in Human Life,* pp. 137, 138).

Before we draw a conclusion regarding the relation of heredity and psalmody in the life of Alexander Campbell, we note that his mother had married a Scotsman to whom the psalms were equally dear. The Reverend Thomas Campbell's family had used the Scotch metrical version of the psalms (1650) by Sir Francis Rouse (1579-1659), which had been received by the General Assembly of the Church of Scotland, and not the version of Nahum Tate and Dr. Nicholas Brady, which the church of England had adopted. Scotsmen considered their version no paraphrase but a more accurate translation than the common prose version. The *Millennial Harbinger* showed its Scottish colors when saying of Rouse's version:

What it sometimes wants in rythmical propriety, is assuredly gained in this correctness. And, moreover, it is hallowed to many by the holiest and tenderest associations. Employing this version in praising God, they sing the songs which of old were sung by martyrs on heath-clad mountains and in lovely caves; the songs, too, which their fathers loved, and which they themselves, in early years had loved and lisped upon a mother's knee. This version had been used and admired, despite its defects, by some of the noblest men that the world has ever produced. With what zest was Dr. Chalmers accustomed to read its sometimes limping stanzas! How much he preferred its simplicity, solidity and sincerety, to that more artistic excellence which many would put in their stead! (*Millennial Harbinger*, December, 1854, p. 707).

Campbell's memory never lost these psalms. He wrote in a December letter of 1856:

You know that I love the Scotch version of the Psalms of David, and that I often quote them because of the veneration I cherish for them (*Millennial Harbinger*, December, 1856, p. 712).

On that May fourth of 1811 at Brush Run—when he was licensed to preach, his father was appointed elder, four deacons were chosen, and that congregation organized—they solemnly had sung Psalm 118:13-29 "in the old metrical version, which, as Seceders, they had been in the habit of using" (*Memoirs of Alexander Campbell*, p. 367). As editor of the *Millennial Harbinger*, Mr. Campbell quoted Psalm 19, Psalm 92, Psalm 103, and other favorites in his pages, as did the later editors. When W. K. Pendleton recorded the "Death of Alexander Campbell," he wrote:

The sublime words of the Psalms were constantly in his mind—and he quoted with remarkable accuracy and propriety from the old metrical version of the Scotch Psalmody, which he memorized in his youth, such as spoke the comfort he needed or the praise he felt (*Millennial Harbinger*, March, 1866, pp. 136, 137).

One would anticipate that Campbell's hymnbook would reflect this heritage by containing many favorite metrical psalms from Rouse or Barton, if not from Tate and Brady or Sternhold and Hopkins. Few, however, even of those he quoted in his magazine, are in his first hymnal. In 1829 at request he added an appendix, at the very end of which is the line, "The following are a few of the pious strains of the ancient saints, in the Scotch version" (p. 165 of 1829 edition).

While the book of Psalms did not contain the subject matter Campbell desired for the "New Testament church," it did help create the high standard he held for religious poetry. Royal Humbert calls the poetry in *Psalms, Hymns, and Spiritual Songs* "sturdy, like a Scotch psalter, with notable absence of doggerel verse" (Alexander Campbell Edits a Hymnal," *The Christian-Evangelist*, December 21, 1936, p. 178).

Scotch Independent Influence

Turning from heredity to a consideration of environment; we know that most histories of that movement influenced by the Campbells include considerations of such names as Erskine, Glas, and Sandeman. Ralph Erskine had become a Seceder in 1737. He was publisher in 1726 of *Gospel Canticles*, which in the 1734 edition was called

Gospel Sonnets or Spiritual Songs. The Synod requested him to place the "songs of Scripture" into meter to enlarge their psalmody. His death in 1752 ended this plan until it was revived by the Synod of 1812. This latter Synod authorized the use of "Paraphrases and Hymns of the Church of Scotland." The growing psalmody was to include only the divinely inspired New Testament songs; but even these, amongst both Burghers and anti-Burghers, were not employed in their worship services.

The move beyond psalmody in Presbyterian Scotland was in the Relief Church. The followers of John Glas (1695-1773) and Robert Sandeman (1718-1771), beyond the psalm singing of their public worship, had used free hymns in their fellowship meetings. At Edinburgh in 1749 they had published a hymnbook, *Christian Songs.* Glassites, or Sandemanians, in Glasgow produced *Hymns and Spiritual Songs* (1781) and *A Selection of Hymns Adapted to Public Worship* (1819). Many of this sect later went in with the Baptists where their Glassite *Christian Songs* mingled with the *Psalms, Hymns and Spiritual Songs in Three Books, Selected for Use in the Scotch Baptist Churches* (1841).

Kentucky Revival Influence

While psalms primarily prevailed for many years in the Calvinistic sphere of influence both in America and abroad, the trend to hymns, which we note in Campbell's book, might have been encouraged by such reformers as those just mentioned.

What were the roads and paths by which the American churches, especially, moved from the one to the other? How much of an influence on the Restoration movement's greatest exponent was the second "great awakening," especially that stemming from Cane Ridge, Kentucky, from August of 1801?

The "awakening" in America in its frontier phase had regarded singing as one of the assets of its revival. It overcame the bias against church songs of human composition. If some of its conversions were not real, that conversion of the church from psalm-singing to hymn-singing was lasting. The revival required a different expression than that afforded by the psalms. Jonathan Edwards of Northampton, Massachusetts, in the earlier "awakening" wanted such singing to abound. With the rise of an evangelical party there came the demand for evangelical song to match the evangelistic preaching.

The Baptists, Methodists, and Cumberland Presbyterians had produced numerous religious songs which reflected the crude frontier conditions. To aid in the dissemination of their peculiar denominational views, hymnbooks began to appear. The nature of the songs was subjective, introspective, and sometimes mystical. The songs themselves were forerunners of the "gospel songs" that became current after the Civil War and Campbell's death, and were popularized by Ira D. Sankey, the song evangelist of Dwight L. Moody.

Alexander Campbell was neither in harmony with the outer manifestations in the American revivals nor happy with the "awakening's" concept of conversion. Rather, he opposed the excesses accompanying such protracted meetings. He favored hymn singing but not the use of what he considered the unfortunately emotional, sectarian, and mystical type. He preferred a more dignified, stately kind of hymn. In this he was like his contemporary, Lowell Mason (1792-1872), America's counterpart to England's George

Whitefield. Mason directed the trend to flow away from the emotionalism in American music, as Whitefield's hymn-book of 1753 had preferred Watt's sober dignity to the fervor and enthusiasm of the Wesleys.

Chapter Thirteen

SOURCES FOR THE HYMNBOOK

From the Presbyterian background Mr. Campbell gained an appreciation for the psalms which effected his taste for the stately. He did not, however, use David's psalms as the sourcebook for his own. From contact with Scotch Independents abroad and revival influences in America, he may have been readied to accept hymns by the church over psalms by David.

Denominational Hymn Sources

We are now ready to suggest an existing forest of books that this pioneer could have explored to find the timber suitable for his hymnal. A family tree of church music might be made to trace Protestant song with its hymns going back to Luther, with the Latin *Breviary* before him; and its psalms reaching to Calvin, with the Hebrew Psalters the origin of that lineage.

From Germany had come many immigrants into Pennsylvania (1690-1750) with their Lutheran hymnals. The 1865 edition of Campbell's work listed three of its songs as "from the German" and a trio of others by the German Lutheran Muhlenberg.

The Baptists of New England had first used the *Bay Psalm Book,* but by 1740 had changed to the New Version, to Watts, or to emotional and denominational hymns of their own. Within one or two decades prior to Campbell's *Psalms, Hymns, and Spiritual Songs* of 1828, they were known to have to their credit *Winchell's Psalms, Hymns, and Spiritual Songs of Watts,* and a second book, *The Psalms and Hymns of Dr. Watts, arranged by Dr. Rippon.*

This Rippon (1751-1836) was a source for two of the hymns in Campbell's 1865 edition. One of these songs had been in the Campbell hymnal from the beginning. Likewise, one hymn in the same 1865 edition is attributed to Baptist James M. Winchell's collection. When the *Psalmist* was added to Baptist achievements in 1843, one of its 1,180 hymns was selected for the Campbell book as were eleven others by one of its compilers, the S. F. Smith who wrote the words of "America."

The Methodists had produced so many hymnbooks on American soil that Coke and Asbury had to caution the use of only those with a bishop's endorsement. Although at least seventeen such books were published between 1805 and 1843, there is evidence of direct borrowing for the early Campbell book only in the case of John Cennick (1718-1755), a Moravian turned Methodist. The line of derivation from Methodism's music appeared in the year 1865 when Campbell's book had come under the Missionary Society's committee. At that late date Methodism was well represented in "Christian church" singing by the Wesley family, with Samuel Wesley contributing a hymn, John Wesley a hymn, and Charles Wesley fifty-six hymns. Only four of Charles Wesley's songs had been included in Campbell's original work.

Since Campbell appreciated Episcopalian worship, it is not surprising to find his generous use of Anglican hymnals. John Newton (1725-1807) curate of Olney, had published *Olney Hymns* in 1779. This early Episcopal hymnal contained two hundred and eighty songs by Newton's own hand and sixty-eight by that of his friend, William Cowper (1731-1800). From the beginning Campbell put to service three hymns by Newton and two by Cowper. By the year prior to Alexander Campbell's death, these had grown to twenty-nine by the former and fourteen by the latter.

The Presbyterians had split in 1741 over the introduction of hymns into church worship. One group was called "Old Side"; the other, "New Side." By 1761 James Lyon, advocating the "New," brought out *Urania: Or a choice collection of psalm tunes, anthems, and hymns.* One of his songs, 104 years later, was accepted into Christian church song.

Isaac Watts

The man most responsible for the movement from "psalms" to "hymns," and the person most often drawn upon in the formation of Campbell's hymnal, was Isaac Watts (1674-1748). He was a member of the Reformed church and has been considered the outstanding nonconformist theologian of his day. His *Psalms Imitated* had been first printed in 1720 by Benjamin Franklin at Philadelphia. One hundred and forty-three of his songs were to be found in Campbell's book by 1865 and eighteen from the start in 1828.

While Campbell squirmed under the often Calvinistic theology of this epoch maker in song, he did call him the "best of lyric bards in Christian psalmody, though not the most evangelical."

Watts could not be ignored. Up to 1840 the book most widely used among the more conservative American churches was Timothy *Dwight's Watts* (Timothy Dwight, 1752-1817). Campbell did not, with advocates of exclusive psalm singing, label Watts vain for thinking he could improve on God and "instruct the Holy Ghost how to write." He admired Watts' gift for creating devotional lyric and for casting the psalms into the mode of free hymnody.

Watts had proposed in his break from literalism "to teach my author to speak like a Christian." This made the psalms of David usable in the New Testament church, and so had riveted Campbell's interest. Campbell included in his hymnal of 1828 Watts' baptized version of Psalm 72 ("Jesus Shall Reign Where'er the Sun"), Psalm 90 ("O God, Our Help in Ages Past"), Psalm 117 ("From All That Dwell Below the Skies") and Psalm 146 ("I'll Praise My Maker While I've Breath"). He had added by 1843 Psalm 122 ("How Pleas'd and Blest Was I"). Other of Watts' hymns used by our editor were such masterpieces as "Awake Our Souls, Away Our Fears," "There Is a Land of Pure Delight," "How Firm a Foundation" or often we hear Campbell quoting: "When I Survey the Wondrous Cross," or "I'm Not Ashamed to Own My Lord."

Next to Watts, Campbell had drawn upon Phillip Doddridge (1702-1751). He used eight of his songs at the beginning and thirty-six at the end of his influence over the hymnal. Doddridge was a friend and follower of Isaac Watts. Watts' hymns were sermonic—"Homilies all, from text to application!" Doddridge's were

> . . . didactic, because he framed them upon the substance of his sermons to be sung by his congregation, line by line, whilst his doctrine was fresh in their memory (Horton Davies, *The English Free Churches;* London, Oxford University Press, 1952, p. 123).

The further names of Wardlaw, Medley, and Mrs. Steele were important to the first work, for they were the source for three or more songs each. In 1865 three hundred and four different authors or books were listed as sources. Beside the persons already discussed these following people were responsible for at least ten of the hymns: Beddome (15), Bonar (23), Bowring (10), Heber (11), Lyte (13),

Kelly (21), W. T. Moore (13), Ray Palmer (10), and Stennett (10). A minimum of one hymn each were found from such persons as Count Zinzendorf (1700-1760), Madame Guyon (1648-1717), the Countess of Huntingdon (1707-1791), and even President Jefferson Davis (1808-1889).

The Influence of Co-workers

We must note also the Campbell hymnbook's reflection of influence by the songs and hymnals of others in the same movement for "unity in truth."

The "New Light" movement sometimes known as the "Christan connection" or "Christian church," had begun almost simultaneously in different places. In North Carolina, James O'Kelly had come out of Methodism; in Kentucky, Barton W. Stone had left Presbyterianism; and in New England, Abner Jones and Elias Smith had ceased to be Baptists. The followers of these different men had combined in 1806 under the common banner "Christian."

One year earlier Elias Smith (1769-1846) had produced for his people *A Collection of Hymns, for the Use of Christians*, which contained camp-meeting type songs. Abner Jones (1772-1841) was joint editor with Smith in 1809 of *Hymns, Original and Selected*. In New England in 1826 *Hymns, Original and Selected for the Use of Christians*, had come from the *Christian Herald* publisher with Robert Foster as editor.

James O'Kelly, who died two years before the Campbell hymnal appeared in 1828, had left behind him at ninety-two years of age a religious body and a song book. This was called *Hymns and Spiritual Songs Designed for the Use of Christians*. Joseph Thomas (1791-1835), who was active in North Carolina and later in Virginia, at about the same time gave the New Lights *The Pilgrims Hymn Book*.

288

In Kentucky, where Barton W. Stone was influential, his co-laborers John Thompson, David Purviance, and others joined in the production of *The Christian Hymn Book* of 1810.

Since Campbell was joined by many from these similar movements, we believe he was aware of their songs after 1828, if not before. Stone, with Johnson and Scott, became coeditor with Campbell in 1834. Campbell had preached in Kentucky in 1824 and the men had been conscious of each other and their similarities for several years before the union.

Barton Warren Stone had not only written some hymns for the Kentucky revival, but had edited two hymnals for his flock. The first hymnbook was coedited by a Thomas Adams in 1829 and was called *The Christian Hymn Book*. The second, in 1832, was by the same title and possibly was a revision of the former. It was put out in cooperation with John T. Johnson (1788-1857), his coeditor of the periodical *The Christian Messenger*.

The other fellow editor with Campbell in hymnbook production after 1834 was Walter Scott (1796-1861). Musically speaking, he could be called more important than the rest. He was born in Scotland to a professional music teacher, and became a flute player before arriving in America in 1818. He met Campbell about four years later and moved within fourteen miles of him (Steubenville, Ohio) about five years later still. This placed him within the area served by the Mahoning Baptist Association. This group appointed Scott to make evangelistic tours. He had exceptional success with his "five-finger exercise" of faith, repentance, baptism, remission of sins, and gift of the Holy Spirit. He was always concerned with improving church music, writing articles in the *Christian Evangelist* and *Millennial Harbinger*, and was one of the first to use a singing evangelist in his work. William Hayden (1799-1863) was appointed by the Mahoning Association to be Scott's song leader, fellow preacher, and soloist.

Walter Scott had produced *Christian Psalms and Hymns,* a hymnbook separate from Campbell's. He published an edition of *Psalms, Hymns, and Spiritual Songs* at Carthage, Ohio, in 1844, called *The Christian Hymn Book, being a collection of Psalms, Hymns, and Spiritual Songs, compiled by the executive committee of the Ohio Christian Book Association.*

William Baxter, biographer of Scott, because of his musical competence was chosen to assist in creating the 1865 hymnal by the editing committee of the American Christian Missionary Society. Baxter's hymn, "I have No Resting Place on Earth," was given to that edition. The editing committee of five contained two men with a great deal to contribute. One was A. S. Hayden of Ohio (1813-1880); the other was W. T. Moore of Kentucky (1832-1926).

Amos Sutton Hayden's works on music included *An Introduction to Sacred Music* (1834), *Sacred Music* (1834), *The Sacred Melodeon* (1849), *The Hymnist* (1863) and *The Christian Hymn and Tune Book* (1870). Campbell always appreciated Hayden and his efforts to improve church music.

> Our confidence in brother A. S. Hayden, as an adept in the science of sacred music, authorizes us to call the attention of the public to the proposals . . . The disciples in Ohio are so well acquainted with the good taste and musical attainments of brother Hayden, that his name is enough to secure their patronage to this undertaking (*Millennial Harbinger,* November, 1834, p. 575).

290

Three of A. S. Hayden's hymns were in Campbell's hymnal of 1865; one can be found in the 1834 edition.

William Thomas Moore had at least thirteen of his songs in the *Christian Hymn Book* of 1865. They ranged from the Christmas carol "Hark! What Joyful Notes Are Swelling" to the new doxology "Praise, God, Ye Heavenly Hosts Above!" All of the songs rang with adoration and proved true to the last half of the final stanza of his "O That I Had Wings Like a Dove,"

> I'll sing of thy wonderful ways,
>   With all of the glorified throng—
> For ever and ever, thy praise
>   Shall be the one theme of my song
>   (p. 826 in 1865 edition).

As in the songs in the Apocalypse, Christ was the object of worship, man the invited guest, love the amazing force, the eternal kingdom the abiding hope, and the crucifixion the awesome fact.

Here and there in the 1865 edition is found the additional name of a Disciple hymn writer such as Augustus Damon Fillmore (1823-1870) or James S. Lamar (1829-1916); but, in the earlier period, when the selections were in Campbell's control, it was from a large collection of hymns—ancient and modern, Catholic and Protestant, American and foreign, Disciples and non-Disciple—that selections were made and words edited to meet the needs of the churches of Christ or Christian churches springing up across the land.

Chapter Fourteen

DOCTRINAL EMPHASIS

If a man's "creed" is a statement of his beliefs, Alexander Campbell, the believer, had a creed; and his hymnal is a testimony of that faith. If, rather, by *creed* we mean a formal statement of doctrines and official interpretation to which assent is required before Christian fellowship is extended and Christian brotherhood acknowledged, then Mr. Campbell would have denied holding or subscribing to one. He steadfastly rejected "human" creeds or "man-made" tests of orthodoxy. The divinely given creed or "good confession" for apostolic times, and for apostolic Christianity in any time, was considered by him to be the acknowledgment that Jesus was the Christ, the Son of the living God.

> The belief of one fact . . . is all that is requisite, as far as faith goes, to salvation. The belief of this *one fact,* and submission to *one institution* expressive of it, is all that is required of Heaven to admission into the Church . . . The one fact is expressed in a single proposition—that Jesus the Nazarene is the Messiah . . . the one institution is baptism into the name of the Father, and of the Son, and the Holy Spirit (*The Christian System,* p. 101).

Yet he, who spoke much against theologies becoming fences of division among Christians, acknowledged his hymnbook as the clearest announcement of his own understanding of the Sacred Oracles.

Theology Proper

"In the beginning God created the heaven and the earth," commenced the Holy Bible. "The Book of Nature open lies," began the spiritual songs in the hymnal of Alexander Campbell. The world of nature was to him a book declaring the glory of God, but the volume of creation was considered closed to the understanding of men who possessed not the further volume of Sacred Scripture. Thus saith the hymn-book:

> The Book of Nature open lies,
>   With much instruction stor'd;
> And when the Lord anoints our eyes,
>   Its pages light afford.
>
> Philosophers have por'd in vain.
>   And guess'd from age to age;
> For reason's eye could ne'er attain
>   To understand a page.
>
> Though to each star they give a name
>   Its size and motions teach,
> The truths which all the stars proclaim,
>   Their wisdom cannot reach.
>
> With skill to measure earth and sea,
>   And weigh the subtile air,
> They cannot, Lord, discover thee,
>   Thou present ev'ry where.
>
> The knowledge of thy saints excels
>   The wisdom of the schools;
> To them his secrets God reveals,
>   Thou men account them fools.
>
> To them the sun and stars on high,
>   The flowers that paint the field,
> And all the artless birds that fly,
>   Divine instruction yield.
>
> The creatures on their senses press,
>   As witnesses to prove
> Their Saviour's power and faithfulness,
>   His providence and love.

Thus may we study Nature's Book,
  To make us wise indeed!
And pity those who only look
  At what they cannot read.
(*Psalms, Hymns, and Spiritual
Songs*, 1844, p. 77).

This song correctly places Campbell outside the camp of deism. He saw the subjectivity in, and the limitations of rationalism. While greatly influenced by the European Enlightenment, he was committed to the defense of revealed religion. Natural science could not be the basis of religion, he insisted, but the scientific method of Bacon ought to be the tool used in the study of revealed religion.

To the man who had come to faith in that self-disclosure of God in events, especially those centering in Jesus Christ, the book of nature became a companion to the book of revelation. Without the light of the second there would have been no instruction regarding God through the first. The believer found every confirmation of his reasonable faith when he looked at a world created and continuing.

Campbell was certain that He who had created, was sustaining that creation. It was ever under His providential care. There was no problem beyond the wisdom of the Omniscient, no place beyond the eye of the Omnipresent, and no burden beyond the capability of the Omnipotent. Campbell referred in the *Millennial Harbinger* of March, 1837 (p. 117), to Newton's Spiritual Song of affirmation which gave confidence to himself and to others:

Though troubles assail, and danger affright,
Though friends should all fail, and foes all unite;
Yet one thing secures us, whatever betide,
The Scripture assures us, *The Lord will provide*.

The birds without barn or store-house are fed;
From them let us learn to trust for our bread:
His saints what is fitting shall ne'er be denied,
So long as 'tis written, *The Lord will provide.*

We may, like the ships, by tempests be tost
On perilous deeps, but cannot be lost:
Though Satan enrages the wind and the tide,
The promise engages, *The Lord will provide.*

His call we obey, like Abrah'm of old,
Not knowing our way, but faith makes us bold;
For though we are strangers, we have a good guide,
And trust, in all dangers, *The Lord will provide.*

No strength of our own, or goodness, we claim;
But since we have known the Saviour's great name,
In this our strong tower for safety we hide—
The Lord is our power—*The Lord will provide.*

When life sinks apace, and death is in view,
The word of his grace shall comfort us through;
Not fearing or doubting, with Christ on our side,
We hope to die shouting, *The Lord will provide.*
(*Psalms, Hymns, and Spiritual Songs,* 1844,
pp. 92, 93).

Most wonderful of all to the editor was the confidence that the Creator-Sustainer was also redeeming love. As Isaac Errett wrote in the *Millennial Harbinger* of September, 1865 (pp. 396-407), "Protestant hymnology" might say with Watts,

> Once 'twas a dreadful seat of wrath,
> And shot devouring flame;
> Our God appeared consuming fire,
> And vengeance was his name.

Or it might join "a choir of grimy demons to sing,"

> His nostrils breathe out fiery streams;
> And from his awful tongue
> A sovereign voice divided the flames,
> And thunder roars along, etc.

Disciple hymnology (as traced, for example, in the index to the *Christian Hymnbook* of 1877), preferred to sing of God's being and perfections, compassion, dominion, eternity, glory and majesty, goodness, greatness, holiness, immutability, invisibility, justice, love, mercy, omnipotence, omnipresence, omniscience, providence, unsearchableness, wisdom, Word and works.

The Holy Spirit became the subject of discussion in several articles on Christian psalmody in Campbellian literature. Besides noting that Scriptural prayers were addressed *to* the Father, *through* the Son, *by* the Spirit's prompting, rather than directly to the Spirit as in many hymns; Campbell pointed to these additional hymnic inconsistencies with Biblical terminology or thought:

(1) The Spirit was addressed as if still in heaven, overlooking the fact that the Spirit descended after Christ had ascended. So Doddridge, in Campbell's opinion, ought not to have sung, "Come, sacred Spirit, from above," any more than Peter at Caesarea Philippi should have said to Jesus, "Come down from heaven and walk on the earth," while He stood before him.

(2) The Holy Spirit was in the same song and the next line told:

> And fill the coldest heart with love;
> O, turn to flesh the flinty stone;
> And let thy sovereign power be known.

This made the assembled congregation a band of un-converted sinners that, because of prayer addressed to the Spirit and by an instant impulse of His sovereign power, would become what through prayer to Father and Son they could not be. Was the Spirit more accessible than the other persons in the Godhead? Need man ask the Spirit to come when He already requests us to come? "As the human body without the Spirit, is dead; so a church, without the Holy Spirit is dead also," wrote Campbell in the *Millennial Harbinger* of August, 1844 (p. 378). The church already had the Holy Spirit or it was not the church.

(3) The Spirit was asked to do what He had already done. Before editing his own hymnal, Campbell had seen the need for such reform on the basis of logic, if nothing else. He first quoted:

> Faith—'tis a precious grace
> Where'er it is bestow'd!
> It boasts of a celestial birth,
> And is the gift of God.

> Jesus it owns a King,
> An all-atoning Priest;
> It claims no merit of its own,
> But looks for all in Christ.

> To him it leads the soul
> When tilled with deep distress,
> Flies to the fountain of his blood,
> And trusts his righteousness.

> Since 'tis thy work alone,
> And that divinely free,
> Lord, send the spirit of thy Son
> To work this faith in me.

297

Then he noted:

> In the conclusion the singer is made to act a singular part; first to declare that he believes that Jesus is a King, an all-atoning priest; that faith leads the soul to him, flies to the fountain of his blood, and trusts his righteousness; and yet, after having sung all this, he represents himself as destitute of such a faith as he has been singing, and prays for the spirit of Jesus Christ to *work* this faith in him! . . . To convert the above sentiments into plain prose, it reads thus: "I believe that faith is a precious grace, the gift of God, of celestial origin. I believe that Jesus is King and an all-atoning Priest; that his righteousness is worthy of my trust, and his blood purifies me from sin. No, I don't believe this but, Lord, send the Spirit of thy Son, who I believe works this grace in men's hearts; and as I don't believe, work this faith in me!" (*Christian Baptist*, August 6, 1827, p. 395).

Emphasis on Christology

Psalms, Hymns, and Spiritual Songs, by its arrangement and content, was strongly Christological. Instead of turning with Calvin to the inspired psalms of David, Campbell chose, with Luther, hymns with Christ at the center. Indeed, in the preface to the 1851 edition, he wrote:

> We have made the divinely inspired psalmody of the sweet Psalmist of Israel our *beau ideal* of Christian psalmody, with the mere difference of dispensation.

But this "mere difference" was, in fact, very major. David's psalms were exemplary for all praise and prayer; yet, as to matter and subject, the mixing of law and gospel would have pleased a "Judaizer" in Paul's day, but not a Disciple of Christ in Campbell's era.

Writing on "Christian Psalmody," he pled that:

Christian faith, Christian hope, Christian love, and Christian devotion, prayer, and praise, differ from every other thing called by the words, faith, hope, love, devotion, prayer, and praise, known or practiced on earth. The Christian horizon is much more spacious and magnificent than was the Jewish, or the Gentile, or the Patriarchal . . . if Psalmody ought to be correspondent with the superior attributes of the dispensation to which we are called. All the parts of Christian worship, public, domestic, and private should be unique, correspondent, harmonious.

He then noted the many topics regarding God's goodness on which saints in 1844 could unite with "fathers Noah, Abraham, Moses, Samuel, and all the patriarchs and prophets" in sympathy and praise. Yet, conscious of the distinction between Christianity and Judaism, he reached this finale:

And, in common with us of this era, could all the Jewish saints participate in the sublime veneration and worship of that bright, and awful, and transcendent justice, truth, and purity, which once irradiated Horeb's proudest summit, and which gleamed in the faces of trembling millions in the rocky desert; and exhorted from infant lips and hoary sires, words of simultaneous terror and alarm, prayers and supplications, unheard before or since, around the base of awful Sinai.

But there are themes connected with another mount which only Christians know, and of which none but Christians can either speak or sing. These are the sublime themes which give to Christian psalmody its peculiar and sacred enchantment. 'Tis in view of these the Christian's heart is enlarged, his soul fired, and his tongue loosed, to tell of things unknown, unfelt, unsung by Noah, Daniel, or Job.

Nothing, then, that keeps not time and melody with these sublime compositions of grandeur, majesty, and love, of which the Holy Spirit is the heaven-inspiring muse, suits the pages of a Christian psalter, and comports with the sweet, touching, melting strains of our Christian Zion.

It is obvious, then, that the first and most striking peculiarity of Christian psalmody is, that Messiah, in His fulness of grace and glory is the all commanding and soul subduing theme. This is the point in which it differs from all the poetry spoken or sung from Adam to Noah, and from Noah to the coronation of Mary's Son in heaven. He is the *Alpha* and the *Omega*, the beginning, middle, and the end of the Christian hymn-book. Whether the compositions are of the narrative, the declarative or ecstatic character, Christ is the theme—'Tis Him first, Him last, Him midst, and without end. Amen and Amen! (*Millennial Harbinger*, February, 1844, p. 83, 84).

A year before producing his first hymnal, Campbell was complaining both of clergymen who preached up "Sinai instead of Calvary, Moses instead of Christ,' and of congregations that sang hymns like "Awaked by Sinai's Awful Sound." Concerning this song he wrote, "I know of nothing more anti-evangelical." He agreed with, and "often commended," the hymn written by Isaac Watts that began,

> 'Tis not the law of ten commands,
>   On holy Sinai given,
> Or sent to man by Moses' hands,
>   Can bring us safe to heaven.

and had the final verse,

> Israel rejoice! Now Joshua leads
>   He'll bring your tribes to rest:
> So far the Saviour's name exceeds
>   The ruler [Moses] and the priest [Aaron].

300

Describing a model service for a typical church in his nine-teenth-century reformation, Campbell recorded the opening hymn "Christ the Lord Is Risen Today!" Reporting a visit to one of the churches (*Millennial Harbinger*, December, 1830, p. 87), he told of the presiding officer saying, "Let us begin the public worship of Almighty *God* by singing—

> *Jesus,* in thee our eyes behold
> A thousand glories more
> Than the rich gems and polish'd gold
> The sons of Aaron wore."

Refuting the charge of Unitarianism he called to witness the hymn "sung in all the churches of the Reformation":

> Jesus, we hail thee Israel's King;
> And now to thee our tribute bring;
> Nor do we fear to bow to thee—
> They worship *God* who worship thee.

Jesus was considered the proper object of praise, as in the "Christian doxologies" found in Paul and the Apocalypse. He was adored as the Christian's example, as heaven's Messiah, and as God incarnate. The name of Jesus Christ was loved and hallowed by the very chosen designations "disciples of Christ," "churches of Christ," "Christians." The voices of former "denominationalists," now could be heard in their frontier churches blending their voices together in the singing of song 20:

> There's no name among men nor angels so bright,
> As in the name of Jesus, the Father's delight;
> The joy of his children, they speak of this name,
> And sweetly its praises in songs they proclaim.
> In all Christian Churches this name is ador'd,
> As their shield and glory, with cheerful accord; . . .
> (*Psalms, Hymns, and Spiritual Songs,* 1843, p. 95).

Chapter Fifteen

SONGS OF SALVATION

An age-old question asks, "What is man?"

Is he a groveling "worm," or God's highest creation? Arthur Schlesinger, Jr., of Harvard University, reminds of the Calvinistic view in "The Age of Alexander Campbell," and relates the incident when:

> John Quincy Adams, hearing a minister quote Isaac Watts' view that men were more base and brutish than the beasts, reflected, "If Watts had said this on a weekday to any one of his parishioners, would he not have knocked him down"? (*The Sage of Bethany: A Pioneer in Broadcloth,* compiled by Perry E. Gresham; St. Louis: The Bethany Press, 1960, p. 29).

Campbell would not have sung with Isaac Watts at this point; but on numerous occasions with head high and shoulders erect, he did join with John Newton:

> And what in yonder world above
> Is ransom'd man ordain'd to be?
> With honor, holiness, and love,
> No angel more adorn'd than he!
> Before the throne, and first in song,
> Man shall his hallelujahs raise;
> While countless angels round him throng,
> And swell the chorus of his praise
> (from "Lord, What Is Man?").

In the *Millennial Harbinger* of May, 1863 (p. 224), Campbell called this "the most sublime verse ever sung by mortal man." Man, indeed, was a sinner and a fallen being, but his depravity was not so absolute that he should sing with the Calvinists, "Our nature's totally depraved—The heart a sink of sin. . . ." Neither was he stone-dead spiritually, and

302

so completely helpless that there remained no freedom of will. Man was able (even if not ready and willing) to respond to God's offer of forgiveness.

God was not to Campbell a capricious Oriental despot, but the heavenly Father; and Jesus was a gracious friend. Prodigal sons needed only to return to their God. The "invitation hymn," therefore held a significant place in churches after the New Testament order. That no man was rejected of God unless he rejected himself was clear from the hymnal:

> Come, sinners, to the gospel feast,
> Let ev'ry soul be Jesus' guest;
> You need not one be left behind,
> For God has bidden all mankind.
>
> Hark! 'tis the Saviour's gracious call,
> The invitation is to all;
> Come, all the world—come, sinner, thou;
> All things in Christ are ready now
> (*Psalms, Hymns, and Spiritual Songs;*
> p. 203 in 1844 edition).

Should some song contain stern warning, as did "Stop, Poor Sinner, Stop and Think," it nevertheless would end with promise:

> But as yet there is a hope,
>   You may his mercy know;
> Though his arm be lifted up,
>   He still forbears the blow:
> 'Twas for sinners Jesus died,
>   Sinners he invites to come;
> None who come shall be denied,
>   He says, "There still is room"
> (Song 134 in 1844 edition).

303

Campbell would not join the "progressive" of his day who would not sing "a hymn indicative of faith in the sacrificial and atoning efficacy of the death of Christ." The grace of God made known in history, especially at Calvary, was now proclaimed to each new generation through the powerful gospel. This good news was the announcement, not only of what God had done, but of what man was to do. Man's part was to respond to God's part. He was neither to be passive and fatalistically to accept his destiny, nor to be overemotional in the experiences of his salvation. The reasonable religion of the book of Acts, as Campbell understood it, revealed not only "acts" done by him by the Lord, but "acts" to be done or steps to be taken to enter into covenant with Him.

> Wisdom divine ordain'd the plan
> To save rebellious, fallen man;
> Attend, you sons of men, give ear;
> The righteousness of God is near.
>
> The Saviour sends the heralds forth,
> From east to west, from south to north,
> Go preach to all—to Israel first,
> *Believe, repent, and be immers'd.*
>
> In spirit Peter preach'd aloud
> To the astonish'd, list'ning crowd;
> Convinc'd, they cry—What shall we do
> T' escape from everlasting woe?
>
> Reform, he cried—in Jesus' name
> Be all immers'd, despise the shame;
> Remission full the Lord will give,
> The Spirit too you shall receive.

This is the way ordain'd by God
To enter his divine abode—
His church on earth—come, enter in,
No longer serve the tyrant sin.

Haste and escape the threat'ning storm;
Believe in Jesus, and reform;
Rise—be immers'd without delay,
And wash your num'rous sins away
(Song 129 in 1844 edition).

Ecclesiology and the Ordinances

Evangelistic meetings in Christian churches, and lecture-ships in Christian colleges, often center their discussions around the topic of "the church." Alexander Campbell held a high view of ecclesiology. He possessed a group consciousness which makes his teachings regarding "the nature of the unity we seek" worthy of study in ecumenical circles today.

As his father had prepared a *Declaration and Address*, which affirmed that "the church on earth is essentially, intentionally, and constitutionally one," he had produced *Psalms, Hymns, and Spiritual Songs* wherein was preached the need of harmony in hearts and of doctrine, as well as the harmony of vocal sounds. No matter what might have been the mental image conjured up by "Campbellites," their hymnbook directed them to sing,

> Come, dear friends, we are all brethren,
>   Bound for Canaan's happy land;
> Come unite and walk together;
>   Christ, our leader, gives command.

> Cease to boast of party merit,
>> Wound the cause of God no more,
> Be united by his spirit,
>> Zion's peace again restore.
>
> Now our hand, our heart, and spirit,
>> Here in fellowship we give;
> Let us love and peace inherit,
>> Show the world how Christians live . . .
> (Part II, Hymn 43, in 1844 edition).

Several songs were directed to the Christians among the sects, such as "Let Christians All Agree, and Peace Among Them Spread"; or, "O May the Saints of Ev'ry Name Unite to Serve the Lamb." There was a "togetherness" to be felt with Christians in every clime and of every color. The individual congregation was a part of the world-encircling church of Christ. Individualism, as common in the "I" and "my" songs, was balanced by the "we" hymns.

A typical service in a church of Christ might have begun, "Bless With Thy Presence, Lord, This Place, Where We Together Meet"; or it might have ended, "Blest Be the Tie that Binds Our Hearts in Christian Love."

Love of God, love of truth, love of each other—these were requisites to spiritual union.

> How sweet, how heav'nly is the sight,
>> When those that love the Lord
> In one another's peace delight,
>> And so fulfil the word:
>
> When each can feel his brother's sigh,
>> And with him hear a part,
> When sorrow flows from eye to eye,
>> And joy from heart to heart:

When free from envy, scorn, and pride,
  Our wishes all above,
Each can his brother's failings hide,
  And show a brother's love
(Song 46 in 1844 edition).

Nowhere could Christian love be manifest more effectively than at the family table in God's house—the Communion table. In Seceder Presbyterian gatherings, as Campbell knew from experience, only those with "Communion tokens" could partake. The Campbell hymnal made clear that amongst disciples of Christ, "None are excluded thence, but those who do themselves exclude" (Song 65 in 1844 edition). The Christian's "Lord" was host at that table, and none else dared debar. Where ecumenicity was proclaimed, but Communion refused, Christian unity did not exist.

How pleasing to behold and see
  The friends of Jesus all agree,
To sit around the sacred board
  As members of one common Lord . . .

To all we freely give our hand,
  Who love the Lord in ev'ry land;
For all are one in Christ our head,
  To whom be endless honors paid.

Here, by the bread and wine, we view
  What boundless curses were our due;
But through the off'ring of our Lord,
  More than was lost is now restor'd.

Let wrath and strife, those seeds of hell
  Ne'er in the Christian bosom dwell
But love and union, by his blood,
  Prove us the chosen heirs of God
(Song 44 in 1844 edition).

The bread and wine were called "memorials," "tokens," and "pledges" in Hymn 158. With backward glance the mind first went to the "upper room," where "'Twas on That Night When Doom'd to Know . . . The Saviour of the World Took Bread."

> Thus assembling, we, by faith,
> Till he come, show forth his death;
> Of his flesh this loaf's the sign,
> And we view his blood in wine
> (Hymn 136, Part II, 1844 edition).

The day of meeting, the first day of every week, the resurrection day, was held to be the ideal "setting" for this "gem" of Communion. The table told of His death for sins; the day spoke of His resurrection for justification. The two facts, death and resurrection, were inseparable. So were the ordinances of the Lord's Supper and the Lord's Day.

> This is the day the first ripe sheaf
> Before the Lord was wav'd, . . .

So began a psalm about the resurrection of Christ, who became the firstfruits of them that slept.

> This is the day the Spirit came
> With us on earth to stay, . . .

and

> This day the Christian Church began, . . .

continued other stanzas, until the distinction was drawn between the "seventh day of the Old Testament" and the "first day of the New":

308

This joyful day let us observe;
  Redemption's work is done;
The Jewish Sabbaths are no more;
  The earthly rest is gone, . . .
(Psalm 28, pp. 38, 39, in 1844
edition).

With Sunday being the memorial of a Christian's hope and the occasion for his confession of faith, it was considered the

Day of all the week the best,
Emblem of eternal rest
("Sanctification of the Lord's
Day," *Millennial Harbinger*,
October, 1850, p. 541).

The psychological response of remembering God's sacrifice on man's behalf was the sacrificial giving on the worshiper's part. It is claimed often that the *Millennial Harbinger* did not say enough on the topic of money stewardship; but the subject of money and giving was not absent from the hymnal.

Hymn 139 (1844), for instance, began, "The gold and silver are the Lord's." In six uncompromising stanzas was declared the importance of giving to finance world evangelism. Hymn 167, beginning "With My Substance I Will Honor," in twenty-four lines asked "the saints of every station" to "gladly join to spread His fame" and promote "His kingdom."

The church and the kingdom were believed to be coextensive. In the weekly Communion service, Jesus was drinking "new" in the Father's kingdom with His fellow-citizens of that kingdom of heaven. If that kingdom was to extend its borders, as Isaiah had predicted, the soldier of the cross not only must give of his money but also of his effort.

> Must we be carried to the skies
>   On beds of flowery ease,
> While others fought to win the prize,
>   And sail'd through bloody seas?

As an editor concerned for the advance of the Christian cause, Campbell often concluded his column:

> Sure I must fight if I would reign;
>   Increase my courage, Lord.   *editor*

The ordinance of immersion, by its action, told of the death which was proclaimed by the Lord's Supper and of the resurrection preached by the Lord's Day. Total immersion implied to Campbell a total surrender to his Lord and total dedication to his cause, as practiced in Christian stewardship.

Hymnologist Louis F. Benson finds the baptismal hymns used by Alexander Campbell a revelation of his opinion on the design and mode of this initiatory rite.

Mr. Campbell used the word "immerse," and not the anglicized Greek word "baptize," and he criticized Silas W. Leonard for accommodating "Methodist friends" in his *Christian Psalmist* by leaving out what would "impinge on 'baby sprinkling.'"

Our example, Jesus, had been immersed, according to Campbell, and in that very instance had declared that He would be the Saviour, and not just a pattern or a teacher.

> In Jordan's tide the Baptist stands
>   Immersing the repenting Jews;
> The Son of God the rite demands,
>   Nor dares the holy man refuse:
> Jesus descends beneath the wave
>   The emblem of his future grave
> (Psalm 9 in 1844 edition).

310

Chapter Sixteen

SONGS OF THE PAST AND THE FUTURE

The *Christian Hymn Book* after 1865, in its first several songs, reflects Alexander Campbell's insistent theme that the revelation that comes through Scripture far outshines the light of nature. Hymn one sounded the pitch in its opening stanza:

> The heavens declare thy glory, Lord!
>   In every star thy wisdom shines;
> But then our eyes behold thy word,
>   We read thy name in fairer lines
> (p. 5 in 1877 edition; the hymn has
> six stanzas).

Hymn two blended in through its second verse:

> All nature shows thy boundless love,
> In worlds below and worlds above;
> But in thy blessed word I trace
> The richer glories of thy grace.

The believer was thought to see the hand of God in the created world; but the nature of God, and the will of God, and the very existence of God, was to be known only through revelation. Campbell believed that knowledge came first from sensation and then from reflection. God had revealed himself in history, especially in Jesus of Nazareth. Historic testimony regarding that revelation was the means of his faith. The witness borne by the apostles, whose eyes had seen and whose ears had heard, enabled every later age to believe on Christ "through their word."

The revelation of God had been progressive. The God, who of olden time had spoken through prophets, had spoken more fully through His Son. The light brought by the gospel of Christ was not to be considered of the same

311

candescense as that light which had come earlier through
the law of Moses.

> The God who once to Israel spoke,
> From Sinai's top, in fire and smoke,
> In gentle strains of gospel grace
> Invites us now to seek his face
> (From Hymn 56 in 1844 edition of
> *Psalms, Hymns, and Spiritual
> Songs*).

Use of the Old Testament

In the Old Testament, the New Testament Christian could
find that which was written for his admonition upon whom
the end of the ages had come. Beside examples of faith and
obedience and insight into God's dealings with men, it contained predictive prophecies and instructive types and shadows
of Christ and His gospel. The typological use made of the
pre-Christian Scriptures is seen in the songs Mr. Campbell
selected.

> When Israel's tribes were parch'd with thirst
> Forth from the rock the waters burst,
> And all their future journey through
> Yielded them drink and gospel too.
>
> In Moses' rod a type they saw
> Of his severe and fiery law;
> The smitten rock prefigur'd him
> From whose pierc'd side all blessings stream.
>
> But let the Saviour's praise resound;
> In him refreshing streams are found;
> Which pardon, strength, and comfort give,
> And thirsty sinners drink and live
> (Pp. 55, 56, Part II, in 1844 edition).

"Finish'd all the types and shadows of the once unfinish'd law!" rang the third verse of Psalm 20 in the edition of 1844, "The types and shadows of the word unite in Christ, the Man, the Lord," resounded the fourth stanza of Hymn 2 of the same arrangement. Verses three and four of Psalm 3 echoed antiphonally:

> The types bore witness to his names
> Obtain'd their chief design and ceas'd—
> The incense and the bleeding lamb,
> The ark, the altar, and the priest.
>
> Predictions in abundance join
> To pour their witness on his head:
> Jesus, we bow before thy throne,
> And own thee as the promis'd seed.

The Bible was considered a dependable record of God's revelation of himself in history, because its penmen had written under inspiration. From the beginning and for the use of the churches, Campbell had chosen the hymn of Fawcett "How Precious Is the Book Divine, by Inspiration Given!" and that hymn of Mrs. Steel, "Father of Mercies! in Thy Word," which sings of "these celestial lines," "these heavenly pages," and "thy sacred word."

Being under the Spirit's control, the prophets of olden times and those of apostolic times had spoken forth information from above and needed not to copy here below from other religions. Cowper was thought to be accurate in his conclusion:

> What glory gilds the sacred page,
>   Majestic like the sun!
> It gives a light to every age—
>   It gives, but borrows none
> (p. 132 in 1829 edition).

313

By following simple "Rules of Interpetation" the believing frontiersman, like "the wayfaring man, though a fool" spoken of by Isaiah, need not err in his understanding of the Book of books.

> Blind unbelief is sure to err,
>   And scan his works in vain:
> God is his own interpreter,
>   And he will make it plain
> (*Millennial Harbinger,* November, 1851, p. 621).

Eschatology and Millennial Optimism

Through the many years of the *Millennial Harbinger,* there was that page which recorded the transference of membership from the portion of the church militant on earth to that section of the church triumphant in the heavens. It seemed only natural that a Christian brother or sister would quote some song about the supernatural, when writing to the editor about the death of a loved one. The "obituary" column often glowed with the hope of immortality:

> Jesus can make the dying bed
>   Feel soft as downy pillows are,
> While on his breast I lean my head,
>   And breathe my life out sweetly there
> (May, 1844, p. 239).

Or again

> Sweet is the scene when Christians die;
>   When holy souls retire to rest!
> How mildly beams the closing eye!
> How gently heaves the expiring breast
> (August, 1851, p. 480).

314

Death, according to the faith expressed in discipledom's song, was natural, certain, and anticipated. Life was fleeting, but not to be grasped. The body was temporal and subject to pain; however it would not be so in its final state. The child of God was to find Christ's death the "antidote" of his own and sing triumphantly with Watts from the earliest to the latest Campbell hymnal, "I'll Praise My Maker While I've Breath."

Heaven was the happy home, the abiding city, the land of rest. John's *Apocalypse*, that painted on the canvas of the imagination with brush dipped in the colors of symbolism, was the basis for a familiar and well-known song about "the heavenly Jerusalem":

> Whose walls are all of precious stones,
>   Most glorious to behold!
> Whose gates are rightly set with pearls,
>   Whose streets are paved with gold.
>
> Those holy gates forever *bar*
>   Pollution, sin, and shame;
> None can obtain admission there
>   But followers of the Lamb
> (*Millennial Harbinger,* September,
> 1839, p. 398).

What made heaven heavenly was the absence of sin's penalties and the presence of Christ, with His eternally satisfying love. From such a fellowship, no retreat could occur; to such a meeting, no earth tie should detain. Since time marched on so rapidly, heaven (beyond death) was considered "not far away." If Christ did not come for the Christian shortly in the second coming, He would come quickly for his soul in death. Alexander Campbell, while believing in the judgment and hell, did not give the subject the large place the Methodists did in their singing. "Day of Judgment, Day of Wonders" appeared in his hymnbook from 1834 onward.

The Millerites had Campbell's attention but not his confidence. He was not a "pre-millennialist" in the Adventist sense of that word, but he did believe in both the "second-coming" and the "millennium." He placed in his early hymnal, and continued to sing:

> When the King of kings comes,
> When the Lord of lords comes;
> We shall have a joyful day
>   When the King of kings comes:
>
> To see the nations broken down,
> And kingdoms once of great renown,
> And saints, now suff'ring, wear the crown
>   When the King of kings comes!

While never doubting the visible return of Jesus Christ, he never thought of this as occurring at the time when the kingdom would come. Jesus had ascended to sit at God's right hand. He had been reigning, since that first Pentecost after His resurrection. He would continue his rule as David's successor until the believers' resurrection.

The millennium of Revelation was believed to be a victory that was to be expected upon earth by the on-marching church. This was neither William Miller's millennium with cataclysmic beginnings nor Robert Owen's millennium with human beginnings. In the nineteenth century, America was a land of utopian dreams, and the church was finding apparent success in planting the banner of Calvary on foreign soil through missionary endeavor. Campbell saw Christian unity on the horizon bringing the dawn of a new day. He

316

picked the name *Millennial Harbinger* for his paper because it was designed to herald the annihilation of sectarianism, the restoration of "pure speech" and the Christian ordinances, and larger measures of the Holy Spirit.

His hymnbook told the same story and shared the same optimism:

> The crystal stream comes down from heav'n
> > It issues from the throne;
> The floods of strife away are driv'n,
> > The church becomes but one:
>
> That peaceful union we shall know,
> > And live upon his love,
> And sing and shout his name below,
> > As angels do above.
>
> A thousand years shall roll around,
> > The church shall be complete;
> Fall'd by the last loud trumpet's sound,
> > Their Saviour's face to meet
> (From song 54 in 1844 edition).

Caught in the flames of enthusiasm, Mr. Campbell visualized "the time not far distant, when—

> No longer hosts encount'ring hosts
> > Shall crowds of slain deplore;
> They'll hang the trumpet in the hall,
> > And study war no more!
> (*Millennial Harbinger*, July, 1848,
> p. 386).

He envisioned the Bible toppling "the atheistic coalition of France," and the church bringing all nations to acknowledge their "Lord." With each victory envisioned, there was a triumphant song waiting to be sung:

The Prince of Salvation in triumph is riding,
And glory attends him along his bright way,
The news of his grace on the breezes are gliding,
   And nations are owning his sway.

Ride on, in thy greatness, thou conq'ring Saviour;
Let thousands of thousands submit to thy reign,
Acknowledge thy goodness, entreat for thy favor,
   And follow thy glorious train.

Ride on, till the compass of thy great dominion
The globe shall encircle from pole unto pole;
And mankind, cemented with friendship and
  union,
   Obey thee with heart and with soul,

Then, loud shall ascend from each sanctified
  nation,
The voice of thanksgiving, the chorus of praise,
And heaven shall echo the song of salvation
   In rich and melodious lays
(From Hymn 14, Part II, 1844 edition).

Joy, optimism, victory, good cheer radiated from every page of Campbell's hymnal, for the suffering Christ always was viewed from *this* side of the empty tomb. Campbell is not visualized fully until we hear his songs, watch him celebrate the fourth of July with "heartfelt joy" in an atmosphere "good for body, soul, and spirit," or see him enjoy a festive meal (*Millennial Harbinger*, September, 1838, p. 431). He had the characters in a story say:

. . . You seem to eat as if it were the performance of a duty you owe yourself, rather than a gratification and a pleasure which was to be enjoyed as one of the kind bounties of nature. Do we not sing in all our churches,

       Religion never was design'd
       To make our pleasures less . . .

(*Millennial Harbinger*, July, 1834, p. 319).

How could the sour note of sadness, or the minor chord of gloom, displace the major gospel sound of victory in a church that met on Christ's resurrection day and proclaimed through its baptism confidence in that resurrection? Rather, they sang:

> I know that my Redeemer lives:
> What comfort this sweet sentence gives!
> He lives, he lives who once was dead,
> He lives, my ever-living head!
>
> He lives to bless me with his love,
> He lives to plead for me above,
> He lives my hungry soul to feed,
> He lives to bless in time of need.
>
> He lives to grant me rich supply,
> He lives to guide me with his eye,
> He lives to comfort me when faint,
> He lives to hear my soul's complaint.
>
> He lives to silence all my fears,
> He lives to wipe my flowing tears,
> He lives to calm my troubled heart,
> He lives all blessings to impart.
>
> He lives, my kind, wise, heav'nly friend
> He lives, and loves me to the end;
> He lives, and while he lives I'll sing,
> He lives, my Prophet, Priest, and King!
>
> He lives, and grants me daily breath;
> He lives, and I shall conquer death;
> He lives my mansion to prepare,
> He lives to bring me safely there.
>
> He lives, all glory to his name!
> He lives, my Jesus, still the same!
> O the sweet joy this sentence gives—
> *I know that my Redeemer lives!*
> (Song 31 in 1844 edition).

Chapter Seventeen

ARRANGING THE HYMNBOOK

Few persons, not experienced in selecting hymns, or in arranging and preparing a book of psalmody, can appreciate the labor and attention necessary to all that is wanting to its perfection in a literary and mechanical point of view, as well as to what is essential to its purity of sentiment and style and adaptation to the wants of a community in all its relations, personal, domestic and congregational (*Millennial Harbinger,* August, 1852, pp. 473, 474).

These words were written by Alexander Campbell after twenty-four years of experience in hymnbook editing. Yet, "labor and attention," energy and thought, are productive only when guided by an established criterion. What was the standard by which a religious community's hymnal ought to be measured? Or what was the ideal toward which such a hymnal should strive?

One Hymnal

It was Campbell's conviction that Disciples of Christ should have but one hymnal as they had but one Bible. To attain this important ideal, he made several concessions. Upon the uniting of forces in the 1832 coalition of "Stonites" and "Campbellites," he pled for merging the hymnbooks of both groups, "making the twain one." While, in the "give and take" demanded by coeditorship, other of Campbell's preferences in hymnody eventually would have to be compromised, this idea of one and only one hymnbook was not to be sacrificed. The singing of any hymn to a variety of tunes, however, was of no serious concern.

When other hymnals began to appear and requests for greater numbers of hymns became general, Campbell donated the copyright of the hymnbook to the American Christian Missionary Society rather than to encourage, by his refusal to yield, the "evil" of a complexity of hymnals in the churches. The movement, it was believed, would be "kept continually in a state of mutation by the introduction of new books" (*Millennial Harbinger,* December, 1848, p. 711).

For Campbell no very large hymnal was considered necessary. A few hymns well learned enabled the congregation to be a worshiping assembly. Divine example indicated that if one hundred and fifty psalms were adequate for the Jew; such a fact should be noted by the Christians.

The number of stanzas in a given hymn, however, needed not to be limited. For mechanical reasons songs were later shortened when the words began to be printed between the staves. Since Campbell's work did not contain musical notes, there was no need to destroy a poet's progression of thought by cutting his work to the "convenient" size of three or four verses.

Scriptural and Poetic

Campbell visualized for his people a Scriptural hymnbook, patterned after the Old Testament psalms "in all points of good taste, good sense, fervor, feeling, profound devotion, divine sentiment, and every praise" (*Millennial Harbinger,* March, 1843, p. 129). The subject matter was to be entirely evangelical. As false doctrines were not to be heard from the pulpits, so they were not to be in the pews.

The hymnal was to be a worship book—not a dictionary. Isaac Watts' four stanzas on Hebrews 11, "Faith Is the Brightest Evidence," was admittedly accurate definition and sound doctrine. But it was no more a proper subject for sacred song than Watts' description of regeneration in "Not All the Outward Forms on Earth." The editor of the *Millennial Harbinger* reasoned:

> The ode to faith, or of faith, is a pretty ode, good poetry, good sense; but is no part of the worship of God to sing the definition of a word or a thing. Christian psalters ought not to be poetic dictionaries, nor rhyming grammars. . . . No one can either praise God or refresh the soul of any one by singing it. . . . Can any one show, in the whole 150 inspired songs, a psalm or hymn of such a category! If not, however useful to sectaries and retailers of definitions such worship be, it has no favor in heaven, and ought to have no place in the Christian worship (June, 1842, p. 279, 280).

Similarly, Isaac Errett, one of the committee of five given the task of editing the Campbell hymnal of 1865, refers to a hymn on the "unpoetical theme" of depravity, remarking:

> I would rather seek poetical inspiration in the fumes and brine of the Dead Sea, or attempt to extract a theme of praise out of the apples of Sodom, than to write hymns on human depravity, to be sung in churches. (*Millennial Harbinger*, September, 1865, p. 401).

As men sing love songs, songs in praise of heroes, or songs of triumph in war, Christian men sing of the love of God, of praise to the hero and captain of their salvation, and of the triumphs of their King's glorious warfare.

While Campbell would not have his hymnbook inaccurate Scripturally, his stress was still not on "orthodoxy." The hymns in the New Testament, he said, have Christ as the theme and not "the speculative theory of a sectarian profession." Attached to the first hymnal, as a conclusion, was an "Essay on Prayer." This began:

When the human mind is indoctrinated into certain modes of thinking and reasoning, every exercise of the mind in religion is tinctured with the distinguishing tenents which constitute the capital points of the system. So that the refined doctrinal Christian thinks, speaks, and acts in religious matters, as if the divine approbation and the enjoyment of heaven were made to depend upon the right opinions or correct speculations on the topics of revelation. Hence we find that the zeal for correct sentiments gives a peculiar turn to every act of devotion . . . as though our acceptance depended upon the ideas or views which the mind takes. . . . It is not uncommon to find our favorite points in speculative theology to engross the whole contents of a prayer as well as of a sermon (p. 172 in 1829 edition).

Simple and Usable

Being an aid for private and corporate worship, the ideal hymnal was to inspire devotion. The poetry was to be grave, chaste, in good taste, and express joyful emotion. The words were to breathe the one spirit of a fervent, humble worshiper of God in sincerity and truth. Jesus had taught His disciples what is called the Lord's Prayer. In this "the manner" was considered by Campbell "as admirable as the matter." Hence, our praise and petition was to be uttered in a "most humble and reverential style," with the language of each psalm, hymn, or ode being appropriate to the feeling of the worshiper and the lyrical sensitivity of the poet.

The language of prayer, spoken or sung, was to be plain and unaffected language. The simplicity in wording was to be accompanied by a simplicity in arrangement or indexing to "afford easy and agreeable reference." To be an "aid" in the worship of God, the book of songs must be helpful and practical. It must contain a sufficient variety of subjects

323

to be adequate for such occasions as arise in a Christian community.

Now and again some news articles in the *Harbinger* noted how appropriate to the reported occasion was the hymn sung, as on the day of the ordination of Charles Louis Loos when the brethren united in singing those "very appropriate lines" beginning—

> Go with thy servant, Lord,
>   His every step attend;
> All needful help to him afford,
>   And bless him to the end
> (*Millennial Harbinger*,
> February, 1850, p. 101).

Basis of Arrangement

Other hymnals, before 1844 by editor Campbell, had been called *Psalms, Hymns, and Spiritual Songs,* but none had placed significance so consciously in each word of that title. As used by Campbell it was more than the announcement that the book was in that historical stream which, since the last half of the eighteenth century, had been flowing from psalmody to hymnody. It was more than an advertisement of return to apostolic phraseology and practice. It declared the existence of a structural blueprint to be followed by any desiring to construct a hymnbook of decency and order. It indicated a confident hope that the songs included in the hymnal would glorify the Divine Architect who had designed man's redemption.

Campbell understood Colossians 3:16 to contain three imperatives and three participles. The former—(1) "Let the word of Christ dwell *in you*"; (2) let it dwell *richly*; (3) let it dwell in you *in all wisdom;*—were to be accomplished in the manner of the latter—(1) through *teaching;* (2) through *admonishing;* (3) and through *praising.*

Mr. Campbell defined the three nouns, *psalms, hymns,* and *spiritual songs* in a unique way, reporting in his early "Preface" the result of his investigation concerning the "precisely intended" meanings.

Gospel Psalms

"Psalms are historic compositions, or poetic narratives," he said. They are "recitations of past favors—of past dispensations" (*Millennial Harbinger,* July, 1844, p. 289). The Presbyterian churches, limiting their song to the psalms of David, had been able to read evangelical implications into the words of their psaltery, but they could not utter Jesus' name. To the contrary. Campbell would make Christ the theme of all song and the Christian "Psalms" could narrate poetically His life.

Mr. Campbell's arrangement began with songs on the incarnation and birth of Jesus and went beyond the resurrection and ascension to the other side of Pentecost and the beginnings of world conquest. In the 1844 hymnal, for example, there were seven songs on the nativity, one on Christ's baptism, two on His ministry, one on His transfiguration, another on the triumphal entry, a pair on the institution of the Lord's Supper, and five on the crucifixion. These were followed by eight on the resurrection. The climax was reached with two songs dealing with the ascension, one with the coronation, and two with the global extension of Christ's kingdom.

In nonliturgical churches, throughout the first half of the nineteenth century, it had become the custom to arrange hymns topically (at least in the index).

In the liturgical church the season was as important as the sermon. In 1827, the year before Campbell's first hymnal, Anglicans had published the *Collection* of Bishop Reginald Heber (1783-1826), from which Campbell borrowed freely. In this work the hymns were arranged according to the Christian calendar. John Keble (1792-1866), founder of the Oxford Revival, had released, also in 1827, his book *The Christian Year*, with its meditative verse upon the feasts and fasts of the church. Alexander Campbell, in his choice of "Psalms," produced a book equally suitable to the homiletically aware and the liturgically conscious.

Hymns to God and Songs to Men

"Hymns," according to the "Preface" of *Psalms, Hymns, and Spiritual Songs,* were "songs of praise, in which the excellencies, glories, and gracious acts of some persons are extolled." Where "Psalms" indirectly praised the Lord, "Hymns" directly addressed God. The Christian hymn, therefore, was a song addressed to the Messiah, adoring "His glory, personal and official, as Prophet, Priest, and King."

"Spiritual Songs," by definition in Campbell's "Preface," were, "either songs, the matter of which was immediately suggested by the Holy Spirit; or sentimental songs, composed on the divine communications to men." Such a song in a Christian hymnal had for its subject matter "the emotion of our souls towards [Christ] and his salvation, declarative of our trust, confidence, hope, and joy in him, and our love to him" (*Millennial Harbinger*, July, 1844, p. 290).

This last category contained a mixture of psalms and hymns, and often carried songs specifically designed for man's edification. The topical scope was broad enough to include eleven subdivisions in the 1844 edition and twenty-one in the edition of 1851. In 1844 the seven songs on nature began with one extolling the wonders of nature's Creator but observing the limits of nature's revelatory power. This song was followed by others on the sun, moon, and stars of the sky, the rivers and oceans, the rain, the trees, and the fish of the sea. The concluding spiritual song, touching the natural world, called all created things to join in the Maker's praise. Five songs were on the "Bible," six on "Providence," nineteen on "Christian Honors and Privileges," and six on "The Christian Hope." Other subtopics were "Christian Love, Union, and Communion." "The Church Triumphant on Earth," "Future Glory," and "Recruiting Songs." Finally, there were both a lengthy group labeled "Miscellaneous"—where three of Campbell's hymns appeared —and a short group called "Songs for Christian Children."

When in 1844 the earlier hymnbook was augmented by a Part II, its songs were neither divided up under a similar arrangement nor added to the existing divisions of "Part I." That rearrangement he felt, could come later, but it never materialized. The 1851 hymnal was "classified and arranged as to subject." The American Christian Missionary Society enlarged the hymnal, combined the parts, and replaced Campbell's divisions by arranging the songs under eleven captions: "Scriptures," "God," "Christ," "Gospel," "Church," "Public Worship," "New Life," "Present and Future," "Home," "Times and Seasons," and the ever present catchall for leftovers: "Miscellaneous."

In 1865 the categories and the hymns of Campbell were gone. The trinity of sacred poetic-composition, with the Campbellian distinctions of "the narrative, the declarative or ecstatic character," had yielded to the more typical ordering according to subject matter.

Chapter Eighteen

LASTING INFLUENCES

How extensive in range and enduring in time was the influence of the Campbell hymnal? Today, a century after Alexander Campbell's death, many of his opinions about music and worship are but little known among the "Christian churches" which claim to have been touched by his reform. Whereas he reasoned against choirs, organs, and inviting the unconverted to join in the worship of God, they favor the use of the choir, an instrument, and at least hymn-singing by children. He preferred a hymnal without musical notes, without songs addressed to the Holy Spirit, and without an extensive number of songs that would seldom be used. They generally have large hymnbooks with musical notes; and several hymns in most of their books are directed not only to the Father and to the Son but to the Holy Spirit.

While some "churches of Christ" distinguish themselves today from "Christian churches" or "Disciples of Christ" in their use of none but vocal music in the praise of God, even they would confess not to follow Campbell on every point. For example no segment of the Restoration movement any longer divides its hymnal into the "psalm," "hymn," and "spiritual song" categories. Neither do they all seek to use one small hymnal of a few, well-known songs; nor do they appear to find detraction if the page contains musical notes as well as meaningful words.

Commenting on the growing size of Disciple hymnals, Louis F. Benson wrote:

> It would be interesting to accept the fact that the committee (i.e. of the American Christian Missionary Society) could find 1320 hymns in current books where Campbell in 1828 found only 125 as evidence that the churches had come

to accept his canons of Praise. But in fact the better part of the additions of 1866 is from XVIIIth century writers (*The English Hymn: Its Development and Use in Worship:* London: Hodder and Stoughton, 1815, p. 392).

If some of the opinions Campbell expressed, like all of the hymns Campbell created, were short-lived, what, if any, of his concepts survive?

Lasting Choices

Campbell believed, and the church confirmed the belief, that worship was of prime importance to the Christian and that the singing of the church merited much careful thought. Some modern churchmen are surprised and pleased at the high standards Campbell had set for the music of the church. Royal Humbert's evaluation that

. . . his approach even today seems modern, accurate, and characterized by permanently valuable standards ("Alexander Campbell Edits a Hymnal," *The Christian-Evangelist*, December 3, 1936, pp. 1696, 1697).

corresponds to the appraisal of organist Charles Huddleston Heaton that

. . . recognition of his high standards of hymnody might result in attention toward improving our own choice of hymns for divine worship ("Our First Hymnal," *The Christian-Evangelist*, June 29, 1955, p. 632).

As early as 1828 Alexander Campbell had his readers singing such enduring compositions as "All Hail the Power of Jesus' Name," "Bless'd Be the Tie That Binds," "Christ the Lord Is Ris'n Today," "Come, You That Love the Lord," "Come Thou Fount of Every Blessing," "From All That Dwell

Below the Skies," "Glorious Things of Thee Are Spoken," "God Moves in a Mysterious Way," "How Firm a Foundation," "Jesus Shall Reign Where'er the Sun," "O God of Bethel, by Whose Hand," "O God, Our Help in Ages Past," "There Is a Fountain Fill'd With Blood," and "What Glory Gilds the Sacred Page."

When Baptists and Disciples joined in 1953 to produce *Christian Worship: A Hymnal,* they included twenty songs that had been sung in the days of *Psalms, Hymns, and Spiritual Songs.* One baptismal-hymn, "Here, Saviour, We Would Come," listed "Alexander Campbell's Christian Hymn Book" as the source. From this early source another ten songs beyond those used in *Christian Worship: A Hymnal* could be found in other modern hymnals. But the question would still remain as to the degree of Campbell's direct and indirect inspiration of those later Disciples who were concerned to write hymns or edit hymnals for that brotherhood.

No such hesitancy exists, however, in rendering the verdict that the Campbell hymnal was the standard hymnbook amongst "Christians only" for three score years. Whether known as *Psalms, Hymns, and Spiritual Songs* (1828-1864), or *The Christian Hymn Book* (1865-1870), or *The Christian Hymnal* (1871-1881), or *The Christian Hymnal, Revised* (1882-1890), Campbell's hymnal enjoyed a popularity beyond all its potential competitors.

Influence Overseas

The Restoration movement in other lands registered some influence from Bethany, West Virginia. The first hymnbook for the British Churches of Christ was made by James Wallis in 1841. He called his work *A Selection of Psalms & Hymns for the Use of the Disciples of Jesus Christ*. This was printed in Nottingham. Hall, Virtue & Co. of London twelve years later printed *Christian Praise: Being a Selection of Psalms, Hymns and Spiritual Songs for the Disciples of the Lord Jesus Christ*. Here we especially note the Campbell mark, not only in the hymnal's title and the designation "Disciple" but by the "Preface" of Alexander Campbell's hymnal printed *in toto*.

Other hymnals followed in Britain. In 1868 David King sent out from Birmingham *Psalms, Hymns and Scripture Chants for Christians*. From the same city in 1908 came the first "official" hymnal, *Hymns for Churches of Christ*. This had been ordered by the annual conference of 1903. Also from the same city, in 1938, the Berean Press published *The Christian Hymnary for Use of Churches of Christ*. This last book was based on the "official" hymnal just mentioned. True to Campbell's preferences, only word editions were made.

For the Australian and New Zealand congregations the Austral Printing and Publishing Co., Ltd., of Melbourne brought from the press *A Collection of Psalms and Hymns for the Use of Christians* (1869), *Psalms and Hymns* (1887), and *Church of Christ Hymn Book* (1931).

In the Mormon Movement

Nearer to the Campbell homestead and sphere of influence geographically than the British Churches of Christ was the American Church of Jesus Christ of Latter Day Saints.

Some ecclesiastical historians have witnessed the occasional striking similarity between these two religious bodies. The names "church of Christ" and "church of Jesus Christ," were similar. Both observed the Lord's Supper the first day of every week. Both railed against "the creeds of human composition" and looked at the Roman Catholic church as an apostasy. Both held that the Protestant Reformation did not go far enough. Both spoke of restoring the ancient order of things, with the Mormons looking to Joseph Smith as God's prophet to bring about that restoration. Both preached immersion as Biblical baptism and its design as the remission of sins. Both called for hearing, faith, and repentance as prerequisites to sharing in a baptism which was an act of obedience. Both defined faith and repentance similarly and uniquely and saw these states of mind produced through the Word of God and not by some mystical operation of the Holy Spirit. Both used the terminology of evangelist Walter Scott in speaking and writing of "the plan of salvation." The Disciples read their *Millennial Harbinger* and the Mormons their *Millennial Star*.

The connecting link theologically is believed by some to be Sidney Rigdon (1793-1876)—once a Baptist, then a "Campbellite," then one of the original twelve apostles of Mormonism, and finally, in the judgment of Mormons, the modern Judas who betrayed that cause. Joseph Welles White, whose thesis, "The Influence of Sidney Rigdon upon the Theology of Mormonism" (University of Southern California, 1947) has not yet been published, compares the fundamental doctrines of Mormons and Disciples, and then asserts that in several of their doctrines "the Mormons varied from the Disciples in just the ways that Rigdon varied" (p. 134). In his *Early History of the Disciples in the Western*

Reserve, A. S. Hayden indicates that jealousy drove Rigdon from his former co-worker.

Whatever the reasons Sidney Rigdon left the Disciples, he took many of their concepts with him. When Joseph Smith with Hyrum Smith was murdered on June 27, 1844, Rigdon expected to take Joseph Smith's place, but was disappointed in this ambition. The apostleship unanimously ousted him on August 8 that year. From about eighty thousand members he succeeded in drawing a small number of followers who held a conference at Pittsburgh in August of 1844. Within eight months, at a later conference on April 9, 1845, they had their own hymnal.

Rigdon's group published a periodical *The Latter-day Saints' Messenger and Advocate,* a semi-monthly printed in Pittsburgh. In April of 1845 it changed its name to *Messenger and Advocate of the Church of Christ.* This journal advertised Rigdon's hymnal (and at 37-1/2¢ per copy) on its last page, as the *Millennial Harbinger* on its final leaf presented Campbell's hymnal. Both journals had a place for poetry, and a sample of a hymn by Rigdon can be found in the Pittsburgh periodical.

Is there a connection between the hymnals of Campbell and Rigdon as there is between their views?

Of the 182 hymns in the Rigdon hymnal thirty-seven are also found amongst the ninety songs in the earliest Mormon hymnal published in 1835 by the wife of Joseph Smith, the prophet. Eleven others are from a Mormon hymnal published in 1844. Fifty-two were in the Campbell hymnal, and only eight of these were also in the Mormon hymnals prior to 1845. It appears that Rigdon wrote some hymns himself, used Mormon hymnals for distinctively Mormon songs and drew from Campbell's hymnal along with other sources for several of the numbers.

Rigdon's hymnal, like Campbell's was small in physical dimension and number of selections, used only words and not tunes, and placed above each song the brief C.M., L.M., 7's or other guide for singers. From the "Preface" one hears the echo of the Bethany sage:

> No saint can engage in this department of the worship of God, and enjoy the spirit of true devotion, unless the composition he sings is true, and such as the Lord approves . . . those which have been selected, are materially altered so as to render them more acceptable to the intelligent saint. . . . It has been one principle object with the compiler, to select such compositions as contained subjects of praise. . . . The compiler never having attended much to poetical compositions, he had little doubt but those of refined practical taste may find many objections, to the various compositions. The object of the compiler was to have the subject matter true, and proper subjects of praise, if the poetry should be defective (*A Collection of Sacred Hymns for the Church of Jesus Christ of Latter Day Saints*, Selected by S. Rigdon, Pittsburgh, 1845, pp. iii, v).

In the Ecumenical Movement

Henry Wilder Foote in dealing with *Three Centuries of American Hymnody* found it easy "to deal with the hymn writers by denominational groups" saying:

> It is only in the present century that such denominational grouping has ceased to have any significance (Harvard University Press, 1940, p. x).

In the third decade of the nineteenth century Alexander Campbell, whose father had sent his *Address of the Christian Association of Washington* (Pennsylvania) "to all that love our Lord Jesus Christ, in sincerity, throughout all the

335

churches," sent out his hymnbook "to the wise and discerning Christians dispersed amongst all the sects of the present day." Campbell hoped that by allowing liberty of opinion and emphasizing universally accepted truths a unity could be manifest. Addressing praise to Christ rather than singing denominational tenets was considered a step toward that goal. However, the sale of the hymnal to nondisciples is, at present, an unknown factor. The book itself seems not to have had any impact among the denominations, but the man himself did kindle a dream for ecumenicity in such men as Charles Clayton Morrison, late-editor of the *Christian Century*, who also edited in 1924 *Hymns of the United Church*.

In a letter writen in May, 1839, by Robert Richardson to Alexander Campbell at Bethany, Mr. Richardson alluded to a meaning for the word *Bethany* in addition to its Hebrew significance, "house of dates." Another derivation he said, would make it mean "house of song."

In this study we hope to have shown that to some degree Bethany was indeed "a house of song" and that the hymnal from its press did joint service with the periodicals in working towards the day when the whole church will be able to sing:

> We are not divided: All one body we,
> One in hope and doctrine, one in charity.

Annotated Bibliography

Bailey, Robert W. *New Ways in Christian Worship.* Nashville: Broadman Press, 1981.

A book written by a minister to help ministers and laypeople prepare for worship.

Barclay, William. *Prayers for Young People.* London: Wm. Collins Sons & Co., Ltd., 1971.

The author's books on the New Testament are very popular; here is a collection of model prayers for youth.

Benson, Louis F. *The Hymnody of the Christian Church.* Richmond, VA: John Knox Press, 1956.

A study of the use of hymns throughout the history of the church.

Blackwood, Andrew W. *The Fine Art of Public Worship.* New York: Abingdon Press, 1939.

One of the old, classic works on the subject of worship by a popular preacher.

Blackwood, Andrew W. *The Funeral: A Sourcebook for Ministers.* Philadelphia: The Westminster Press, 1942.

For the individual who sees worship possibilities in the funeral situation.

Blackwood, Andrew W. *Leading in Public Prayer.* New York: Abingdon Press, 1958.

A good study of the role of prayer in public worship, written by one of the great preachers of the twentieth century.

Bradshaw, Paul F. *Daily Prayer in the Early Church.* New York: Oxford University Press, 1982.

The first two chapters discuss the role of prayer in first century Judaism and Christianity.

Burkhardt, John E. *Worship.* Philadelphia: The Westminster Press, 1982.

This book is for the rare individual who wishes for a strong theological statement about worship that he/she might ponder.

Coffin, Henry Sloane. *The Public Worship of God.* Philadelphia: The Westminster Press, 1946.

Written to fill a niche in a series of books that includes some by Andrew Blackwood, this work pursues a more liturgical view of worship.

Colquhoun, Frank. *Hymns that Live.* Downers Grove, IL: InterVarsity Press, 1980.

Excellent studies of the meaning and message of a number of the great hymns.

Cullmann, Oscar. *Early Christian Worship.* Philadelphia: The Westminster Press, 1953.

The author focuses on worship in the first century, particularly as it is reflected in the New Testament writings.

Cully, Iris V. *Christian Worship and Church Education.* Philadelphia: The Westminster Press, 1967.

Written by one whose interests are in the area of Christian education.

Davies, Horton. *Christian Worship.* New York: Abingdon Press, 1957.

The author devotes half of the book to an examination of the historic worship practices of a number of mainline Christian bodies as a foundation for considering worship today.

DeWelt, Don. *The Church in the Bible.* Joplin, MO: College Press, 1958.

Chapter 18 treats the topic of worship in the early church.

DeWelt, Don. *If You Want to Preach.* Joplin, MO: College Press, 1957.

The book contains material helpful to effective communication in preaching—and effective communication is essential to valid worship.

DeWelt, Don. *Prayertime: A Guide to Daily Worship.* Joplin, MO: College Press, 1982.

A book designed to be used as a personal daily devotional guide throughout the entire year.

DeWelt, Don. *Sweet Hour of Prayer.* Joplin, MO: College Press.

A book designed to help an individual in the daily experiences of prayer.

Dobbins, Gaines S. *The Church at Worship.* Nashville: Broadman Press, 1962.

After considering at some length the improvement of public worship the author relates worship to Christian education and evangelism.

Doran, Carol, and Thomas H. Troeger. *Renewing Worship in the Congregation.* Valley Forge, PA: Judson Press, 1983.

The authors discuss some effective but non-traditional ways of approaching the worship service.

Fields, Wilbur. *Let Us Draw Near.* Privately printed by the author, 1965; reprinted by College Press.

An extensive collection of calls to worship, stewardship meditations, and communion meditations.

Fisher, Fred L. *Prayer in the New Testament.* Philadelphia: The Westminster Press, 1964.

A topical study of the different kinds of prayer that are recorded in the New Testament writings.

Fosdick, Harry Emerson. *The Meaning of Prayer.* London: Collins, 1964. (Available in other editions as well.)

An insightful book on prayer that may be studied through in a few sittings or used as a daily devotional guide; very helpful.

Gobbel, A. Roger, and Phillip C. Huber. *Creative Designs with Children at Worship.* Atlanta: John Knox Press, 1981.

Contains an introductory section about the nature of children's worship and then presents a large number of brief, model worship sketches for children.

Hahn, Ferdinand. *The Worship of the Early Church.* Trans. David E. Green. Philadelphia: Fortress Press, 1973.

The author examines worship in the early communities. i.e. Judaism, Aramaic-speaking, Hellenistic Jewish, Gentile, subapostolic, and the early Fathers.

Hardin, H. Grady, Joseph D. Quillian, Jr., and James F. White. *The Celebration of the Gospel.* New York: Abingdon Press, 1964.

Considers worship as celebration, and also has an interesting chapter on weddings and funerals as occasions of worship.

Hardin, Grady. *The Leadership of Worship.* Nashville: Abingdon, 1980.

A book designed to instruct church leaders in securing more complete involvement of congregational participation in worship.

Harms, John W. *Prayer in the Market Place.* St. Louis: The Bethany Press, 1958.

A collection of contemporary, model prayers that were offered on secular as well as religious occasions.

Heaton, Charles Huddleston. *A Guidebook to Worship Services of Sacred Music.* St. Louis: The Bethany Press, 1962.

A good study of the serious use of music in the worship service of the church.

Hedley, George. *Christian Worship: Some Meanings and Means.* New York: The Macmillan Company, 1953.

Includes a good historical study of early biblical worship.

Heimsath, Charles H. *The Genius of Public Worship.* New York: Charles Scribner's Sons, 1944.

An older book but yet a good comparative study of the various cultural or denominational approaches to worship.

Henry, Ed. *In Remembrance.* Joplin, MO: College Press, 1977.

A collection of model communion meditations for each Sunday of a year.

Hopper, Myron Taggart. *The Candle of the Lord.* St. Louis: The Bethany Press, 1957.

A collection of brief worship services designed for older young people.

Horton, Douglas. *The Meaning of Worship.* New York: Harper & Brothers, Publishers, 1959.

Suffice it to say that the contents represent the Lyman Beecher Lectures for 1958.

Jones, Ilion T. *A Historical Approach to Evangelical Worship.* New York: Abingdon Press, 1954.

The author builds a philosophy of worship on the basis of a thorough study of the historical development of worship.

Keir, Thomas H. *The Word in Worship.* London: Oxford University Press, 1960.

Presented first as the Warrack Lectureship in 1960, this book while liturgically oriented treats a very important theme.

MacDonald, Alexander B. *Christian Worship in the Primitive Church.* Edinburgh: T. & T. Clark, 1935.

An old book—but then the topic is old also, and it is a good study.

McDormand, Thomas Bruce. *The Art of Building Worship Services.* Nashville: Broadman Press, 1958.

The author carefully considers the various parts of the worship service, thus providing a very helpful book.

Marshall, Catherine (ed.) *The Prayers of Peter Marshall.* New York: McGraw-Hill Book Company, Inc., 1954.

One can be introduced to the sheer beauty of the language of public prayer by reading this collection of prayers composed by one of the great preachers of the twentieth century.

Martin, Ralph P. *Worship in the Early Church.* Grand Rapids: William B. Eerdmans Publishing Company, 1974.

A scholarly study of the major themes of worship, such a study being based primarily on the biblical texts.

Martin, Ralph P. *The Worship of God.* Grand Rapids: William B. Eerdmans Publishing Company, 1982.

The author considers each part of the worship service, presenting what the sub-title calls "some theological, pastoral, and practical reflections"; an excellent book.

Massey, James Earl. *The Worshiping Church.* Anderson, IN: The Warner Press, 1961.

A book designed to help people understand public worship so that they might participate more fully in it.

Maxwell, William D. *A History of Christian Worship.* Grand Rapids: Baker Book House, 1982.

One of the very best historical studies of the development of worship, this book is an update of the author's *An Outline of Christian Worship*, first published in 1936.

Moule, C. F. D. *Worship in the New Testament*. Richmond, VA: John Knox Press, 1961.

The book includes sections on the Lord's Supper and baptism.

Murch, James DeForest. *Christian Minister's Manual*. Cincinnati: The Standard Publishing Company, 1937.

A very helpful guide on many topics for the minister but especially an excellent worship manual to assist in the planning of weddings, funerals, and various special services of worship.

Murch, James DeForest. *Teach Me to Pray*. Cincinnati: Standard Publishing, 1958.

There are several points on public prayer scattered through this book written by one of the noted leaders of the Restoration Movement.

Nakarai, Toyozo W. *An Elder's Public Prayers*. Hicksville, NY: Exposition Press, 1979.

A collection of prayers, written and delivered by one of the great biblical scholars of the Restoration Movement.

Nathan, Walter L. *Art and the Message of the Church*. Philadelphia: The Westminster Press, 1961.

Considers Christian art through the centuries but also has some good suggestions for modern worship.

Northcott, Cecil. *Hymns in Christian Worship*. Richmond, VA: John Knox Press, 1964.

A study of the use of hymns both in history and in the present church.

Oesterley, W. O. E. *The Jewish Background of the Christian Liturgy*. Gloucester, MA: Peter Smith, 1965.

A serious study written by one of the most respected scholars of Jewish studies.

Palmer, Albert W. *The Art of Conducting Public Worship.* New York: The Macmillan Company, 1953.

A good guide to worship preparation, written from a lightly liturgical perspective.

Palmer, Albert W. *Come, Let Us Worship.* New York: The Macmillan Company, 1941.

An older book yet has some good ideas for our perusal.

Payne, O. E. *Instrumental Music is Scriptural.* Cincinnati: The Standard Publishing Company, 1920.

An old, yet important book on a continuing controversy within the Restoration Movement.

Peaston, A. Elliott. *The Prayer Book Tradition in the Free Churches.* London: James Clarke & Co. Ltd., 1964.

A comparative study of the worship practices of different churches, including a chapter on the Churches of Christ.

The Pioneers on Worship. Kansas City, MO: The Old Paths Book Club, 1947.

A collection of statements on the subject of worship written by early leaders of the Restoration Movement, including Alexander Campbell.

Randolph, David James. *God's Party.* Nashville: Abingdon Press, 1975.

The author proposes that new forms are needed in worship and then proceeds to suggest such forms; a helpful book.

Rayburn, Robert G. *O Come, Let Us Worship.* Grand Rapids: Baker Book House, 1980.

The author discusses the topic of corporate worship after first examining it in the Old and New Testaments; he also has two chapters on weddings and funerals as acts of worship.

Ream, Guin. *Come Worship*. St. Louis: The Bethany Press, 1957.

The author presents forty-seven model worship services for youth suitable to various occasions.

Reed, Luther D. *Worship: A Study of Corporate Devotion*. Philadelphia: Muhlenberg Press, 1959.

While the book is liturgically oriented it does contain an excellent section (over half of the book) on the use of music in worship.

Routley, Erik. *Hymns and the Faith*. Grand Rapids: William B. Eerdmans Publishing Company, 1968.

A book containing individual analyses of some of the great hymns of the church.

Schilling, S. Paul. *The Faith We Sing*. Philadelphia: The Westminster Press, 1983.

This book stresses the importance of the study of the message of the hymns we use with a view to enhancing Christian belief.

Sclater, J. R. P. *The Public Worship of God*. Grand Rapids: Baker Book House, 1970.

A reprint of the Lyman Beecher Lectures of 1927, stating a Britisher's views on the role of the word in worship.

Segler, Franklin M. *Christian Worship: Its Theology and Practice*. Nashville: Broadman Press, 1967.

A good, all-purpose study of worship, discussing the history, the means of expressing, and the actual conducting of worship.

Shedd, Charlie W. *The Exciting Church Where People Really Pray*. Waco, TX: Word Books, Publishers, 1974.

A very elementary book by a popular writer—but nonetheless a helpful book.

Shedd, Charlie W. *How to Develop a Praying Church.* Nashville: Abingdon Press, 1964.

Another book by the author, brief but excellent, on the topic of prayer as it relates to the congregation.

Simpson, Robert L. *The Interpretation of Prayer in the Early Church.* Philadelphia: The Westminster Press, 1965.

A careful study of the effect that the Lord's Prayer had on the church in the first several centuries.

Spencer, Donald A. *Hymn and Scripture Selection Guide.* Valley Forge: Judson Press, 1977.

An excellent sourcebook for cross-referencing 380 hymns and gospel songs to thousands of biblical texts.

Standard Manual for Funeral Occasions. Cincinnati: The Standard Publishing Company, 1953.

A helpful, pocket-sized manual to be used in preparing for the funeral service—an occasion that can be an opportunity for praise and worship.

Stone, Sam. *The Christian Minister.* Cincinnati: Standard Publishing, 1980.

Chapter 20 of this excellent book treats the subject of conducting the worship services of the congregation.

Underhill, Evelyn. *Worship.* New York: Harper & Brothers, 1936.

While many readers will feel uncomfortable with this book it needs to be listed as one of the classics in the field of worship.

Verkuyl, Gerrit. *Enriching Teen-Age Worship.* Chicago: Moody Press, 1950.

A small but helpful book discussing the theory and practice of worship for young people.

Vonk, Idalee Wolf. *Growing in Stature.* Cincinnati: The Standard Publishing Company, 1951.

A collection of fifty-two representative worship services for young people.

Wallis, Charles L. (ed.) *Worship Resources for the Christian Year.* New York: Harper & Brothers, 1954.

An extensive sourcebook of material for use in worship services; leans toward the liturgical.

Watkins, Keith. *The Breaking of Bread.* St. Louis: The Bethany Press, 1966.

A good study of worship, based on an initial discussion of the contribution of the Campbellian heritage to worship theory.

Watkins, Keith. *The Feast of Joy.* St. Louis: The Bethany Press, 1977.

The observance of the Lord's Supper should be a time of highest joy for the body of believers even as the biological family finds its greatest joy in celebrated observances.

Watkins, Keith. *Liturgies in a Time When Cities Burn.* Nashville: Abingdon Press, 1969.

An examination of the influence of the traumatic years of the 60s upon worship and what worship has to say to the age in which we live.

Webber, Robert E. *Worship Old and New.* Grand Rapids: Zondervan Publishing House, 1982.

A study of the historic origins as well as the theology of worship.

White, James F. *Introduction to Christian Worship.* Nashville: Abingdon Press, 1980.

This book claims to be both a survey of worship as well as a careful examination of the Christian way of life.

347

White, James F. *New Forms of Worship*. Nashville: Abingdon Press, 1971.

The serious student of worship should study carefully the material written on the subject by James White; this book focuses on the role of the physical senses in worship.

White, James F. *The Worldliness of Worship*. New York: Oxford University Press, 1967.

A book written for laypeople to cause them to think about the central concerns of worship.

Williamson, Robert L. *Effective Public Prayer*. Nashville: Broadman Press, 1960.

An excellent study, written by a minister, on an important phase of worship—public prayer.

Willimon, William H. *The Bible: A Sustaining Presence in Worship*. Valley Forge: Judson Press, 1981.

A good study of worship, prayer, the Lord's Supper, and preaching, based on biblical texts.

Wohlgemuth, Paul W. *Rethinking Church Music*. Carol Stream, IL: Hope Publishing Company, 1981.

A basic study of music as it relates to the worship and spiritual life of a congregation.

Topical Index

As arranged in *Monser's Topical Index and Digest of the Bible* edited by Harold E. Monser with A. T. Robertson, D. R. Dungan and Others.

LORD'S SUPPER (Gr. *Eucharist*).— I Cor. 11:20. Called "Communion of blood of Christ"—I Cor. 10:16. Called "The breaking of bread"— Acts 2:42, 20:7.

Instances of.—Appointed by Christ— Mt. 26:26-30; Mk. 14:12-17; Lu. 22:15-18. *Cf.* Lu. 22:15-18 and Lu. 22:19, 20. Enjoined by apostles —Acts 2:42. Observed by disciples —Acts 2:42; 20:7; I Cor. 11:20-26.

Its purpose.—To proclaim the Lord's death—I Cor. 11:26. To commemorate Jesus—Lu. 2:19; I Cor. 11:24, 25. For a communion of brethren— I Cor. 10:16, 17. For spiritual sustenance—Mt. 26:26-28; Mk. 14:22-24; Lu. 22:19, 20; John 6:52-57.

Paul's teaching respecting it.—Was direct from Christ—I Cor. 11:23. The reason for assembling—I Cor. 11:20. Must eat worthily—I Cor. 11:27. Was abused in Corinth—I Cor. 11:21ff. Must prove himself— I Cor. 11:28-31. Must partake jointly —I Cor. 10:17; 11:33. No communion with demons—I Cor. 10:20, 21.

PRAISE: Is due to God for His lovingkindness.—II Chr. 20:21; Ps. 138:1-2. For all His benefits—Ps. 103:2-18; 145:2-9; 107:8-14; 108:3-4; Is. 63:7-9. For His holiness—Ps. 99:3; Is. 6:3.

How offered: With the understanding —Ps. 47:6-7; I Cor. 14:15-16. With the whole heart—Ps. 9:1-2; 111:1-2. With uprightness of heart—Ps. 119:7. With the lips—Ps. 63:3-5; 119:171-172. With gladness—II Chr. 29:30; Jer. 33:11; Ps. 98:4-9; Acts 2:46-47.

Why offered: For the gift of Christ— Rom. 15:8-13; John 12:12-13; Heb. 13:12-15; Rev. 5:12. For being planted in Christ—Is. 61:2-3; Eph. 1:3-6; Phil. 4:8; I Pet. 1:3-5; 2:9-10.

Old Testament: Instances of.—Melchizedek—Gen. 14:19-20. Moses— Ex. 15:1-21. Jethro—Ex. 18:10-11. Deborah—Ju. 5:1-11. Asaph and his brethren—I Chr. 16:8-36. Hannah—I Sam. 2:1-10. David—I Chr. 29:10-13; Ps. 119:164; II Sam. Ch. 22. At laying foundation of temple—Ezra 3:10-11. Placing ark in temple—II Chr. 5:13-14. Hezekiah—Is. 38:19-20. Daniel— Dan. 2:20-23.

New Testament instances.—Mary— Lu. 1:46:55. Shepherds—Lu. 2:20. Zacharias—Lu. 1:68-69. Anna— Lu. 2:36-38. Disciples—Lu. 19:37-38. The people—Lu. 18:43. The apostles—Lu. 24:53. Those first obedient to the faith—Acts 2:47. Lame man—Acts 3:8. Paul and Silas —Acts 16:25.

References from Old Testament.— Enter His courts with—Ps. 100:4. Praise is good—Ps. 147:1. Thou shalt call thy gates—Is. 60:18. The garment of praise for spirit of heaviness—Is. 61:3. Bringing sacrifices of thanksgiving—Jer. 17:26. Earth full of His—Hab. 3:3.

From New Testament.—Out of mouth of babes Thou hast perfected—Mt. 21:6. Give God the praise—John 9:24. Whose praise is not of men —Rom. 2:29. Do that which is good and thou shalt have—Rom. 13:3. Brother whose praise is in gospel— II Cor. 8:18. In this I praise you not —I Cor. 11:17.

PRAYER. What is prayer? It is the soul's desire for God—Ps. 42:1, 2; 63:1-3; 84:2; 143:6-9.

It is as universal as man—Ps. 65:2; 86:9; Is. 66:23. Began with Seth— Gen. 4:23.

It is a cry—a supplication—Ex. 22:23, 27; Job 23:3, 4; Ps. 34:15, 17; 86:3; 88:1, 2, 9, 13; Is. 19:20; 30:19; 58:9.

It is an instinct that must have utterance —Ps. 51:1-3; Is. 44:17; 45:20; Mt. 27:46; Mk. 15:34; Lu. 18:7, 13.

It is an appeal from the child to the father—Hos. 14:3; Mt. 6:6-13; Lu. 11:2-4.

It is a necessity—Hos. 14:1-3; Amos 5:6; Heb. 4:16.

Enjoined.—I Chr. 16:11, 35; 28:9; II Chr. 7:14, 15; Ps. 35:6; 62:8; 105:3, 4; Is. 55:6; 58:9; 65:24; Jer. 29:12, 13; 33:3; Lam. 2:10; 3:41; Ez. 36:37; Hos. 14:2; Zeph. 2:3; Zech. 10:1, 6; Mt. 7:7; 24:20; 26:41; Mk. 13:33; 14:38; Lu. 11:5-13; 18:1; 21:36; John 16:24-27; Acts 8:22; Rom. 12:12; Eph. 6:17, 18; Phil. 4:6; Col. 4:2; I Thess. 5:17; I Tim. 2:1, 8; Heb. 4:16; Jas. 1:5-7; 5:13; I Pet. 4:7.

Confession.—Duty of—Lev. 5:5; Num. 5:6, 7; Jer. 3:13; Mt. 10:32; Lu. 12:18; 15:21; John 9:22; Rom. 10:9; 14:11; Phil. 2:11; Jas. 5:16.

Blessedness of—Lev. 26:40-42; Job 33:27, 28; Pr. 28:13; I John 1:9.

Individual—Gen. 32:9, 10; II Sam. 24:17; I Chr. 21:8; Job 40:4, 5; Ps. 32:5; 38:4; 40:11, 12; 41:4; 51:3, 4; 69:5; 119:176; 130:3; Is. 6:5; Dan. 9:20; Lu. 18:13.

National—Num. 14:40; Ju. 10:10, 15; I Sam. 7:6; 12:10; Neh. 9:2, 33-35; Ps. 106:6, 7; Jer. 3:25; 14:7, 20; Lam. 5:16; Dan. 9:5-15. *Moses* for Israel—Ex. 32:31, 32; 34:9; Num. 14:19. *Ezra* for Israel— Ezra 9:5-15; 10:1. *Nehemiah* for Judah—Neh. 1:4-11. *Isaiah* for Judah—Is. 64:6, 7. *Daniel* for Israel —Dan. 9:7-23. *Daniel* for Judah— Dan. 9:3-19.

Intercession.—Gen. 20:7; Jer. 27:18; 29:7; II Cor. 9:14; Eph. 6:18; I Tim. 2:1; II Tim. 4:16; Heb. 13:18-21; Jas. 5:14-16; I John 5:16. Priestly—Ex. 28:9-12, 29, 30, 38.

Instances of—Old Testament: *Abraham* for Abimelech—Gen. 20:7, 17, 18. For Ishmael—Gen. 17:18. For Sodom and Gomorrah—Gen. 18:23-32. *Boaz* for Ruth—Ruth 2:12. *Daniel* for Israel and Judah—Can. 9:3-23. *David* for the Child of Bathsheba—II Sam. 12:16. For Israel— II Sam. 24:17; I Chr. 29:10-19; Ps. 25:22; 28:9. For the righteous—Ps. 7:9; 36:10. For Solomon—I Chr. 29:19. *Eli* for Hannah—I Sam. 1:17. *Elisha* for the Shunammite's son—II Ki. 4:33. *Ezekiel* for Israel— Ez. 9:8. *Ezra* for Israel—Ezra 8:21-23; 9:5-15. *Hezekiah* for Judah— II Ki. 19:14-20. For those who had cleansed themselves for the passover —II Chr. 30:18-20. *Isaiah*—Is. 37:4; 63:16-19; 64:1-12. *Job* in behalf of his friends—Job 42:8-10. *Joshua for Israel*—Josh. 7:6-9. *Moses for Israel*—Ex. 32:11-14, 31, 32; 34: 9; Num. 11:1, 2; 14:13-24; 21:7; Deut. 1:11; 9:18-20, 25-29; 10:10; Ps. 106:23. God's model for Moses—Num. 6:22-27. *Moses for Aaron*—Deut. 9:20. For Miriam—Num. 12: 13. For Pharaoh—Ex. 8:12, 30, 31; 9:33, 34; 10:18, 19. *Naomi* for Ruth—Ruth 1:8, 9. *Nehemiah* for Judah—Neh. 1:4-11. *Samuel* for Israel—I Sam. 7:5-8; 12:19-23. *Solomon* for Israel—I Ki. 8:22-54; II Chr. 6: 12-42. New Testament: *Jesus*: For Peter—Lu. 22:32. For His disciples—John 17:9-24. For those who crucified Him—Lu. 23:34 *Epaphras* for the Colossians—Col. 4:12. *Paul* for Israel—Rom. 10:1. For Christians of Rome—Rom. 1:9. For Ephesians—Eph. 1:16-21; 3:14-21. For Philippians—Phil. 1:3-7, 9. For Colossians—Col. 1:3, 9. For Thessalonians—I Thess. 1:2; 3:10-13; 5:23; II Thess. 1:11, 12; 2:16, 17; 3:5, 16. For Onesiphorus—II Tim. 1:16, 18. For Philemon—Philemon 4-6. *Philemon for Paul*—Philemon 22. *The Church in Jerusalem* for Peter—Acts 12:5. For the Sick—Jas. 5:14, 15. Paul asks for prayers of disciples—Rom. 15:30; II Cor. 1:11; Eph. 6:19; Col. 4:3; I Thess. 5:25; II Thess. 3:1; Heb. 13:18. See Phil. 1:19, 20. Forbidden to pray for—Jer. 7:13-16; 14:10-12.

Praise.—Ps. 30:4; 59:16; 63:3; 92: 1-2; 95:2; 106:1; 107:8, 21, 31; 147:7; Is. 12:5; 63:7; Jer. 20:13; Dan. 2:23; Lu. 1:64; 2:13, 28; 18: 43; 19:37; Acts 2:47; 3:8; 16:25; Heb. 13:15; Rev. 4:9-11; 5:12.

Supplication.—Ex. 33:12-16, 18; I Ki. 8:22-53; II Ki. 20:3; II Chr. 6:12-42; Ezra 8:21-23; Job 8:5; Ps. 6:9; 22:19, 21; 28:2; 40:11-17; 69:1, 2, 13-18, 29; 70:5; 88:1-18; Jer. 36:7; Dan. 6:11; Jonah 1:14; Rom. 10:1; II Cor. 1:11; 9:14; Eph. 6:18; Phil. 1:4, 19; 4:6; I Tim. 5:5; II Tim. 1:3.

Thanksgiving.—Gen. 24:27; Ex. 18: 10; I Sam. 2:1; I Ki. 8:15, 56; I Chr. 16:8; II Chr. 20:21-28; Neh. 12:31-40; Ps. 18:17-49; 75:1; 118: 1-4; 140:13; Dan. 2:19, 23; Rom. 1:8; I Cor. 15:57; II Cor. 2:14, 15; 9:15; Eph. 1:3; Phil. 1:3-7; Col. 1:3, 12, 13; I Thess. 1:2; I Pet. 1:3.

HOW SHALL WE PRAY? Should be offered to God.—Deut. 6:13; Ps. 5:2. **As to a Father.**—Mt. 6:9-13; Lu. 11:2-4. **To Jesus.**—Acts 7:59.

In the name of Jesus.—Mt. 18:19-20; 28:18-20; John 14:13, 14; 15: 16; 16:23-26; Eph. 2:18; 5:20; Col. 3:17; I Pet. 2:5. See Lu. 23:42. Continually—Ps. 55:17; 88:1; Rom. 12:12; I Thess. 5:17. Faith, In—Ps. 56:9; 86:7; Mt. 21:21, 22; Mk. 11: 24; Heb. 10:22; Jas. 1:6; I John 5:14. Fasting, With—Neh. 1:4; Dan. 9:3; Acts 13:3. Forgiving spirit, With—Mt. 6:11-15; 18:21-35; Mk. 11:25. Hasty, Not—Eccl. 5:2. Heart, With the—Lam. 3:41. Heart, With the whole—II Chr. 22:9; Ps. 119: 58, 145; Jer. 24:7; 29:12, 13. Heart, With preparation of—Job 11:13; Heb. 10:22. Humility—II Chr. 7:14; 33:12. Importunity—Gen. 32:26-28; Mt. 7:7-11; Lu. 11:8; 18:1-7. Model—Mt. 6:9-13; Lu. 11:2-4. Repetitions, Avoid vain—Mt. 6:7. Righteous, must be—Ps. 34:15, 17, 18; John 15:7,

351

16. Secret, In—Mt. 6:6. Sincerity—Mt. 6:5; Heb. 10:22. Spirit and understanding, With—John 4:22-24; I Cor. 14:14-19. Truth, In—Ps. 145:18; John 4:24. Unfeigned lips, With—Ps. 17:1. Watch and pray—Neh. 4:9; Ps. 5:3; Mt. 26:41; Lu. 21:36; Eph. 6:18; Col. 4:2, 3; I Pet. 4:7. Will of God, According to—I John 5:14-16. *Jesus in Gethsemane* —Mt. 26:39; Lu. 22:32.

Described as: Beseeching the Lord—Ex. 32:11. Calling on the Lord—Acts 7:59; Rom. 10:12-14; II Tim. 2:22. Calling on the name of the Lord—Gen. 4:26; 12:8; Ps. 116:4; Acts 22:16; I Cor. 1:2. Crying unto God. See "What is Prayer?" Drawing near to God—Ps. 73:28; Heb. 10:22. Lifting up the heart—Lam. 3:41. Lifting up the soul—Ps. 25:1. Pouring out the heart—Ps. 62:8. Pouring out the soul—I Sam. 1:15. Seeking the face of the Lord—Ps. 27:8. Seeking unto God—Job 8:5.

Postures in prayer.—Bowing down—Gen. 24:52; Ps. 95:6. Bowing the knees—Is. 45:23; Rom. 14:11; Eph. 3:14; Phil. 2:10. Bowing the head—Gen. 24:26, 48; Ex. 4:31; 12:27; II Chr. 20:18. Falling on face—Num. 16:22, 45; 20:6; Josh. 5:14; 7:6; I Chr. 21:16; II Chr. 20:18; Ez. 9:8; Mt. 26:39; MK. 14:35. Kneeling—I Ki. 8:54; II Chr. 6:13; Ezra 9:5; Ps. 95:6; Dan. 6:10; Lu. 22:41; Acts 7:60; 9:40; 20:36; 21:5. Looking up—Ps. 5:3. Standing—I Sam. 1:26; I Ki. 8:14, 22, 55; II Chr. 20:9; Mk. 11:25; Lu. 18:11-13. Toward the temple in Jerusalem —I Ki. 8:35, 48, 49; II Chr. 6:38;

Ps. 5:7; Dan. 6:10; Jonah 2:4. Lifting up the hands—Neh. 8:6; Ps. 28: 2; 134:2; 141:2; Lam. 2:19; 3:41; I Tim. 2:8. Spreading out the hands —Ex. 9:29; I Ki. 8:22, 38, 54; Ezra 9:5; Job 11:13; Ps. 28:2; 63:4; 88:9; 143:6; Is. 1:15; Lam. 1:17.

Answers to prayer.—Ex. 22:23, 27; II Chr. 7:14; Job 12:4; 33:26; 34: 28; Ps. 21:2, 4; 34:15, 17; 38:15; 55:16, 17; 56:9; 65:2, 5; 69:33; 86:5; 91:15; 99:6; 102:17, 18; 118:5; 138:3; 145:18, 19; Pr. 15: 8, 29; Is. 19:20; 30:19; 55:6, 7; 58:9; 65:24; Jer. 29:12, 13; Lam. 3:57; Ez. 36:37; Dan. 9:20-23; 10:12; Joel 2:32; Jonah 2:2; Zech. 13:9; Mt. 6:6; 18:19; Lu. 11:13; 18:7; John 15:7; 16:23-27; Acts 4:31; II Cor. 12:8; Jas. 5:16-18; I John 3:22; 5:14, 15. Christ received answer—John 11:42; Heb. 5:7. Christ answers—John 14:13, 14.

Examples: Abraham—Gen. 15:1-20; 17:20. Lot—Gen. 19:19-21. Abraham's servant—Gen. 24:12-21. Isaac Gen. 25:21. Jacob—Gen. 32:24-30. Israelites—Ex. 2:23, 24; 14:10; Ju. 3:9, 15; 4:3, 23; 6:7-14; 10:10, 15, 16; I Sam. 12:10, 11; II Chr. 15:4; Neh. 9:27; Ps. 106:15. Gideon—Ju. 6:36-40. Manoah— Ju. 13:8, 9. Samson—Ju. 15:18, 19; 16:28-30. Hannah—I Sam. 1:10-17, 27. Samuel—I Sam. 7:9. David—I Sam. 23:10-12; Ps. 18:6. Solomon—I Ki. 3:1-13; 9:2, 3. Man of God—I Ki. 13:6. Elijah—I Ki. 18:36-39; Jas. 5:17, 18. Elisha—II Ki. 4:33-35; 6:18, 19. Jehoahaz—II Ki. 13:4. Hezekiah and Isaiah—II Ki. 19:14-20; 20:1-6, 10, 11; II Chr. 32:20, 21, 24. Jabez—I Chr. 4:10. Abijah's army—II Chr. 13:14-18. Asa—II Chr. 14:11-15; 15:16. Jehoshaphat —II Chr. 18:31; 20:6-27. Levites— II Chr. 30:27. Manasseh—II Chr. 33:13, 19. Ezra—Ezra 8:21-23. Nehemiah—Neh. 4:9, 15. Job— 42:10. Jeremiah—Lam. 3:55, 56. Daniel—Dan. 9:20-23. Jonah— Jonah 2:2, 10. Reubenites—I Chr. 5:20. Jews—Ezra 8:21, 23; Zech. 7:1-4. Zacharias—Lu. 1:13. Apostles —Acts 4:29-31. Ananias—Acts 10: 4. Cornelius—Acts 10:4, 21. Disciples—Acts 12:5, 7. Paul—Acts 28:8. Paul and Silas—Acts 16:25, 26.

Christ as a mediator.—Rom. 8:34; Eph. 2:18; 3:12; I Tim. 2:5; Heb. 4:14-16; 13:15.

Aid of Holy Spirit.—Zech. 12:10; Rom. 8:26; Eph. 2:18; 6:18; Jude 20.

Assurances.—Ps. 37:4; 81:10; Is. 65:24; Jer. 33:3; Mt. 9:29; Mk. 11: 24; John 14:14; 15:7, 16; Eph. 3:20; Jas. 5:16; I John 3:20.

Private prayer.—Job 22:27. Commanded—Mt. 6:6.

Examples of: Lot—Gen. 19:20. Abraham's servant—Gen. 24:12. Jacob— Gen. 32:9-12. Moses—Deut. 9:18-20. Gideon—Ju. 6:22, 36, 39. Hannah—I Sam. 1:9-15. David— II Sam. 7:18-29. Hezekiah—II Ki. 20:2, 5. Isaiah—II Ki. 20:11. Manasseh—II Chr. 33:12, 13. Ezra 9:5, 6. Nehemiah—Neh. 1:4; 2:4. Jeremiah—Jer. 32:16-25. Daniel—Dan. 9:3, 17-20. Daniel and companions —Dan. 2:17-23. Jonah—Jonah 2:1. Anna—Lu. 2:37.

Public prayer.—God hears—II Chr. 7:14, 16. God accepts—Is. 56:7.

Christ sanctions—Mt. 18:20. Form of prayer—Mt. 6:9-13; Lu. 11:2-4. Should be understood—I Cor. 14: 14-16. **Examples.**—Joshua—Josh. 7:6-9. David—I Chr. 29:10-19. Solomon—II Chr. Ch. 6. Jehoshaphat—II Chr. 20:5-13. Levites— Neh. Ch. 9. Jews—Lu. 1:10. Disciples—Acts 2:46; 4:24; 12:5, 12; 13:3; 16:16.

Prayers of Jesus.—Mt. 19:13; Lu. 3:21; 11:1; John 12:27, 28; Heb. 5:7. Of thanksgiving—Mt. 11:25, 26; 14:19; 15:36; 26:27; Mk. 6: 41; 14:22; Lu. 22:17; John 11:41, 42; I Cor. 11:24. In a mountain— Mt. 14:23; Mk. 6:46; Lu. 6:12. In the upper room—John 17:1-26. For Peter—Lu. 22:32. In Gethsemane —Mt. 26:36-42; Mk. 14:32-39; Lu. 22:41-45. On the cross—Mt. 27: 46; Lu. 23:34, 46.

Paul's prayers.—Rom. 1:3; 10:1; I Cor. 1:3; II Cor. 13:7; Eph. 1:16-19; 3:14-19; Phil. 1:3-10; Col. 1: 3, 9; I Thess. 1:2; 3:10-13; 5:23; II Thess. 1:11; 2:16, 17; 3:5, 16; II Tim. 1:3, 18; Philemon 4-6; Heb. 13:20, 21.

WORSHIP: Of Jehovah.—Ex. 20:3; I Chr. 29:30; II Chr. 7:3; Neh. 8:6; 9:3; Job 1:20; Is. 27:13; John 12: 20; Acts 24:11; I Cor. 14:25; Heb. 1:6; Rev. Ch. 4.

Of Jesus.—Mt. 2:2, 8, 11; 8:2; 9:18; 14:33; 15:25; 28:9, 17; Mk. 5:6; Lu. 24:52; John 9:38; Rev. 7:9, 10.

With an offering.—Gen. 22:5; Ex. 24:1, 5; Deut. 26:10. Before one altar—II Chr. 32:12; Ps. 95:6; 99: 5; 132:7; Jer. 7:2; 26:2.

Toward the temple.—Ps. 5:7; 138:2; Ez. 46:2, 3.

In the beauty of holiness.—I Chr. 16:

29; Ps. 27:4; 29:2; 96:9.

With song and music.—Ps. 66:4; 100:1-4; II Chr. 5:12-14; 29:27-30; Ezra 3:10, 11; Is. 30:29; Rev. 5:8-14; 15:2-4.

In spirit.—John 4:23, 24; Phil. 3:3.

Universal.—Ps. 22:27-29; 86:9; Is. 49:7; 66:23; John 4:20-24; Phil. 2:10, 11. From the gods—Ps. 97:7.

Works of men's hands.—Ps. 115:4-8; Is. 2:8, 20; 44:15; 46:6; Jer. 44:15-19; Mic. 5:13; Acts 19:24-27; Rev. 9:20.

Vain.—Mt. 15:9; Mk. 7:7; Col. 2:18.

Ignorant.—John 4:22; Acts 17:23-25.

Host of heaven.—II Ki. 21:3; II Chr. 33:3; Ez. 8:16; Zeph. 1:4, 5; Acts 7:42.

Index of Scriptures

INDEX OF SCRIPTURES

357

INDEX OF SCRIPTURES

Index of Subjects